LEARN TO PROGRAM WITH
SMALL BASIC

LEARN TO PROGRAM WITH SMALL BASIC

An Introduction to Programming with Games, Art, Science, and Math

by Majed Marji and Ed Price

no starch press

San Francisco

Printed in USA
First printing

20 19 18 17 16   1 2 3 4 5 6 7 8 9

ISBN-10: 1-59327-702-4
ISBN-13: 978-1-59327-702-4

Publisher: William Pollock
Production Editor: Laurel Chun
Cover Illustration: Josh Ellingson
Developmental Editors: Hayley Baker and Tyler Ortman
Technical Reviewer: Vijaye Raji
Copyeditor: Anne Marie Walker
Compositors: Laurel Chun and Kathleen Miller
Proofreader: Lisa Devoto Farrell
Indexer: BIM Indexing & Proofreading Services

For information on distribution, translations, or bulk sales, please contact No Starch Press, Inc. directly:

No Starch Press, Inc.
245 8th Street, San Francisco, CA 94103
phone: 415.863.9900; info@nostarch.com; www.nostarch.com

Library of Congress Cataloging-in-Publication Data

```
Names: Marji, Majed, author. | Price, Ed, 1978- author.
Title: Learn to program with small basic : an introduction to programming
   with games, art, science, and math / by Majed Marji and Ed Price.
Description: San Francisco : No Starch Press, [2016] | Includes index.
Identifiers: LCCN 2015039128| ISBN 9781593277024 | ISBN 1593277024
Subjects:  LCSH: BASIC (Computer program language)
Classification: LCC QA76.73.B3 M3743 2016 | DDC 005.1/3--dc23
LC record available at http://lccn.loc.gov/2015039128
```

BRIEF CONTENTS

CONTENTS IN DETAIL

FOREWORD

Computer programming is magical. Programmers make computers come to life, and with the right tools, the possibilities are limitless. But even today's skilled programmers started with something very small and simple.

I have often wondered what exactly makes programming exciting. The answer, I think, is how even tiny programs can make things happen instantly. When I was twelve, I was introduced to BASIC for the first time. The sheer simplicity of it struck me. It was inviting, not intimidating. And at the time, BASIC was everywhere—it had taken the new world of micro-computers by storm.

My first program worked flawlessly and gave me the instant gratification that kept me wanting to do more. This is what it looked like:

```
10 PRINT "Hello"
20 GOTO 10
```

These two lines of code just printed Hello again and again and again—but that's all it took to get me hooked.

Fifteen years later, while working at Microsoft, I signed up to teach programming to a group of fifth graders. It was then I realized that as programming as a discipline had gotten more and more sophisticated, the simplicity of BASIC had been lost. There was no easy way for children to experience the same instant gratification that I experienced using BASIC.

When researching tools that could make learning computer science fun and welcoming, I stumbled across the article "Why Johnny Can't Code"[1]). The article, published by Salon in 2006, argues that today's children are missing out on computer science because there aren't easy-to-use languages like BASIC readily available.

This inspired me to create Small Basic, a simple and easy way for children to learn programming.

But it's been far from an individual effort. Since launching Small Basic in 2011, the outpouring of support from the community has been incredible. The programming environment has extended in ways I couldn't have imagined—sensing hands and faces with Kinect, talking to robots, and even integrating with enterprise databases. Small Basic has been translated into more than twenty languages, and at the time of this writing, more than 280,000 programs have been uploaded to *http://www.smallbasic.com/* by children around the world.

The original vision of Small Basic is now being carried on by Ed Price and Michael Scherotter, along with the support of active community members like Nonki, LitDev, and many more.

Majed Marji is no stranger to teaching programming. Following his success with *Learn to Program with Scratch*, I was really excited to hear he was going to author this book along with Ed Price. I'm happy to see *Learn to Program with Small Basic* come alive and be available for everyone who wants to take their first step into programming. The book does a great job of introducing beginners to programming concepts while keeping the content fun and engaging.

Welcome to the magical world of programming. What do you want to create today?

Vijaye Raji
Creator of Small Basic
Director of Engineering, Facebook
Former Principal Software Architect, Microsoft

---

1. *http://www.salon.com/2006/09/14/basic_2/*

ACKNOWLEDGMENTS

This book represents the culmination of hard work from many people to whom I owe my thanks. I'd like to begin by recognizing the editorial and production departments at No Starch who have done an outstanding job in bringing out this book to life. In particular, it is a pleasure to acknowledge the help of our editor, Hayley Baker, and our production editor, Laurel Chun, who worked hard to ensure that everything came together like it was supposed to.

I'd also like to thank the book's technical editor, Vijaye Raji, for his thorough review and numerous constructive comments. Many thanks go to my coauthor, Ed Price, for making this book far better than it could have been without him.

And above all, my gratitude goes to my wife, Marina, and my two sons, Asad and Karam, who provided endless personal support. To them I owe an apology for the time this project has taken and my greatest thanks. The book is theirs too, and so is the spirit behind it. I dedicate this book to them as a sincere expression of appreciation and love.

Majed Marji

Firstly, I'd like to thank Majed for bringing me on this amazing journey with him. In college, I had a tough time learning C++, so with this book, Majed and I tried to write the programming learning experience that I wish I had had when I started programming.

I found Small Basic in 2012, while helping run Microsoft's MSDN forums, and was excited to see that the community was being led by the teachers. Thank you to Vijaye for creating Small Basic and to the Small Basic community for their passion, which inspired me to write for the Small Basic blog and work on two new releases of Small Basic with Kinect and LEGO® MINDSTORMS® support.

Thanks to my wife, my four daughters, and my infant son, Asher, who was raised during this book. I'd also like to thank Tyler Ortman and Bill Pollock from No Starch Press for their support and for sticking with us.

I dedicate this book to the Small Basic team (Michael, Ray, Li Xin, François, Deva, and Liz) and Community Council (Nonki, Steve, Rick, Yan, and Liam) for keeping the dream going!

Ed Price

INTRODUCTION

Have you ever wondered how people create computer programs? Have you ever wanted to conjure up your own video game? Have you ever flipped through a programming book and been discouraged by its dull language and boring examples? If so, there may be a computer programmer lurking inside you, waiting to be unleashed. Welcome to *Learn to Program with Small Basic*!

Microsoft Small Basic is a free, text-based programming language designed for beginners. It provides a complete programming environment that helps you write, test, and fine-tune your creations. This book shows you how to install Small Basic and how to use it to do amazing things. We'll show you that programming can be fun, rewarding, and—best of all—easy!

Who Should Read This Book?

You! This book introduces you to Small Basic in a fun, engaging, and interactive way. We offer an abundance of sample programs that you can run, explore, and tweak to make your own. Try every exercise and dig in to the extra online resources, review questions, and practice exercises. By the time you're done with this book, you'll be creating your own games!

If you're feeling inspired, you can share your Small Basic creations on the Small Basic MSDN forum, where the Small Basic Community Council will be waiting to answer any questions and check out all your awesome work.

What's in This Book?

Each chapter builds on the last one to help you hone your programming skills. We'll start you with the basics, and by the end, you'll be a total whiz!

- **Chapter 1: Introducing Small Basic** explains Small Basic's features and gets you set up. Then you'll create your first program.

- **Chapter 2: Getting Started** walks you through creating simple programs using Small Basic's built-in text window.

- **Chapter 3: Drawing Basics** shows you how to write programs that draw shapes in the graphics window.

- **Chapter 4: Using Variables** explains how variables keep track of information. Variables play a huge role in programming, and you'll use them throughout the book.

- **Chapter 5: Drawing Shapes with Turtle Graphics** teaches you how to command your own artistic turtle. You'll draw intricate geometric shapes and patterns that would be tiresome to do by hand.

- **Chapter 6: Getting User Input** shows you how to bring your programs to life by making them interactive. You'll write a program that can greet you by name.

- In **Chapter 7: Empowering Programs with Math**, you'll use math to make games, like a dice game that uses a random number generator.

- **Chapter 8: Making Decisions with If Statements** shows you how to control the logic and flow of your programs. With If statements under your belt, you'll be able to create even more powerful and exciting programs.

- In **Chapter 9: Using Decisions to Make Games**, you'll build on your knowledge of If statements and use them to make complex games.

- In **Chapter 10: Solving Problems with Subroutines**, you'll break down your code into simple sections that you use again and again. Then you'll put all your code together to make a game where you battle a fire-breathing dragon!

- In **Chapter 11: Event-Driven Programming**, you'll make interactive programs, such as a simple drawing program, that respond to user input.

- **Chapter 12: Building Graphical User Interfaces** covers how to create a full application with buttons, labels, and all the bells and whistles of a professional program. You'll build on your simple drawing program and create buttons that let your user change the pen color.

- **Chapter 13: Repeating For Loops** will show you how to use For loops in your programs to avoid repeating code. You'll learn how to automate boring tasks and draw a bunch of pictures in just a few lines of code.

- **Chapter 14: Creating Conditional While Loops** discusses more advanced conditional programming and ends with making a game of rock-paper-scissors you can play against the computer.

- **Chapter 15: Grouping Data in One-Dimensional Arrays** introduces arrays and how to store large amounts of data. Storing and manipulating data is another important aspect of programming, and you'll take advantage of it to program a magic 8 ball.

- **Chapter 16: Storing Data with Associative Arrays** shows you how to store strings in descriptive arrays. You'll transform your computer into a poet by writing a program that generates poems all on its own.

- Once you have a handle on arrays, in **Chapter 17: Expanding to Higher-Dimension Arrays**, you'll take arrays up to two or more dimensions, which lets you put a lot more data in them. At the end you'll create your own treasure-hunting game.

- **Chapter 18: Advanced Text Magic** teaches you how to handle and process text in your programs. Then you'll use your knowledge to write a simple spell-check program.

- **Chapter 19: Receiving File Input and Output** helps you build bigger programs by teaching you how to handle files full of data. You'll then use that knowledge to create a program featuring a math wizard.

Online Resources

Visit *http://www.nostarch.com/smallbasic/* to download the extra book resources and to find updates. You'll find these additional resources and review questions for teachers and students:

Book Programs and Solutions   Download the finished programs, all the images you'll need, some skeleton code for the Programming Challenges, and the solutions to the Programming Challenges and Try It Out exercises. This will save wear and tear on your typing fingers!

Additional Resources   These are online articles that relate to the topics covered in this book. Many of these were written just to supplement the book!

Review Questions   Test your knowledge (or your student's knowledge).

Practice Exercises   In addition to the Try It Out exercises and the Programming Challenges in the book, you can even find more exercises to practice. This is also great for teachers who want more options for assignments.

A Note to the Reader

When learning a new skill, there's nothing more important than practice. Reading this book is only the first step. To become a great programmer, you must program! The more of the book's resources you use, the more you learn. Don't be afraid to experiment. No matter what buttons you press or what commands you give, you won't hurt the computer. We promise.

With a little patience and dedication, you'll soon amaze your friends with the wonderful things you'll create. We want to empower you to make fun games and even to change the world!

1

INTRODUCING SMALL BASIC

Bill Gates once had a goal to get a computer into every home. Now, nearly every desk has a personal computer—so just about anyone can learn to code, too. In this book, you'll learn to program with a language called Microsoft Small Basic.

We'll start this chapter by explaining some general computing concepts and Small Basic itself. Then we'll show you how to set up everything you need to use Small Basic and top it off with writing your first program!

What Is a Computer?

A computer is an electronic device that processes data according to a set of instructions—it's that magical device in your pocket or on your desk or lap. Computers can perform calculations (like your math teacher) and compare numbers (like in fantasy football), and they can store, retrieve, and process data at high levels of speed and accuracy (like parents remembering a curfew).

A computer's hardware is everything you can touch on your computer—inside the guts of every computer are hundreds of interconnected electronic pieces. If you want to imagine data inside your computer, picture a massive mall with hundreds of stores and tens of thousands of shoppers moving like clockwork between the stores.

But without something more, all that hardware couldn't do anything useful. Every computer requires programs to tell it what to do—we call these instructions *software*. The people who can write software are called *programmers*—and you're about to become one today.

What Is a Computer Program?

A computer program is a set of instructions given to a computer to perform a task (like a list of homework from your teacher). Your web browser, your favorite video games, word processors—these are all computer programs.

A program tells the computer what data to read (like numbers or text), where to read the data from (like from a user, file, or the Internet), how to process this data (it might search, sort, or calculate the data), what kind of information to produce (like paragraphs, reports, or graphs), where to store the produced output (like a disk, network, or database), and how to display the results (like through a monitor, printer, or plotter). Whoa, that's a lot!

A computer program specifies every detail along the way. Computers communicate in machine language, which is a bunch of 1s and 0s. (Can you imagine talking 1s and 0s to your friends?) A long time ago, the first computer programs ever written were actually entered into to the computer by flipping some switches on the computer's front panel (on for 1, off for 0). Would you want to flip switches all day? Imagine the errors!

Luckily, computer scientists invented programming languages, which are a lot easier to use than machine language. Today there are hundreds of programming languages, but Small Basic is the programming language you'll learn in this book!

What Is Small Basic?

Small Basic is a free programming language that Microsoft created for anyone who wants to learn programming. You can write all kinds of applications with Small Basic, including games, simulations, animations, and more.

How did the language come about? It started with a programmer at Microsoft named Vijaye Raji. Raji had just read David Brin's article, "Why Johnny Can't Code,"[1] which describes how valuable it is to learn and teach coding in BASIC. In his article, Brin challenged Microsoft to make a new

---

1. *http://www.salon.com/2006/09/14/basic_2/*

BASIC language that would help kids learn to code, and Raji accepted that challenge. Although BASIC was crucial to Microsoft's success in the 1970s, 1980s, and 1990s, there really wasn't a great programming language suitable for beginners in 2007.

So Raji wondered if he could create a smaller version of BASIC using only the simplest parts of the original language. On October 23, 2008, he released Microsoft Small Basic v0.1, the first version of Small Basic.

The Vision of Small Basic

Small Basic's four goals will help make your learning experience as awesome as possible:

- **It's Simple.** Small Basic is a simple programming language with a helpful code Editor and a Help Area to make coding easy.
- **It's Fun.** Small Basic lets you create games and other cool programs right away. It also lets you command a turtle to make art, and it's fun to use!
- **It's Social.** With Small Basic, you can publish your game to the Web on the Microsoft gallery, show it to your friends, and embed it on your blog or website. Your friends can import your program and collaborate with you to make it better.
- **It's Gradual.** Once you learn the fundamentals of programming with Small Basic, it's easy to export your code into the free Visual Studio Community and start a new adventure with Visual Basic .NET, a programming language that's used by millions of professional programmers and an important next step in your learning journey.

We'll cover everything you need to get started with Small Basic in this book!

The Basics of Small Basic

The three main parts of Small Basic are the language, the supporting library, and the *programming environment*, which is the interface you'll use to write your own programs. Let's explore each element now.

The Small Basic Language

To form a valid sentence in English, you need to follow its grammatical rules. In the same way, to write a valid Small Basic program, you must follow the grammatical rules of Small Basic, which are called *syntax rules*. Syntax includes punctuation, spelling, statement ordering, and so on. When you break these rules, Small Basic detects all the *syntax errors* in your program and reports them to you so you can fix them.

The Small Basic Library

The Small Basic *library* contains hundreds of methods that you can use in your programs to perform different tasks. For example, you can use these methods when you want to tell the computer to display an image on the screen, draw a circle, download a file from the Internet, or even compute the square root of 275,625.

The Small Basic Development Environment

Small Basic comes with an *integrated development environment (IDE)*, which is the application you'll use to write your programs. The IDE contains a text Editor (in which you'll type your program) and a Toolbar. The Toolbar has buttons that let you save and run your program, open a program so you can modify it, share your program on the Web, graduate your program to Visual Basic, and much more.

Installing Small Basic

The first step in your learning journey is to install Small Basic on your computer. Open your web browser, go to Microsoft's Small Basic website at *http://www.smallbasic.com/*, and click the **Download** button in the upper-right corner. You'll go to the Download page to pick your operating system and language. When you start the download, a dialog appears asking for your permission to open the *SmallBasic.msi* file. Click the **Run** or **Open** button to start the setup wizard.

When the wizard starts, click **Next** on the first page, accept the License Agreement, click **Next** again, click **Next** for the default setup, and then click **Install**. (If a User Access Control dialog pops up and asks for your permission to install the program, click **Yes**.) Click **Finish** when the installation is done. If you need to see these steps in detail, check out *http://tiny.cc/installationguide/*.

The Small Basic IDE

Now that your installation is complete, let's take a look at the Small Basic IDE. Open the Windows Start menu, and either type **Small Basic** to search for it (and click to open it) or select **All Programs ▸ Small Basic ▸ Microsoft Small Basic**. When you run the program for the first time, you'll see something like Figure 1-1 (enter `Prog` in the Editor to see the IntelliSense menu).

The IDE contains four main parts. The Editor ❶ is where you enter your Small Basic programs. You can open and work with multiple Editor windows at the same time, but only one Editor is active at once. Right-click the Editor to see a pop-up menu with options like Cut, Copy, Paste, and Find. The menu also has a Format Program option that indents the lines in your program to make it easier to read.

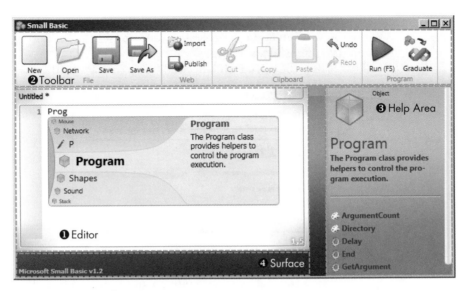

Figure 1-1: The Small Basic IDE

The Toolbar ❷ contains buttons that let you edit and run your program, and the Help Area ❸ provides instant information about the code you enter into the Editor. The Surface ❹ is an open area where you can move and organize your Editor windows for each Small Basic program.

You'll use the Toolbar a lot, so let's explore it in detail.

Opening and Saving Your Work

In the Toolbar's File group, click **New** (CTRL-N) to start programming from scratch, or click **Open** (CTRL-O) to pick up where you left off in writing a program. **Save** (CTRL-S) often so you don't lose your work, and click **Save As** to save your program in a new file.

Sharing Your Work and Importing Games

Let's say your friend just published a new game to the Small Basic website, and you want to check it out. In the Web group, click **Import** to enter the Import ID (which you get from your friend) and download your friend's code. Then you can make the game even cooler with your own modifications.

Let's try opening a game that someone has already made. Click **Import**, and then enter the code **TETRIS**. You'll see the code someone wrote to re-create the famous game, and you can see how it was made. To play the game now, click **Run**.

Later, when you're ready to share your own programs, you can click **Publish**, and Small Basic will publish your program to the Web so your friends can play your game or app online and see your code. You can also share your program in the Small Basic forum to get direct help from the community. Small Basic even gives you the option to embed your code snippet so you can add the project to your website. You'll find the embed code on the published web page.

When you click **Publish**, you'll see a dialog like the one in Figure 1-2.

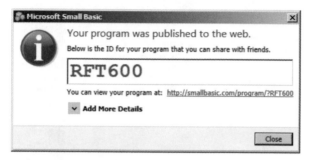

Figure 1-2: The Publish to Web dialog

When you Publish your code, in addition to getting the Import ID and the web page URL, you can also click **Add More Details** to enter a title, description, and category (like *game, sample exercise, example, math, fun,* or *miscellaneous*) for your program.

Copy and Paste; Undo and Redo

In Small Basic, you can edit your code like you're editing any kind of text. From the Clipboard group, click **Cut** (CTRL-X) to remove a piece of code from one place in the Editor to paste it somewhere else. To avoid retyping code, click **Copy** (CTRL-C). To select all your code, press CTRL-A, and then cut or copy it.

After you cut or copy, click **Paste** (CTRL-V) to paste the contents into the Editor. If you make a mistake, no worries! Just click **Undo** (CTRL-Z). If you click **Undo** too many times, click **Redo** (CTRL-Y) to reverse the change. You can also look for a bit of code in a large file. To open the Find window and search for your text, just press F3, press CTRL-F, or right-click in the Editor and click **Find** in the context menu.

Running Your Program and Graduating

When you finish a program, click **Run** (F5) in the Program group to *compile* it; the Small Basic compiler, which is part of the IDE, checks if you have any errors, and if not, builds your program. When you've mastered Small Basic, just click **Graduate** to export your code into Visual Basic in Visual Studio Community and go on to learn your next language.

Writing and Running Your First Program

Now that you know your way around the IDE, let's write a Small Basic program. First, create a new folder on your computer called *Small Basic*; this is where you'll save all the programs you create throughout this book.

Then click the **New** button to open a new Editor window, and follow these steps:

1. Enter the program in Listing 1-1 into the Editor. You'll need to enter it exactly as you see it.

```
1 ' Greetings.sb
2 TextWindow.WriteLine("Greetings, Planet!")
```

Listing 1-1: Your first program

NOTE *When you enter a listing to try it out, don't include the line numbers at the left! These numbers are just for reference; we'll use them to explain the code. You'll see them in your Editor, too, but they aren't part of your code.*

2. Click the **Save** button on the Toolbar (or press CTRL-S), browse to the *Small Basic* folder you just made, and save your program as *Greetings.sb*.

3. Click **Run** on the Toolbar. If you didn't make any typing mistakes, you'll see an output window like the one in Figure 1-3.

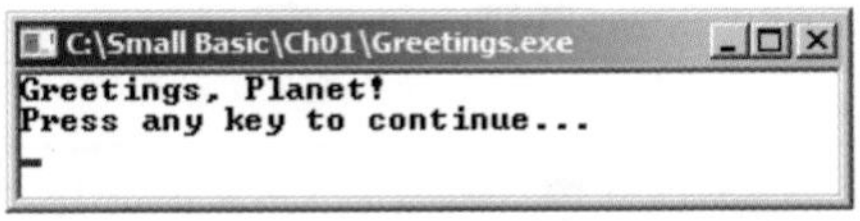

Figure 1-3: The output of Greetings.sb

NOTE *When you run this program, your window will have a black background; that is the default background color for the text window. The images in this book were created with a white background to make it easier for you to read them.*

Even though it's short, this is a complete Small Basic program! But what does each piece of the program do? Let's dissect it.

Objects and Methods

The window in Figure 1-3 is the *text window*, and it can only display text. You told Small Basic to bring up the text window using TextWindow, one of the many *objects* in the Small Basic library. You can think of an object as a little toolbox for a specific job, such as doing math problems, defining words, or drawing pictures.

Objects in Small Basic can perform predefined tasks using *methods*. Methods are like the tools in your object toolbox. To get most methods to do something, you have to give them one or more values (such as text or numbers) to act on. Each value is called an *argument*.

WriteLine() is one method of the TextWindow object, and the message "Greetings, Planet!" is an argument that goes in the parentheses. The statement TextWindow.WriteLine() instructs the computer to display the message Greetings, Planet! in the text window.

Throughout this book we'll include parentheses with the names of the methods, like WriteLine(), so you can easily tell that they're methods.

Naming Your Programs

Project names can make it easy for you to identify what your project is about; these names don't really matter much to Small Basic. Although we asked you to save this program as *Greetings.sb* because it was what the program was about, you could save it as *SecretGarden.sb*, *FuzzyKittens.sb*, or even *HungerBoardGames.sb*, if you really wanted to. Just don't change the *.sb* part of the filename, which is called the *extension*. Small Basic programs use that extension by default, and there's no reason to change it!

Files Generated by Small Basic

When you click the Run button, Small Basic creates other files in order to run your program. Open the folder where you saved your *Greetings.sb* program. Table 1-1 lists the files you should find in that folder if you clicked Run earlier.

Table 1-1: Files Generated by the Small Basic Compiler

File	Description
Greetings.sb	This is your *source code* file, which contains everything you entered into the IDE. If you want to edit your code and make it better, you edit this file.
Greetings.exe	This is the executable file created by Small Basic. This file is what your computer actually runs. Double-click this file, and your program will run.
SmallBasicLibrary.dll	You can ignore this file for now. The dynamic link library (.*dll*) file contains executable code that supplements your *Greetings .exe* file. The *Greetings.exe* file won't run without this file!
Greetings.pdb	You can ignore this file for now, too. This program database (.*pdb*) file contains information that is used by advanced tools to *debug*, or fix any errors, in the program.

Now that you've compiled your source code, you can also run your *Greetings.sb* program without using the IDE. You do this by double-clicking the *Greetings.exe* file.

NOTE *When you click Run after editing your source file, Small Basic overwrites the .exe, .dll, and .pdb files. If you want to keep these files, you need to manually copy them to a different location before you click Run. Also, don't forget to click Save to save the changes to your .sb file.*

Helping Hands: IntelliSense and Syntax Coloring

If you're following along and typing in Small Basic, you've seen how it analyzes what you type, even before you finish the word. Small Basic offers a list of suggestions that could help you complete what you're typing. You can scroll through this list by pressing the up and down arrows on your keyboard. Press ENTER or double-click your selection to insert the highlighted text into your code. This technology is called *intelligent sense* or *IntelliSense* for short. Use it to speed up your typing time and reduce your syntax errors.

TIP   *You can make IntelliSense transparent by just holding down the* CTRL *key to see your code underneath it.*

You might have also noticed that the Small Basic Editor used different colors for some words in the program. This feature is called *syntax coloring.* *Keywords*, which are reserved words with special meanings to Small Basic, are shown in blue-purple. S*trings*, which are sequences of characters enclosed in quotes, are orange, and so are numbers. Method names are dark red, object names are blue-green, and so on. Syntax coloring helps you distinguish the different parts of the code and makes your program easier to read. You'll learn more about these parts of code later in the book.

Drawing with Small Basic

The TextWindow object we used earlier works well for applications that don't have a *graphical user interface (GUI)*, which is a user interface that contains buttons, text boxes, and images, like Microsoft Word or Angry Birds (or Angry Words). For example, you can use TextWindow to write applications that perform math problems or that process data, where the input and output use only characters (like text). This is called a *text-based user interface.* If you want to create an application with a GUI (pronounced *gooey*, like a candy bar), complete with buttons and images, you can use the Small Basic library's GraphicsWindow object. Using GraphicsWindow, you can create applications that show buttons, images, and more for your users to interact with. Let's try it out!

Enter the program in Listing 1-2 into the Editor, and then click **Run** in the Toolbar.

```
1  ' Graphic.sb
2  GraphicsWindow.DrawText(100, 50, "Greetings, Planet!")
```

Listing 1-2: Your first graphical program

This program uses the DrawText() method of the GraphicsWindow object to display a message. The DrawText() method requires three arguments. The first two arguments tell Small Basic the horizontal (*x*) and vertical (*y*) positions of the output message, starting in the upper-left corner of the window. The third argument tells Small Basic what text to display. The output of this program is shown in Figure 1-4. As you can see, the message is displayed at position (100, 50).

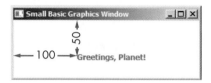

Figure 1-4: The output of Graphic.sb

The GraphicsWindow object contains many other methods that let you create GUI applications; explore a few of them in Try It Out 1-1.

TRY IT OUT 1-1

Enter the following program into the Editor, and then run it to see what happens:

```
GraphicsWindow.DrawEllipse(20, 20, 100, 100)
GraphicsWindow.DrawRectangle(140, 20, 100, 100)
GraphicsWindow.FillEllipse(260, 20, 200, 100)
```

The output of the program is shown in Figure 1-5. The numbers illustrate how Small Basic followed your code.

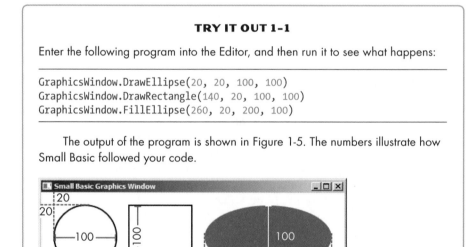

Figure 1-5: The output of the program

Programming Challenges

If you get stuck, check out *http://nostarch.com/smallbasic/* for the solutions and for more resources and review questions for teachers and students.

1. Identify the objects, methods, arguments, and keywords in the following code snippet. (Hint: the Small Basic editor shows keywords in blue-purple.)

```
If (today = "Friday") Then
  TextWindow.WriteLine("Today is Friday.")
Else
    TextWindow.WriteLine("I lost track of what day it is.")
EndIf
```

2. Write a program to display your name in the text window.

3. Write a program to display your name in a message box using the GraphicsWindow object. (Hint: use the ShowMessage() method.)

2

GETTING STARTED

Now we'll walk through some code
step-by-step, so you can learn about
the important pieces. As you read, enter
the examples, and we'll explain how to run
them and modify them. But don't stop there: experiment to give your programs a personal touch. We've
included exercises at the end of each section to help
you become a programming master (like a Jedi, but
without the dangerous lightsabers). Try out the exercises to hone your skills.

The Parts of a Program

Let's explore the different parts of a program by looking at a simple example. Listing 2-1 shows a program similar to the *Greetings.sb* program you wrote in Chapter 1. Enter this program into the Small Basic Editor, and then click the **Run** button on the Toolbar (or press F5 on your keyboard) to run it.

```
1  ' Welcome.sb
2  TextWindow.WriteLine("Welcome to Small Basic.")
```

Listing 2-1: Writing a welcome message

These two lines are the *source code* of your *Welcome.sb* program. When you run this code, you'll see an output window that looks like Figure 2-1. (Note that the window's title shows where we saved the file, so yours could be different.)

Figure 2-1: The output window for Welcome.sb

NOTE   *Your console window will look slightly different from this one, since the window has a black background by default. For the rest of the book, we'll show the output as text, except when it's necessary to see the window.*

Small Basic automatically adds the text Press any key to continue... to the window to give you a chance to view the output (there isn't an *any* key on your keyboard, so don't look for it). Otherwise, the screen would flash your output and disappear.

Comments and Statements

The line that starts with a single quote (') is called a *comment*. You can add comments to explain what your program does, and Small Basic just ignores them. The comment on line 1 is the name of the file that contains your source code.

NOTE   *You should get into the habit of commenting your code, because you'll often head to the forums or to friends for help, and they'll need to understand what your code is trying to do.*

The Small Basic Editor shows all comments in green so you can easily tell them apart from lines of actual code, which are called *statements*. Comments make programs easier to read, and you can add them anywhere! But be careful not to use too many comments, or you might make your code even harder to read! It's a good practice to write comments at the beginning of your code to describe your program or to explain any tricky parts.

If you add a blank line that separates the comments from the code, Small Basic also ignores it, so add as many empty lines as you need to make your program easier to read! Line 2 in *Welcome.sb* is your program's first statement, and that's where the program begins executing. (Don't worry: nobody dies!)

Figure 2-2 shows the parts of our statement. Let's break it down and see what each part does!

Figure 2-2: The statement in Welcome.sb

TextWindow is an object built into Small Basic that takes text input and sends text output to your screen. WriteLine() is a method of the TextWindow object. This method displays the data passed to it in the output window. When you use TextWindow.WriteLine(), you tell the TextWindow object to execute its WriteLine() method. This is known as *dot notation* because of the dot between the object and the method. Dot notation is used to access an object's method and follows this format: ObjectName.MethodName(Arguments). In this example, "Welcome to Small Basic." is an argument to the WriteLine() method. It tells the method exactly what you want to write.

Characters and Strings

Letters, numbers, punctuation marks (dot, colon, semicolon, and so on), and other symbols are called *characters*. A sequence of these characters surrounded by double quotes is called a *string*. The quotation marks show where the string starts and ends.

In our *Welcome.sb* program, the text that reads "Welcome to Small Basic." is a string.

Arguments and Methods

You pass *arguments* to a method inside its parentheses. An argument can be a string, a number, or some other value. The WriteLine() method accepts only one argument, and in your *Welcome.sb* program you pass it the string "Welcome to Small Basic." as its argument.

Click the WriteLine() method in the Editor, and check Small Basic's Help Area (Figure 2-3). It'll show you what kind of data to pass to that method.

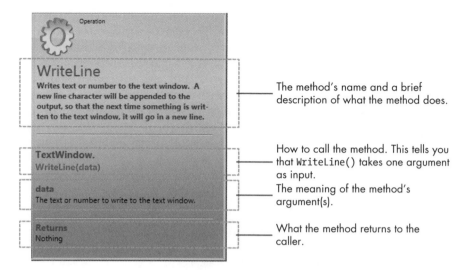

The method's name and a brief description of what the method does.

How to call the method. This tells you that WriteLine() takes one argument as input.

The meaning of the method's argument(s).

What the method returns to the caller.

Figure 2-3: The Help Area information for the WriteLine() method

The Help Area is your friend! Read it to avoid needless mistakes and frustration.

TRY IT OUT 2-1

Point out the object, method, and arguments in these calls:

1. Shapes.AddRectangle(100, 50)
2. Math.Max(5, 10)
3. Sound.PlayBellRing()

Exploring Other Features

In this section, you'll explore other key features of Small Basic by making small changes to the *Welcome.sb* program. Each example highlights a different feature, so let's jump right in! Small Basic is warm and inviting!

Case Sensitivity

You originally entered TextWindow.WriteLine("Welcome to Small Basic."), but Small Basic wouldn't care if you changed the case of any letter in TextWindow or WriteLine. For example, you could write: TextWindow.writeLINE("Welcome to Small Basic."). This gives you the same output as before because Small Basic is *case insensitive*, which means that it doesn't matter if your code is written in uppercase or lowercase letters.

Identifiers like Writeline, writeline, and WRiTeLiNe are all interpreted the same way by the *compiler*, which reads each line of code and builds the application. But you should get into the habit of respecting the case of identifiers because other languages are *case sensitive*. Small Basic is like a friendly coach who won't yell at you for improper capitalization. It'll even fix your typing mistakes for you, thanks to IntelliSense's autocorrect function.

But what happens if you change the string? Try entering the welcome message in all capital letters:

```
TextWindow.WriteLine("WELCOME TO SMALL BASIC.")
```

When you run this program, WELCOME TO SMALL BASIC. is displayed in all capital letters in the output window. Why? The reason is that Small Basic's WriteLine() method displays anything between the quotes exactly as you wrote it!

Sequential Execution

Listing 2-1 displays only one line of text, but you could display as many lines as you want. Let's follow Listing 2-2 to extend the program to display three lines!

```
1  ' ThreeLines.sb
2  TextWindow.WriteLine("Welcome to Small Basic.")
3  TextWindow.WriteLine("")
4  TextWindow.WriteLine("Anyone can code!")
```

Listing 2-2: Displaying more lines

When you run this program, you'll see this output:

```
Welcome to Small Basic.

Anyone can code!
```

Your program's output shows that each line is executed in the order it's listed in the program, from top to bottom. Do you see that empty line in the output? That was made by the statement in line 3 where you gave WriteLine() a pair of double quotes with no characters inside them. Because "" contains no characters, it's called an *empty string*. Empty strings are useful when you want to display empty lines to break up the program's output and make it easier to read.

Displaying Numbers and Doing Math

You can also use WriteLine() to display numbers. Try out Listing 2-3.

```
1  ' TextAndNum.sb
2  TextWindow.WriteLine("5 + 7")
3  TextWindow.WriteLine(5 + 7)
```

Listing 2-3: Showing the difference between strings and numbers

Here's the output of this program:

```
5 + 7
12
```

When you pass anything to WriteLine() in double quotes, the output window shows exactly what's inside the quotes. So, when you pass "5 + 7" to WriteLine() in line 2, Small Basic treats the plus sign inside the string like any other character and doesn't see it as an addition problem!

The WriteLine() command on line 3, however, is different. You passed 5 + 7 to WriteLine() *without* double quotes. In this case, Small Basic understands that these are numbers, not parts of a string. Behind the scenes it adds 5 to 7 to get 12 and passes the sum to WriteLine().

Joining Strings

You can also add strings together to build sentences or add to phrases, as shown in Listing 2-4. Combining strings is called *concatenation*.

```
1  ' JoinString.sb
2  TextWindow.WriteLine("Hello," + " oblate spheroid!")
```

Listing 2-4: Explaining concatenation

In line 2 of Listing 2-4, the WriteLine() method takes two strings, "Hello," and " oblate spheroid!", with a plus sign (+) between them. In this case, because you're not performing addition, the plus sign has a different meaning: it's called a *concatenation operator*, which joins two strings together into a single string. Notice the extra space in " oblate spheroid!". It makes your message display with a space between the words.

The plus sign (+) glues "Hello," onto " oblate spheroid!" and creates the new string "Hello, oblate spheroid!".

You can also join strings and numbers together. Small Basic automatically converts any number to a string so that concatenation can do its thing! Take a look at Listing 2-5 and its output in Figure 2-4.

```
1  ' JoinNum.sb
2  TextWindow.WriteLine("Let's concatenate: 5 + 7 = " + 12)
```

Listing 2-5: Adding a number to text

The WriteLine() method needs a string as an argument. To create that string, Small Basic turns the entire argument into a string, as shown in Figure 2-4. It converts the number 12 to a string ("12") and then glues it to "Let's concatenate: 5 + 7 = " to make a new string: "Let's concatenate: 5 + 7 = 12".

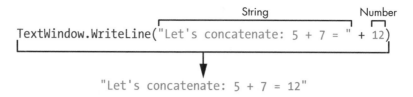

```
TextWindow.WriteLine("Let's concatenate: 5 + 7 = " + 12)
```

                    String   Number

"Let's concatenate: 5 + 7 = 12"

Figure 2-4: Using the plus sign to join a string and a number

---

TRY IT OUT 2-2

Write a program to display Figure 2-5.

```
 *------*
_|(.)(.)|_
\|  /\  |/
 | \_/ |
 *--||--*
  __/\__
```

Figure 2-5: Making a face

Object Properties

Small Basic objects can have *properties* (or attributes) that you can change. If you change these properties, the object's methods may give you different outcomes when you call them.

For example, let's imagine a new object named Frog that contains two methods, Jump() and Eat(), and one property called EnergyLevel. When you call the Jump() method, Frog jumps, but each jump causes its EnergyLevel to go down. You can call the Eat() method to restore its energy. If you keep ordering the Frog to jump without feeding it, the Frog runs out of energy and can't jump anymore. The outcome of calling the Jump() method depends on the current value of the EnergyLevel property. The property changes the *state* of the Frog object (whether it can jump or not). Calling Jump() at one state (when EnergyLevel is high) gives a different output than calling Jump() at a different state (when EnergyLevel is low). Poor hungry frog!

Setting and Changing Property Values

Here's the general format for setting or changing a property of an object:

ObjectName.PropertyName = Value

For example, to make the TextWindow object output yellow text, you would enter:

```
TextWindow.ForegroundColor = "Yellow"
```

That statement changes the TextWindow object's state: after this statement, any text printed by calling WriteLine() is displayed in yellow. But any text that has already been displayed in the text window won't be affected. The statement tells the TextWindow object, "From this point on display text using a yellow color."

Working with Properties

Listing 2-6 shows some ways you can put the TextWindow properties to use.

```
1  ' Properties.sb
2  TextWindow.Title = "Discovering Properties..."
3  TextWindow.BackgroundColor = "Yellow"
4  TextWindow.Clear()
5
6  TextWindow.CursorLeft = 4
7  TextWindow.CursorTop = 1
8  TextWindow.ForegroundColor = "Blue"
9  TextWindow.Write("BLUE TEXT")
10
11 TextWindow.CursorTop = 3
12 TextWindow.ForegroundColor = "Red"
13 TextWindow.Write("RED TEXT")
14
15 TextWindow.CursorLeft = 1
16 TextWindow.CursorTop = 5
17 TextWindow.BackgroundColor = "Green"
```

Listing 2-6: Placing and coloring your text

Running this code gives you the output in Figure 2-6.

Figure 2-6: The output of Properties.sb

Now let's walk through the code. Figure 2-7 will help you visualize what's happening. It illustrates the text window as a rectangular grid of characters and shows the position of the cursor after Small Basic completes each statement.

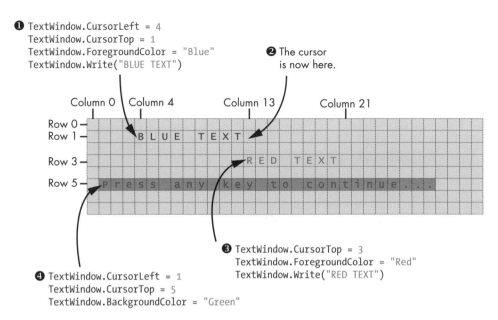

```
❶ TextWindow.CursorLeft = 4
  TextWindow.CursorTop = 1
  TextWindow.ForegroundColor = "Blue"
  TextWindow.Write("BLUE TEXT")
```

❷ The cursor
   is now here.

Column 0   Column 4   Column 13   Column 21

Row 0 —
Row 1 —   B L U E   T E X T

Row 3 —   R E D   T E X T

Row 5 —   P r e s s   a n y   k e y   t o   c o n t i n u e . . .

❸ TextWindow.CursorTop = 3
  TextWindow.ForegroundColor = "Red"
  TextWindow.Write("RED TEXT")

```
❹ TextWindow.CursorLeft = 1
  TextWindow.CursorTop = 5
  TextWindow.BackgroundColor = "Green"
```

Figure 2-7: Illustrating the output of Properties.sb

Line 2 sets the Title property, which tells Small Basic the title of the text window. Line 3 sets the BackgroundColor property to "Yellow" for all the upcoming text outputs. The Clear() method (line 4) tells TextWindow to repaint itself using its BackgroundColor property, which is what makes the window's background yellow. Try removing this line from the program to see what changes in your program's output.

Lines 6–8 set the cursor position to column 4, row 1 and set the foreground color (the text color) to blue for the next output. The Write() method at line 9 writes the string "BLUE TEXT", starting at the current position of the cursor. The Write() method is just like the WriteLine() method, except it doesn't move the cursor to the next line after it displays the string. After this call, the cursor is at column 13 but still in row 1.

Line 11 moves the cursor down to row 3. Line 12 sets the foreground color to red, and line 13 calls Write() to display the string "RED TEXT".

Lines 15 and 16 move the cursor to column 1, row 5; line 17 sets the background color to green. This is the last statement, so the program *terminates* at this point (because there's no more code to run). Because the foreground color of the text window is still set to red, the Press any key to continue... message is displayed in red on a green background.

TIP   *For a complete list of colors you can use in the text window, see* http://tiny.cc/twcolors.

Arithmetic Operators

Computers are excellent for crunching numbers (they megabyte!) and work great as glorified calculators. Small Basic includes the four basic arithmetic operations: addition, subtraction, multiplication, and division, which are represented by +, -, *, and /, respectively. Those symbols are called *operators* because they operate on values, which are called *operands*. Let's look at a few examples. These math operations will be familiar to you. Try entering these lines in the Editor:

```
TextWindow.Writeline(4 + 5)
TextWindow.Writeline(3 / 6)
TextWindow.Writeline(8.0 / 4)
TextWindow.Writeline(3 * 4)
TextWindow.Writeline(9 - 3)
```

When you run this program, each answer appears on a new line, like this:

```
9
0.5
2
12
6
```

But how would Small Basic find the result of an expression like this: 6 * 2 + 3? Does this mean multiply 6 times 2 and then add 3, which equals

15, or multiply 6 times the sum of 2 and 3, which equals 30? When an arithmetic expression contains different operators, Small Basic completes the expression using the same *priority* used in algebra, as shown in Figure 2-9.

❶	( )	Parentheses come first, then . . .
❷	* /	multiplication and division are performed in order of occurrence (from left to right), then . . .
❸	+ –	addition and subtraction are performed in order of occurrence (from left to right).

Figure 2-9: The order of operations in Small Basic

So, for 6 * 2 + 3 with no parentheses, Small Basic would multiply 6 times 2 and then add 3, for a result of 15.

As in ordinary math, each left parenthesis in a Small Basic program must have a matching right parenthesis. For example, the expression (6 + 4) is valid, but (6 + (8 - 2))) isn't valid because it has an extra right parenthesis.

To make sure you get the results you want, use parentheses to clarify the order of operations. This helps you avoid mistakes and makes your code easier to understand. For example, enter the following:

```
TextWindow.WriteLine((3.5 + 6.5) - (5 - 2.5))
```

If you placed your parentheses correctly, you should get 7.5.

Adding a single space on both sides of an operator is also a good idea. For example, the expression 5 + 4 * 8 is easier to read than 5+4*8. Although Small Basic can read two consecutive arithmetic operators, as in 3*-8, it's best to put the negative number in parentheses, such as 3 * (-8) to make your code easy to read and avoid any confusion.

TRY IT OUT 2-4

In Lewis Carroll's *Through the Looking Glass*, the Red Queen and the White Queen ask Alice to do some addition and subtraction in Wonderland. Using the WriteLine() method, create Small Basic programs to help her solve these two problems:

"Can you do Addition?" the White Queen asked. "What's one and one and one and one and one and one and one and one and one and one?"

"I don't know," said Alice. "I lost count."

"She can't do Addition," the Red Queen interrupted, "Can you do Subtraction? Take nine from eight."

"Nine from eight I can't, you know," Alice replied very readily: "but—"

Programming Errors

Just because a program runs doesn't mean it's correct. All programmers make errors at some point, especially when they write long programs. But don't worry! You'll make fewer errors the more you practice. Three main types of errors in programming are syntax errors, logic errors, and runtime errors; we'll teach you how to find and fix them.

Syntax Errors

Errors pop up whenever a program breaks one of the language's syntax rules. Examples of syntax errors include the following:

- Missing punctuation, such as in `TextWindow.WriteLine("Hello)`, which includes a string without an ending quote
- Extra punctuation at the end of a statement
- Misspelled keywords, such as `Whle` instead of `While`
- Arithmetic operators used incorrectly, such as `5 ** 2`
- Mismatched parentheses in arithmetic expressions, such as `5 * (6 - (3 + 2)`

NOTE   *A keyword is a special word that tells Small Basic to do something, like to repeat a statement. We'll explain each one in later chapters.*

Fortunately, the minute you click the Run button, Small Basic discovers any syntax errors and describes them in an *error message*. The error message lists the line numbers in your source code where the errors were found (see Figure 2-10). If your program contains a syntax error, look at the line that contains the error and see if you can fix it!

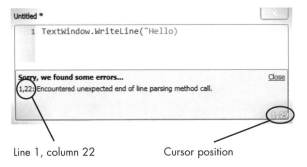

Figure 2-10: An example of a syntax error

Need to find the problem fast? Just double-click the error message to jump to the line that contains the error. (Pretty awesome, huh?)

Logic Errors

Sometimes, you might make a mistake in your program's logic. These *logic errors* cause your programs to produce the wrong results. For example, if you accidentally used a minus sign instead of a plus sign, you've made a logic error. Your program runs normally, but the output's incorrect!

Logic errors are called *bugs*, and *debugging* is the process we use for finding and fixing these bugs. For short programs, you might be able to locate the bugs by *hand tracing*, which means you read the program line by line and write down the output you expect for each step. Another common technique is to insert additional WriteLine() statements to display the output at different parts of the program. This helps you narrow down the lines where the program might have gone wrong.

Runtime Errors

Runtime errors happen after you run your program, when it experiences a problem that's not solved in your code. For example, your user may enter bad numbers that can cause your program to stop working, or crash. You'll discover these errors yourself when you start tinkering with Small Basic.

Programming Challenges

If you get stuck, check out *http://nostarch.com/smallbasic/* for the solutions and for more resources and review questions for teachers and students.

1. Write a program that displays your name and age, similar to the following output. Use colors to make the output fit your own style!

    ```
    My name is Sandra Wilson
    I am 12 years old
    ```

2. Replace the question marks in the following program with strings that give your user information about the order of an element in the periodic table. Run the program to check its output.

    ```
    TextWindow.Write("?" + " is the " + "?")
    TextWindow.WriteLine(" element in the periodic table.")
    ```

3. Cathy wrote the following program to figure out how much money she earned from babysitting. But there's a problem: her program doesn't work. Help Cathy find the bug in her program and fix it.

    ```
    ' This program computes my earnings from babysitting.
    ' Hours worked: 20
    ' Pay rate: $4 per hour

    TextWindow.WriteLine("I earned: $" (20 * 4))
    ```

4. Write a program that creates a Christmas card similar to the one shown here. Use any colors to decorate the tree.

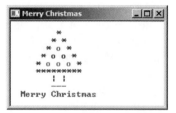

3

DRAWING BASICS

With Small Basic you can become a masterful artist. Instead of a paintbrush, you've got the power of code. Let's jump in so you can start creating your very own masterpiece! We showed you the `TextWindow` object, but in this chapter, you'll explore the `GraphicsWindow` object, which includes methods that draw lines, triangles, rectangles, ellipses, and even fancy text.

The Graphics Coordinate System

Think of the graphics window as a rectangular grid. Every point on this grid is described with two numbers, called *coordinates*. The x-coordinate tells you a point's horizontal position, and the y-coordinate tells you a point's vertical position. You specify the point's location using parentheses, like this: (x, y).

In the system you use at school, point (0, 0) is in the middle of the graph, but things are a little different in the graphics window. Figure 3-1 shows you that point (0, 0) is in the upper-left corner of the graphics window, which means you can only see the points that have positive x- and y- values.

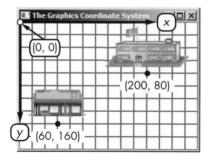

Figure 3-1: The coordinate system of the graphics window

Now that you know how the graphics window's coordinate system works, let's play around with it. The next sections take you on a tour of some methods you can use to draw simple pictures. Throughout the chapter, we'll show you drawings to create with Small Basic, and we'll include the gridlines to help you visualize the coordinates involved in each shape.

Drawing Lines

To draw a line, you can use the DrawLine() method:

```
GraphicsWindow.DrawLine(x1, y1, x2, y2)
```

The arguments *x1, y1* and *x2, y2* are for the x- and y-coordinates of the two end points of the line. To put this method into action, run the program in Listing 3-1, which draws two parallel lines.

```
1 ' ParallelLines.sb
2 GraphicsWindow.Title = "Parallel Lines"
3 GraphicsWindow.DrawLine(40, 50, 100, 50)   ' Top line
4 GraphicsWindow.DrawLine(40, 70, 100, 70)   ' Bottom line
```

Listing 3-1: Drawing parallel lines

In line 3, Small Basic starts at the upper-left corner and then jumps to the right 40 and down 50. From there, it draws the line to the right, to the (100, 50) end point. Then, in line 4, it hops down to (40, 70) and draws a second line to the right, at the (100, 70) end point. Each pair of end points uses the same x-coordinates; the different y-coordinates draw the second line below the first line.

Great job! But lines by themselves aren't very exciting (unless they're short lines at Disneyland). Let's use several different lines to draw a sailboat like the one in Figure 3-2.

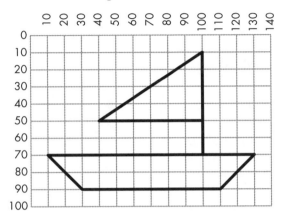

Figure 3-2: A sailboat drawn entirely with line segments

This shape's made up of seven line segments, and your program includes seven DrawLine() statements. The code for this program is in Listing 3-2, and you can see its output in Figure 3-3.

```
1 ' SailBoat.sb
2 GraphicsWindow.Title = "SailBoat"
3 GraphicsWindow.DrawLine(10, 70, 130, 70)   ' Top of the boat
4 GraphicsWindow.DrawLine(130, 70, 110, 90)  ' Right side
5 GraphicsWindow.DrawLine(110, 90, 30, 90)   ' Bottom of the boat
6 GraphicsWindow.DrawLine(30, 90, 10, 70)    ' Left edge
7 GraphicsWindow.DrawLine(100, 70, 100, 10)  ' Mast
8 GraphicsWindow.DrawLine(100, 10, 40, 50)   ' Slanted sail edge
9 GraphicsWindow.DrawLine(40, 50, 100, 50)   ' Bottom edge of sail
```

Listing 3-2: Drawing a boat with seven lines

Congratulations, you've just drawn your first picture in Small Basic. You're well on your way to becoming a great artist.

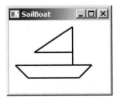

Figure 3-3: The output of SailBoat.sb

Drawing Shapes

You can draw lots of cool pictures using lines, but that can be super slow. You can simplify your code by drawing geometric shapes with built-in methods, which also saves you a lot of time!

Triangles

Use the DrawTriangle() and FillTriangle() methods to draw triangles:

```
GraphicsWindow.DrawTriangle(x1, y1, x2, y2, x3, y3)
GraphicsWindow.FillTriangle(x1, y1, x2, y2, x3, y3)
```

These methods take the x- and y-coordinates of the three corners of the triangle.

The DrawTriangle() method draws the triangle's outline, and the FillTriangle() method fills the inside of the triangle with whatever color you set the BrushColor property to.

TIP   *For a complete list of colors you can use in the graphics window, please see* http://tiny.cc/hexcolors/.

For example, to fill a triangle with blue, use these two statements:

```
GraphicsWindow.BrushColor = "Blue"
GraphicsWindow.FillTriangle(100, 10, 40, 50, 100, 50)
```

If you want to see the border, then add a call to DrawTriangle():

```
GraphicsWindow.BrushColor = "Blue"
GraphicsWindow.FillTriangle(100, 10, 40, 50, 100, 50)
GraphicsWindow.DrawTriangle(100, 10, 40, 50, 100, 50)
```

Experiment with these methods to draw all kinds of triangles. Check your understanding with Try It Out 3-1.

TRY IT OUT 3-1

Write a program that draws the shape in Figure 3-4. (Hint: start by drawing the four blue triangles, and then draw the four yellow triangles.)

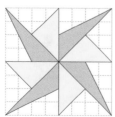

Figure 3-4: A fancy pinwheel

Rectangles and Squares

Using the DrawRectangle() and FillRectangle() methods, you can draw rectangles or squares of different sizes:

```
GraphicsWindow.DrawRectangle(x, y, width, height)
GraphicsWindow.FillRectangle(x, y, width, height)
```

In both methods, the first two arguments (*x* and *y*) are the coordinates of the upper-left corner of the rectangle. The third argument sets the width, and the fourth argument sets the height. Use the same number for the third and fourth arguments to draw a square.

To try out these methods, let's write a program that draws the house shown in Figure 3-5.

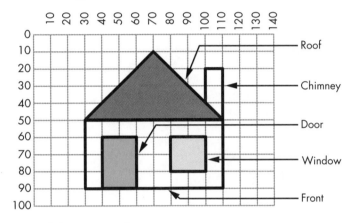

Figure 3-5: Drawing a house

The complete program is shown in Listing 3-3.

```
1  ' House.sb
2  GraphicsWindow.Title = "House"
3  GraphicsWindow.DrawRectangle(30, 50, 80, 40)      ' Front of the house
4
5  GraphicsWindow.BrushColor = "Orange"              ' Door is light orange
6  GraphicsWindow.FillRectangle(40, 60, 20, 30)        ' Door
7  GraphicsWindow.DrawRectangle(40, 60, 20, 30)        ' Door border
8
9  GraphicsWindow.BrushColor = "Lightblue"            ' Window is light blue
10 GraphicsWindow.FillRectangle(80, 60, 20, 20)        ' Window
11 GraphicsWindow.DrawRectangle(80, 60, 20, 20)        ' Window border
12
13 GraphicsWindow.DrawRectangle(100, 20, 10, 30)       ' Chimney
14
15 GraphicsWindow.BrushColor = "Gray"                 ' Roof is gray
16 GraphicsWindow.FillTriangle(30, 50, 70, 10, 110, 50)  ' Roof
17 GraphicsWindow.DrawTriangle(30, 50, 70, 10, 110, 50)  ' Roof border
```

Listing 3-3: Building the house of your dreams

Figure 3-6 shows what the output looks like. The front side is a rectangle with its upper-left corner at (30, 50), a width of 80, and a height of 40 (line 3). The door is a filled rectangle with its upper-left corner at (40, 60), a width of 20, and a height of 30 (line 6).

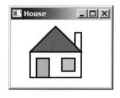

Figure 3-6: The output of House.sb

The window is a filled square with its upper-left corner at (80, 60) and a side length of 20 (line 10). The roof is a filled triangle whose three corner points are at (30, 50), (70, 10), and (110, 50).

The chimney is also a rectangle with its upper-left corner at (100, 20). Its width is 10 and height is 30 (line 13). However, part of this rectangle is covered by the roof, so you need to draw the chimney first, and then draw the roof on top of it to cover the bottom of the chimney.

Now you have the house of your dreams!

TRY IT OUT 3-2

Now that you can draw lines, triangles, rectangles, and squares, write a program that draws the fox shown in Figure 3-7. Add some colors.

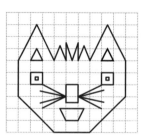

Figure 3-7: Drawing and coloring the fox

Ellipses and Circles

GraphicsWindow also has methods for drawing ellipses (ovals) and circles. Here are two ellipse methods that use four arguments:

```
GraphicsWindow.DrawEllipse(x, y, width, height)
GraphicsWindow.FillEllipse(x, y, width, height)
```

Figure 3-8 explains these four arguments. The first two arguments, x and y, set the upper-left coordinate of the ellipse. The third argument, $width$, sets the width of the ellipse, and the fourth argument, $height$, sets the height of the ellipse. To draw a circle, just set the width and the height of the ellipse to the same value.

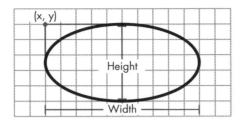

Figure 3-8: The four arguments for the ellipse-drawing methods

To use these drawing methods, let's write a program that draws the face shown in Figure 3-9.

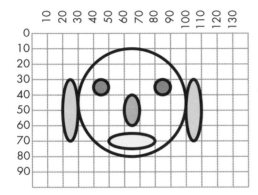

Figure 3-9: Drawing a face

To draw the face, you just have to draw a circle and some different ellipses using the right parameters. The full program is shown in Listing 3-4.

```
1  ' Face.sb
2  GraphicsWindow.Title = "Face"
3
4  GraphicsWindow.BrushColor = "Yellow"        ' Color of the two ears
5  GraphicsWindow.FillEllipse(20, 30, 10, 40)  ' Left ear
6  GraphicsWindow.DrawEllipse(20, 30, 10, 40)  ' Left ear border
7
8  GraphicsWindow.FillEllipse(100, 30, 10, 40) ' Right ear
9  GraphicsWindow.DrawEllipse(100, 30, 10, 40) ' Right ear border
10
11 GraphicsWindow.BrushColor = "Lime"          ' Color of the two eyes
12 GraphicsWindow.FillEllipse(40, 30, 10, 10)  ' Left eye
13 GraphicsWindow.DrawEllipse(40, 30, 10, 10)  ' Left eye border
14
15 GraphicsWindow.FillEllipse(80, 30, 10, 10)  ' Right eye
16 GraphicsWindow.DrawEllipse(80, 30, 10, 10)  ' Right eye border
17
18 GraphicsWindow.BrushColor = "SandyBrown"    ' Color of the nose
19 GraphicsWindow.FillEllipse(60, 40, 10, 20)  ' Nose
20 GraphicsWindow.DrawEllipse(60, 40, 10, 20)  ' Nose border
21
```

```
22 GraphicsWindow.BrushColor = "LightCyan"        ' Color of the mouth
23 GraphicsWindow.FillEllipse(50, 65, 30, 10)     ' Mouth
24 GraphicsWindow.DrawEllipse(50, 65, 30, 10)     ' Mouth border
25
26 GraphicsWindow.DrawEllipse(30, 10, 70, 70)     ' Face border
```

Listing 3-4: Drawing the most awesome ellipse face ever

The output of this program is shown in Figure 3-10. All of the ellipses in this picture use the same pen size and color, but you can add even more detail to your Small Basic drawings by changing those properties. Let's see how.

Figure 3-10: The output of Face.sb

Pen Size and Color

To change the pen size and color, you can set the following properties before you draw a line or a shape:

```
GraphicsWindow.PenWidth = 20           ' Sets line width
GraphicsWindow.PenColor = "Green"      ' Sets line color
```

If you want to mix things up, you can change your pen color every time you run your program by using the GetRandomColor() method of the GraphicsWindow object. Check it out:

```
GraphicsWindow.PenColor = GraphicsWindow.GetRandomColor()
```

This method doesn't have any arguments, which is why there's nothing in the GetRandomColor() method's parentheses; it returns a randomly selected color. Go ahead and try it out!

Pen Width and Shape Size

When drawing triangles, rectangles, and ellipses, the width of the pen you use in the drawing affects the size of the shape. Listing 3-5 shows you what we mean.

```
1 ' PenWidthDemo.sb
2 GraphicsWindow.Title = "Pen Width Demo"
3
4 GraphicsWindow.PenWidth = 20          ' Width of circle
5 GraphicsWindow.PenColor = "Lime"      ' Color of circle
```

```
 6 GraphicsWindow.DrawEllipse(20, 20, 100, 100)      ' Circle border
 7
 8 GraphicsWindow.PenWidth = 1                        ' Width of square
 9 GraphicsWindow.PenColor = "Black"                  ' Color of square
10 GraphicsWindow.DrawRectangle(20, 20, 100, 100)     ' Square border
```

Listing 3-5: Using pen width to change the size of the shape

This program uses a pen with a width of 20 to draw the border of the circle. Figure 3-11 shows that the border extends 10 pixels out from the perimeter of the square, even though the circle and the square have the same dimensions. When measured across the outside edges, the diameter of the output circle is 120 pixels instead of the specified value of 100.

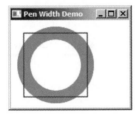

Figure 3-11: The output of PenWidthDemo.sb

TRY IT OUT 3-3

Write a program that draws a bike like the one shown in Figure 3-12. (Hint: use the given grid lines to figure out the coordinates of the different shapes to make them easier to code.)

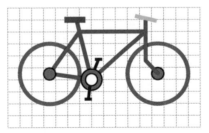

Figure 3-12: Drawing a bike

Drawing Text

A picture might be worth a thousand words, but you can also draw text in the graphics window, like this:

```
GraphicsWindow.DrawText(x, y, "text")
```

DrawText() takes three arguments. The first two arguments set the x- and y-coordinates of the upper-left corner of the text, and the third argument takes a string of the text (or numbers) you want to draw. Remember to put the string in quotes.

If you want to change how the text appears, use the GraphicsWindow object properties in Table 3-1.

Table 3-1: GraphicsWindow Properties for the Font Name, Size, Style, and Color

Property	Default	Description
FontName	"Tahoma"	The name of the font
FontSize	12	The size of the font
FontBold	"True"	Whether or not the font's bold
FontItalic	"False"	Whether or not the font's italic
BrushColor	"SlateBlue"	The color of the brush that draws the text

If you don't change any of these properties, Small Basic uses the default values listed in Table 3-1. The program in Listing 3-6 changes these properties to draw some fancy text.

```
1  ' Fonts.sb
2  GraphicsWindow.Title = "Fonts"
3  GraphicsWindow.BackgroundColor = "LightYellow"
4  GraphicsWindow.FontName = "Times New Roman"
5  GraphicsWindow.FontSize = 120
6  GraphicsWindow.FontItalic = "True"
7
8  GraphicsWindow.BrushColor = "Silver"       ' Text shadow color
9  GraphicsWindow.DrawText(5, 5, "Hello!") ' Shadow position/text
10
11 GraphicsWindow.BrushColor = "RosyBrown" ' Text color
12 GraphicsWindow.DrawText(0, 0, "Hello!") ' Position and text
```

Listing 3-6: Trying out some fonts

In line 3, the BackgroundColor property changes the background color of the graphics window. Lines 4–6 set the name, size, and italics properties of the font you use in any calls to DrawText(). Line 8 sets the color of the font using the BrushColor property, and line 9 draws the string "Hello!" starting at point (5, 5). This line draws the background shadow you see in Figure 3-13. In line 11, the program changes the BrushColor property, and then line 12 draws the same string in a slightly different position. This creates the appearance of text with a background shadow, as shown in Figure 3-13.

Figure 3-13: The output of Fonts.sb

By layering text on top of other text like this, you can create some cool effects. Try playing with this code to see what you can come up with!

You can also draw text to fit a certain width by using the `DrawBoundText()` method:

```
GraphicsWindow.DrawBoundText(x, y, width, "text")
```

The parameters *x*, *y*, and *"text"* mean the same as they do in the `DrawText()` method: *x* and *y* are where you start to draw, and *"text"* is the string of text or numbers to draw. The third argument, *width*, tells Small Basic the maximum available width for the text in the output. If the text doesn't fit in the given width, then it continues on a new line. Even though the rectangle that the text appears in has a fixed width, the text keeps going, so the rectangle text area stretches vertically for as long as it needs to. But if one word's too long to fit in your *bound* rectangle (which happens, especially if the font's too big), then it gets clipped! The program in Listing 3-7 and its output in Figure 3-14 show you what we mean.

```
1  ' BoundTextDemo.sb
2  GraphicsWindow.Title = "DrawBoundText Demo"
3
4  ' No clipping
5  GraphicsWindow.FontSize = 15        ' Smaller font
6  GraphicsWindow.DrawBoundText(10, 10, 70, "Today is my birthday")
7
8  ' With clipping
9  GraphicsWindow.FontSize = 18        ' Larger font
10 GraphicsWindow.DrawBoundText(150, 10, 70, "Today is my birthday")
11 GraphicsWindow.DrawRectangle(150, 10, 70, 80)
```

Listing 3-7: Boundaries that contain the text

The text in the invisible rectangle on the left automatically wraps to make sure it doesn't go beyond the width you specified. In the *bound* rectangle on the right, the text gets clipped because it's too long to fit. Small Basic displays three dots, called an *ellipsis*, indicating that text has been clipped.

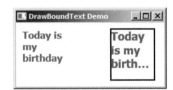

Figure 3-14: The output of BoundTextDemo.sb

Inserting Images

Some images might be too complicated to draw with basic shapes, or they might just take too long to code. Instead, you can draw those images ahead of time with a paint program and then use them in your application.

GraphicsWindow provides two methods to insert images. Although these methods start with *Draw*, they actually insert an existing image in the graphics window:

```
GraphicsWindow.DrawImage(imageName, x, y)
GraphicsWindow.DrawResizedImage(imageName, x, y, width, height)
```

Both methods take the image pathname and the x- and y-coordinates to determine the image's location in the graphics window. DrawResizedImage() takes two additional arguments (*width* and *height*) so you can resize the input image.

Listing 3-8 shows the DrawImage() method with an example image.

```
1  ' ImageDemo.sb
2  GraphicsWindow.Title = "Image Demo"
3  GraphicsWindow.Width = 320     ' Same width as background image
4  GraphicsWindow.Height = 240    ' Same height as image
5  GraphicsWindow.DrawImage("C:\Small Basic\Ch03\BkGnd.bmp", 0, 0)
6
7  GraphicsWindow.BrushColor = "White"     ' Text color
8  GraphicsWindow.FontSize = 50
9  GraphicsWindow.DrawText(10, 120, "Hello Moon!")
```

Listing 3-8: Inserting your first image

The program starts by setting the width and height of GraphicsWindow to 320 and 240 pixels, respectively, to match the size of the image. Line 5 calls DrawImage() and passes in the pathname where the image is saved. In lines 7–9, the program draws the white text Hello Moon! on top of the background image. When you run this program on your computer, make sure you set the path in line 5 to the correct location of the *BkGnd.bmp* file on your computer. Figure 3-15 shows the output.

Figure 3-15: The output of ImageDemo.sb

NOTE   *Small Basic can also draw images from the Web. Here's an example:*

```
GraphicsWindow.DrawImage("http://smallbasic.com/bkgnd.jpg", 0, 0)
```

Programming Challenges

If you get stuck, check out *http://nostarch.com/smallbasic/* for the solutions and for more resources and review questions for teachers and students.

1. Write a program that connects the following six points with line segments: (20, 110), (110, 50), (10, 50), (100, 110), (60, 20), (20, 110). What shape do you get?

2. What's the output of the following program?

```
GraphicsWindow.DrawLine(50, 18, 61, 37)
GraphicsWindow.DrawLine(61, 37, 83, 43)
GraphicsWindow.DrawLine(83, 43, 69, 60)
GraphicsWindow.DrawLine(69, 60, 71, 82)
GraphicsWindow.DrawLine(71, 82, 50, 73)
GraphicsWindow.DrawLine(50, 73, 29, 82)
GraphicsWindow.DrawLine(29, 82, 31, 60)
GraphicsWindow.DrawLine(31, 60, 17, 43)
GraphicsWindow.DrawLine(17, 43, 39, 37)
GraphicsWindow.DrawLine(39, 37, 50, 18)
```

3. What's the output of the following program?

```
GraphicsWindow.DrawRectangle(10, 10, 90, 50)
GraphicsWindow.DrawRectangle(15, 60, 75, 4)
GraphicsWindow.DrawRectangle(34, 64, 6, 6)
GraphicsWindow.DrawRectangle(74, 64, 6, 6)
GraphicsWindow.DrawRectangle(30, 70, 75, 10)
GraphicsWindow.DrawRectangle(20, 80, 80, 2)
```

4. What's the strangest thing in your house? Draw it using the DrawLine() method.

The following problems show a grid to make it easier for you to draw the shapes. You can use any size you like for the grid. We recommend 20 pixels.

5. Write a program that draws this star.

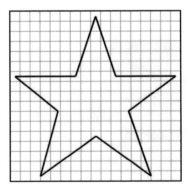

6. Write a program that draws this bank, using any colors you'd like.

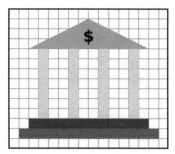

7. Write a program that draws this truck. For extra credit, add front wheels.

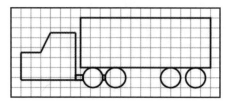

8. Write a program that draws a traffic light like this one.

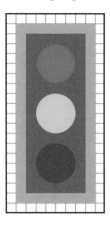

9. Write a program that draws a train like this one.

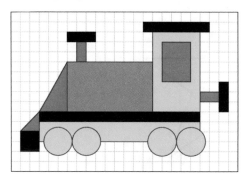

10. Write a program that draws the following shape.

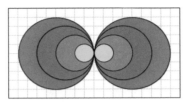

11. Write a program that draws this person.

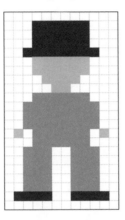

12. Write a program that draws a soccer field similar to this one.

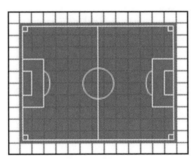

4

USING VARIABLES

Have you ever wanted to be a doctor, astronaut, firefighter, animator, mayor, botanist, or ninja? What if you could be all of them but just one at a time? A *variable* can be anything in your programs, like a string or a number, but it can only be one thing at a time. For example, a number-guessing game might ask the player to enter their name (a string) and then greet the player using that name. Next, the program might ask them to enter their first guess for the game (a number) and then check to see if they guessed correctly.

For the game to work, it must remember, or *store*, the data entered by the player. It also might need to track how many rounds it took the player to guess the secret number. You can do all this using variables!

In this chapter, you'll learn how to define variables and use them to store text or numbers. You'll then use variables in programs that solve practical problems.

What's a Variable?

A variable is used to store values, like numbers or text. You can use it similarly to how you might use a treasure chest to store valuables if you were a pirate. Think of a variable as a box. You can put different things inside your box to use later on. You can change the value of your variable, just like you can put something new inside your box, like your gum collection. Variables are called variables because their contents can vary.

To create a variable in Small Basic, use an *assignment statement* like this:

```
treasureChest = "My booty!"
```

This statement creates the variable treasureChest and assigns it the string "My booty!" The equal sign is an *assignment operator*. Assigning a value to a variable for the first time is called *initializing* the variable.

Now let's explore how to use variables in your programs. Anchors aweigh!

The Basics of Using Variables

Karen has 12 stuffed bears. Her sister, Linda, has half as many. How many bears does Linda have? You could do the math in your head or with a calculator, but let's follow Listing 4-1 to do this problem the Small Basic way!

```
1 ' Variables.sb
2 karenBears = 12              ' Karen has 12 bears
3 lindaBears = karenBears / 2 ' Linda has half as many bears as Karen
4
5 TextWindow.Write("Karen's " + karenBears + " bears aren't as ")
6 TextWindow.WriteLine("fancy as Linda's " + lindabears + " bears!")
```

Listing 4-1: Demonstrating variables

The statement karenBears = 12 at line 2 creates a variable named karenBears and assigns the value 12 to it. Line 3 divides karenBears by 2 and then stores the result in a new variable named lindaBears. When line 3 runs, lindaBears holds the value 12 ÷ 2, which is 6.

Line 5 outputs the string "Karen's ", and then the plus sign concatenates the value of karenBears, which is 12, after the string. Then it concatenates " bears aren't as " after the 12. (For a refresher on concatenation, refer to "Joining Strings" on page 18.) Similarly, line 6 outputs the string "fancy as Linda's " and then the value stored in the variable lindaBears. Finally, it adds " bears!".

Now, let's run the program to see the result. You should see this:

```
Karen's 12 bears aren't as fancy as Linda's 6 bears!
```

Try changing the value in karenBears and running the program again to see what happens. Neat, huh? Changing the value of karenBears will also change the value of lindaBears. Variables can make your programming life so much easier!

Let's check out some other important concepts you need to know for when you want to use your own variables.

Assigning Expressions to Variables

Arithmetic expressions are combinations of variables, operators, and numbers. They can be constant numbers (such as 3, 6.8, or -10), arithmetic operations (such as 3 + 6 or 10 / 3), or algebraic expressions (karenBears / 2). Evaluating an arithmetic expression in Small Basic is just like evaluating an expression in math. For example, the expression 4 * 3 + 6 / 2 is evaluated as (4 × 3 + 6 ÷ 2) = 12 + 3 = 15. You can also use parentheses in expressions to decide the order of operations.

You can set variables to the result of an arithmetic expression using an assignment statement. Your program grabs the value to the right of the equal sign and assigns that value to the variable on the left of the equal sign. You already did this in Listing 4-1; let's build on that knowledge and write some more variables set to arithmetic expressions!

Here's an example:

```
barbies = 5                      ' You have 5 Barbies
ponies = barbies + 7             ' You have 7 more My Little Ponies than Barbies
donate = (barbies * ponies) / 10 ' Total toys you need to donate
```

When you run this program, the variables barbies, ponies, and donate are 5, 12, and 6, respectively. Time to donate 6 toys!

You need to set the variable on the left of an assignment operator, as you've seen in every assignment example so far. So this statement is incorrect:

```
5 = barbies  ' This is backwards, like the Twilight Zone
```

Try running it yourself to see if you get an error!

Passing Variables to Methods

A method's arguments can be constants, variables, or even expressions. For example, the argument to WriteLine() in the following statement is an arithmetic expression:

```
TextWindow.WriteLine((3 * x + y) / (x - y))
```

If x = 7 and y = 5, this statement displays 13 on the screen. See if you can figure out how to write and run this code. Remember to set x and y first!

Changing the Value of a Variable

When you create a new variable in your program, you assign it an initial value using the assignment operator. You can also use the assignment operator to *change* the value of an existing variable, which wipes out the old value, like this:

```
ferrets = 5
ferrets = 15
TextWindow.WriteLine("There are " + ferrets + " ferrets in my bed!")
```

The first line in this example creates a new variable named ferrets and assigns 5 to it, but the second line changes its value to 15. So the WriteLine statement will output There are 15 ferrets in my bed!

Behind the scenes, the variable ferrets points to a storage area in the computer's memory. When you write ferrets = 15, you tell Small Basic to go into the space in the memory reserved for ferrets and replace the 5 with a 15. When you display the value of ferrets, you grab whatever's stored in the space at that moment.

You can also add to a variable to change its value. Imagine you're programming a game in which the player has to shoot attacking airplanes. When the player shoots an airplane, you want to increase their score (stored in a variable named score) by five points. How would you update the score variable? Here's one way:

```
score = 10        ' Assumes the player already has 10 points
temp = score + 5  ' temp = 10 + 5 (= 15)
score = temp      ' Now the player has 15 points
```

The second line uses a temporary variable named temp to store the result of adding five to the current value of score. The value of temp is then assigned to score.

But you can do this faster in one statement:

```
score = score + 5
```

Do you see how the same variable, score, is on both sides of the assignment? This statement adds 5 to the current value of the variable score and then stores the result back into the same variable. The old value of 10 is replaced by the new value, 15. See Figure 4-1.

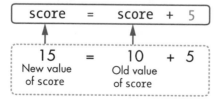

Figure 4-1: Illustrating the statement
score = score + 5

These two ways of updating the score variable are basically the same, but the second method's more common, and you'll see it all the time in other people's programs.

Using Spaces for Readability

Add tabs and spaces to make your expressions more readable. For example, look at these two expressions:

```
x=y+10*(x-3)-z
x = y + 10 * (x - 3) - z
```

They're the same to Small Basic, but the spaces in the second line make it easier for humans (and other nonrobots) to read.

TRY IT OUT 4-1

The following program finds the average of the weekly hours you spend on homework for two classes. First, identify all the variables in this program. What does this program display when you run it? Try it out!

```
mathHours = 8
scienceHours = 6
avgHours = (mathHours + scienceHours) / 2
TextWindow.Write("I spend " + mathHours)
TextWindow.Write(" hours a week on math homework and " + scienceHours)
TextWindow.WriteLine(" hours a week on science homework.")
TextWindow.Write("The average of " + mathHours + " and ")
TextWindow.WriteLine(scienceHours + " is " + avgHours + ".")
```

Now swap in the actual weekly hours you spend on two classes. How long do you spend on homework? Show the results to your parents—it might be a good primer before you discuss your report card!

Rules for Naming Variables

The names you give to variables are called *identifiers*. Variable names can include letters (lowercase and uppercase), digits (0 to 9), and underscore characters (_). You can name variables anything, as long as you follow a few rules:

1. The name must start with a letter or underscore. It can't start with a number.

2. Don't use any of Small Basic's keywords, like If, Else, Then, And, or While. These keywords have special meanings, and they can't be used for anything else. You'll learn more about them later in this book.

3. Variable names in Small Basic are case insensitive; side, SIDE, and siDE are the same variable.

Based on these rules, MyAddress, totalScore, player1, sum, room_temperature, and _x123 are all valid variable names.

In addition to the rules we mentioned, programmers also use other guidelines when naming variables. These *conventions* are good programming practices, and you should follow them, too. Let's look at these additional conventions.

Say What You Mean

Although you can name a variable anything, we recommend you choose a name that explains what the variable is for. For example, using a variable named address to store a person's address makes more sense than using a variable named xy123 or TacoTruck.

Find the Right Length

Avoid single-letter names like m, j, x, and w, unless their meanings are very clear, or you'll just make your program harder to read and understand. But don't use names that are so long that they put your friends to sleep, either!

Choose short, meaningful names instead. For example, use name or presidentName instead of the_name_of_the_president.

Stick with Your Style

It's currently popular to name variables by starting with a lowercase letter and then capitalizing the first letter of each additional word, like sideLength, firstName, roomTemp, variablesAreAwesome, and scoobyDoo. This naming style is called *camel case* because it has a hump in the middle. But don't worry—camel-cased variables won't spit!

This book uses camel case, but if you prefer a different style, that's okay. Just use one naming convention and stick to it! Although Small Basic is case insensitive when it comes to variable names, you should be consistent about casing when you name your variables. If you name a variable firstName, use the same capitalization throughout your program. This makes it easier for you to find variables and for others to understand your code. The IntelliSense autocomplete feature can help you. Let's see how.

Let IntelliSense Work for You

When you create a variable in your program, the name of that variable is added to the IntelliSense drop-down menu. When you want to reuse a variable (or check its case), just type the first few letters and look for it in IntelliSense, shown in Figure 4-2. Small Basic finishes your variable names, just like a best friend who finishes your . . . sandwiches!

```
1  interestRate = 5
2  amount = in
```

Figure 4-2: How a variable is added to the IntelliSense menu

Note how the name of the variable created in the first statement (interestRate) appears in the menu. When I started to type in on the second line, the IDE highlighted the name of the variable. Pressing the ENTER key autocompletes what I started to type. Thanks, IntelliSense!

Avoid Naming Variables After Methods and Objects

Method names aren't reserved keywords, so you could use them as variable names. For example, Small Basic won't complain if you write this:

```
writeline = 5
TextWindow.WriteLine(writeline)
```

Although this is valid, we strongly recommend you don't name your variables after existing methods. The world is confusing enough already.

TRY IT OUT 4-2

1. Which of these variable names are invalid? If the name is invalid, explain why.

   ```
   _myBooK
   1MoreRound
   $FinalScore
   Level2
   ```

2. For each of the following values, what would you name a variable that represents it, and why?

   - The score of a player in a game

   - The hypotenuse of a right triangle

   - The number of floors in a building

   - The number of miles a car can drive per gallon of fuel

   - The number of licks it takes to get to the center of a Tootsie Pop

---

Simplifying Expressions

Variables can make calculating arithmetic expressions easier. Let's say you want to write a program that evaluates this expression:

$$\frac{\frac{1}{5} + \frac{5}{7}}{\frac{7}{8} - \frac{2}{3}}$$

You can write a bunch of different programs that would all give you the right answer. For example, you could write a statement that evaluates the whole expression at once:

```
TextWindow.WriteLine((1 / 5 + 5 / 7) / (7 / 8 - 2 / 3))
```

Or you might evaluate the numerator and the denominator separately and then display the result of their division:

```
num = (1 / 5) + (5 / 7)        ' Finds the numerator
den = (7 / 8) - (2 / 3)        ' Finds the denominator
TextWindow.WriteLine(num / den) ' Does the division
```

You could also evaluate each fraction separately and then display the result of the combined expression:

```
a = 1 / 5
b = 5 / 7
c = 7 / 8
d = 2 / 3
answer = (a + b) / (c - d)
TextWindow.WriteLine(answer)
```

Although these three programs give you the same answer, each program uses a different style. The first program is the "chubby bunny" of programming: it crams everything into one statement. If the original expression was more complex, the statement would be really hard to follow. The third program does the opposite: it represents every fraction in the expression with a variable, and that can also be hard to read.

If you're Goldilocks, the second solution is your "just right." It breaks down the expression into just enough parts to make the program easier to understand. The variables num and den clearly represent the numerator and the denominator.

As these examples show, there's often more than one way to solve a problem. If you ever get stuck on a problem, try breaking it into more manageable pieces!

Using Variables to Solve Problems

People often solve problems without really thinking through every step of the process. But computers can't do this: they need you to think through each step *for them* (at least until *The Terminator* or *The Matrix* come true). That's why it takes some planning to use a computer to solve a problem. When developing a solution to a programming problem, you should do this:

1. Understand what the problem is.
2. Design a solution.
3. Write the program.
4. Test the program to make sure it works as you expect it to.

Let's say you want to create a program that computes the area of a circle with a given radius. To solve the problem, you need to answer these basic questions:

1. What do you need the program to output?
2. What input do you need, and where will the program get this input from?
3. What processing will the program have to do to turn the input into the output?

For this problem, here's how you'd answer those questions:

1. Your program needs to output the area of a circle. It'll show this output to the user in the text window.
2. This program needs a single input from your user: the radius of the circle.
3. Your program will need to compute the area using this formula, which might be familiar from math class:

$$\text{area} = \pi \times (\text{radius})^2$$

NOTE   *The Greek letter π, pronounced* pi, *is a special number that can be rounded to 3.1416. We gave you free pi!*

Now that you've defined your problem, let's design a step-by-step solution, which is called an *algorithm*. First, we'll break down each part of the problem (the input, processing, and output) into detailed steps.

Get in the habit of writing an outline of the program that puts each step in order. This outline is called *pseudocode* because it's not a real program, but it explains what the code should do. Looking at your pseudocode should give you a clear idea of the real code you'll need to write for each step. For complex problems, pseudocode helps you express your thought process in simple terms that you can then translate into real code. Figure 4-3 shows our algorithm and pseudocode for the circle area problem.

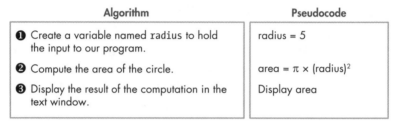

Figure 4-3: Algorithm and pseudocode for calculating the area of a circle

The final step is to translate your pseudocode into a Small Basic program. Because we haven't shown you how to get values from the user yet, you'll use a fixed number for the radius. Enter the program in Listing 4-2.

```
1 ' CircleArea.sb
2 radius = 5
3 area = 3.1416 * radius * radius
4 TextWindow.WriteLine("Area = " + area)
```

Listing 4-2: Computing the area of a circle

In line 2, you create a variable named radius and assign it a value of 5. In line 3, you compute the area of the circle using the formula from page 51 and assign the result to a new variable named area. In line 4, you display the value of the variable area after the text "Area = " to make it clear what the displayed number means.

When you run the code, you'll see this:

```
Area = 78.5400
```

TRY IT OUT 4-4

Write a program that calculates and displays the circumference of a circle with a radius of 5 units. We'll give you a hint: the equation for the circumference of a circle is $2 \times \pi \times radius$.

Two Kinds of Data

Programs use all different types of data: applications that do calculations use numbers, but others might use text.

Small Basic uses very simple data types. It has built-in support for just two data types: numbers and strings. Numbers can be integers, like –2 and 2365, or decimal numbers, like 0.25 and –123.78. As you know, strings are characters strung together between double quotation marks, like "The Declaration of Independence" or "She sells seashells by the seashore."

You don't need to tell Small Basic what type of data you're going to store in a variable. This is a beginner-friendly way of programming.

Global Variables

Variables in Small Basic are *global* in scope. This means you can define a variable and access a variable from anywhere in your program. This feature is helpful because it lets you define variables just when you need them (instead of having to put all your variables at the top of your program). But you have to be careful! Because Small Basic reads your programs in order, it's possible to create logical errors. Try the program in Listing 4-3.

```
1  ' LogicError.sb
2  y = x / 10
3  x = 20
4  TextWindow.WriteLine("y = " + y)
```

Listing 4-3: Logic error with global variables

If you're reading this code closely, you've already noticed that, in line 2, we're using the variable x *before* we've assigned it any particular value. When we run this code, we get the following output:

```
y = 0
```

Does that answer surprise you? Here's what's happening. When the Small Basic compiler reads this code, it first makes a list of all the variables you defined in the program. The initial values for these variables are left empty, like empty boxes. As long as the expressions in the program use variable names from that list, the compiler's happy and the program will run.

When the program runs the expression x / 10 in line 2, it interprets x as a number because division only makes sense for numbers. That's why it fills the empty box for x with 0. It then assigns the result of the division (which is 0) to y. The variable x is changed to 20 in line 3, but it's too late! You get the wrong output.

Most other programming languages would report a syntax error because the expression x / 10 in line 2 uses a variable x that hasn't been defined yet in the program. Small Basic lets you define variables anywhere in your program; just don't expect to get away with it in other languages.

Be careful when you order your statements because Small Basic runs top to bottom. Make sure you define your variables before you use them for the first time.

TRY IT OUT 4-5

What's the output of this program? Explain what you see.

```
TextWindow.WriteLine("Before: x = " + x + " and y = " + y)
x = 10
y = 10
TextWindow.WriteLine("After: x = " + x + " and y = " + y)
```

Programming Challenges

If you get stuck, check out *http://nostarch.com/smallbasic/* for the solutions and for more resources and review questions for teachers and students.

1. Do you like knock-knock jokes? Try the following program to see how to tell them in Small Basic! Which program lines do you need to change to tell a different joke? Make the change and run the program again to see what happens:

```
' KnockKnock.sb
' Small Basic can tell knock-knock jokes!

name = "Orange"
reply = "you going to answer the door?"

TextWindow.WriteLine("Knock Knock")
TextWindow.WriteLine("Who's there?")
TextWindow.WriteLine(name)
TextWindow.WriteLine(name + " who?")
TextWindow.WriteLine(name + " " + reply)
TextWindow.WriteLine("")
```

2. Translate this pseudocode into a Small Basic program:
    a. Set *quantity* to 10.
    b. Set *item price* to 15 dollars.
    c. Compute *total price* by multiplying *quantity* by *item price*.
    d. Display *total price*.

5

DRAWING SHAPES WITH TURTLE GRAPHICS

In Chapter 3 you learned how to draw pictures using code, but in Small Basic you can program a friendly turtle to draw pictures for you! In this chapter, you'll explore the Turtle object. You'll also learn how to use a For loop to repeat lines of code a set number of times to draw beautiful designs.

Meet the Turtle

Enter this statement in the Small Basic Editor:

```
Turtle.Show()
```

Now click **Run**. Presto! A turtle should appear in the center of the graphics window (Figure 5-1), waiting for your commands.

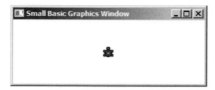

Figure 5-1: Hello, turtle!

You might wonder how useful this slow creature can be, but don't underestimate its powers. Once upon a time a turtle won a race against the fastest hare on Earth!

Small Basic's turtle uses the GraphicsWindow object's pen to draw lines. It always carries this pen (perhaps it's hidden in its shell next to the turtle wax), and you can decide if the pen is up or down! When the pen is down, the turtle draws as it moves. When the pen is up, the turtle moves without leaving a trace. You can command the turtle to put down or lift up its pen by using the PenDown() and PenUp() methods (see Figure 5-2).

Turtle.PenDown()   Turtle.PenUp()

Figure 5-2: Illustrating the PenUp() and PenDown() methods

The default pen state is down, so the turtle's ready to draw from the day it's born. Now let's explore what it can do.

Moving the Turtle

You can enter commands to tell your turtle what to do. Just like Ash Ketchum commands Pikachu, you'll command your turtle. First, let's use the Turtle object to tell the turtle to move!

Give it a push by entering these lines in the Editor. Then click **Run**.

```
Turtle.Show()
Turtle.Move(100)
```

Go, turtle, go! The Move() method in this example commands the turtle to move forward 100 pixels.

Now let's look at the two different ways of moving your turtle: absolute motion and relative motion.

Absolute Motion

With *absolute motion,* you tell your turtle to go to a point on the graphics window. No matter where the turtle is, it moves to the exact point you choose.

One way to move the turtle to a particular point on the graphics window is to change its X and Y properties. To see how, run the program shown in Listing 5-1.

```
1 ' SetTurtle.sb
2 Turtle.Show()
3 Program.Delay(1000)
4 Turtle.X = 100
5 Turtle.Y = 140
```

Listing 5-1: Setting the turtle's position

The Show() method (line 2) causes the turtle to appear near the center of the graphics window (320, 240). The Delay() method on line 3 makes the program sleep for 1,000 milliseconds (which is 1 second), so you can see the turtle's initial position. Line 4 sets the turtle's X position to 100, and line 5 sets the turtle's Y position to 140. After running lines 4 and 5, the turtle will appear at point (100, 140) on the graphics window, as illustrated in Figure 5-3. Note that the turtle moved to the new location without leaving any trace; it's like the turtle got picked up and placed at (100, 140).

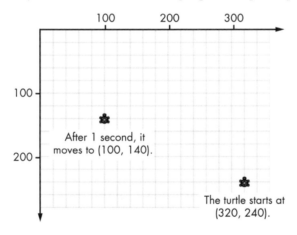

Figure 5-3: Moving the turtle by setting its X and Y properties

Another way to move the turtle to an absolute position on the graphics window is to use the MoveTo() method. This method takes the x- and y-coordinates of the desired position as arguments. Run the program in Listing 5-2 to see what this method does.

```
1  ' MoveTo.sb
2  Turtle.Show()
3  Program.Delay(1000)
4  Turtle.MoveTo(100, 140)
```

Listing 5-2: Moving the turtle using absolute motion

You can see the output of this program in Figure 5-4. Again, the turtle starts at (320, 240) pointing north (line 2), and the program sleeps for 1 second so you can watch the turtle in action (line 3). After 1 second, the turtle turns toward (100, 140) before it starts its slow journey toward that point. This time, the turtle draws a line while moving (because the turtle's pen is down by default). If you add Turtle.PenUp() anywhere before calling MoveTo(), the turtle moves to (100, 140) without leaving any trace.

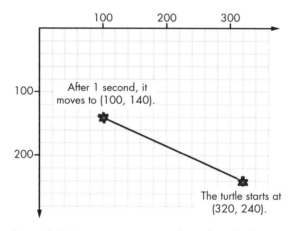

Figure 5-4: Using MoveTo() to set the turtle's absolute position

Note that when it stops moving, the turtle stays pointed in the direction it turned to. It doesn't reset to face north again. Compare this figure to Figure 5-3, where the turtle remains pointing north, like it's been picked up and moved to the new position.

Let's say you want your turtle to face north after it completes its journey. Add the following statement at the end of Listing 5-2:

```
Turtle.Angle = 0
```

When the turtle reaches point (100, 140), it'll turn in place to point north. Try it out! See Figure 5-5 to understand the relationship between the Angle property and the direction in which the turtle's facing.

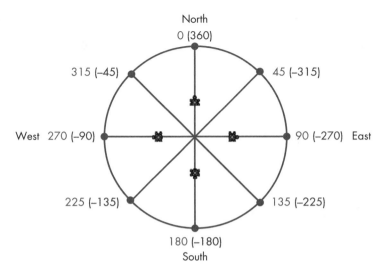

Figure 5-5: For the turtle, 0 is north, 90 is east, 180 is south, and 270 is west.

As you can see in Figure 5-5, when you set your turtle's Angle to 0 or 360, it faces north. You can set the turtle's Angle to 45, to make it face northeast; 90, to make it face east; 135 (southeast); 180 (south); 225 (southwest); 270 (west); 315 (northwest); and 360 (back to north again). Of course, you can set the turtle's Angle to any number you want. Experiment by setting the Angle property of the Turtle object to different numbers to see which directions the turtle will face. Don't forget to try negative numbers.

Relative Motion

With *relative motion* you tell the turtle how far to move from its current position; that is, you tell it how far to move *relative to* its current position.

Let's practice by making the turtle hit an imaginary target. Listing 5-3 shows one way to program the turtle to hit the target.

```
1 ' RelativeMotion.sb
2 Turtle.Show()
3 Turtle.Move(150)
4 Turtle.TurnRight()
5 Turtle.Move(100)
```

Listing 5-3: Moving the turtle using relative motion

The output is illustrated in Figure 5-6. Line 3 moves the turtle up 150 pixels, line 4 turns the turtle to the right, and line 5 moves the turtle forward 100 pixels.

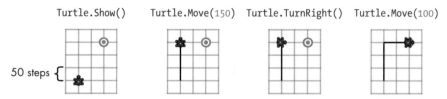

Figure 5-6: Moving the turtle using relative motion commands

Relative motion differs from absolute motion because we told the turtle to move a certain distance instead of telling it to go to a set of coordinates.

When you pass a negative number to Move(), your turtle will move backward. You can also use the Turn() method to command your turtle to turn in place by any angle you desire. Enter the code shown in Listing 5-4 to play around with these options, and run the program to see the results in action.

```
1 ' Turn.sb
2 Turtle.Show()
3 Turtle.Turn(45)
4 Turtle.Move(100)
5 Turtle.Turn(-90)
6 Turtle.Move(-100)
```

Listing 5-4: Turning the turtle using relative motion

Line 3 turns the turtle to the right by 45 degrees. Line 4 moves the turtle forward 100 pixels (see the left image in Figure 5-7). The −90 in line 5 turns the turtle to the left by 90 degrees. Line 6 moves the turtle backward 100 pixels (see the right image in Figure 5-7).

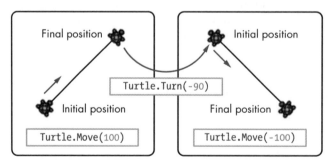

Figure 5-7: Illustrating the turtle's Move() and Turn() methods

Coloring Your Steps

You can set your turtle's pen size and color using GraphicsWindow's PenWidth and PenColor properties. For example, the following code makes your turtle draw with a red pen that's 5 pixels wide.

```
GraphicsWindow.PenColor = "Red"
GraphicsWindow.PenWidth = 5
```

Add this code before commanding your turtle to move, and then observe what happens.

Controlling Your Speed

The Turtle object has one more property that you need to know. The Speed property sets how fast the turtle moves. The possible Speed values are 1 to 10. Follow along with Listing 5-5 to watch your turtle race around your screen.

```
1  ' TurtleSpeed.sb
2  Turtle.Show()
3  Turtle.Speed = 2      ' Sets the initial speed to 2
4  Turtle.Move(100)      ' Moves the turtle forward 100 pixels
5  Turtle.Speed = 5      ' Changes the speed to 5
6  Turtle.TurnRight()    ' Turns the turtle to its right
7  Turtle.Move(100)
8  Turtle.Speed = 9      ' Changes the speed to 9
9  Turtle.TurnRight()
10 Turtle.Move(100)
```

Listing 5-5: Setting the turtle's speed

Line 3 sets the turtle's speed to 2. The turtle slowly moves 100 pixels (line 4) and then gets faster in line 5. You can already see the speed increase as the turtle turns right (line 6) and darts forward 100 pixels (line 7). Then you set the turtle to a speed of 9 (line 8). The turtle quickly turns right (line 9) and sprints forward another 100 pixels (line 10). If you don't want to watch the turtle move slowly while drawing, set the Speed property to 10 at the start of your program. The turtle will move so fast that you'll barely see it. It's superturtle!

TRY IT OUT 5-1

Write a program that makes your turtle draw this star (Figure 5-8). The coordinates of each point are included.

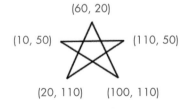

(60, 20)

(10, 50)   (110, 50)

(20, 110)   (100, 110)

Figure 5-8: A star pattern

Introducing the For Loop

As you start writing longer programs, you'll need to repeat some statements. For example, let's make the turtle draw a square: enter the code shown in Listing 5-6.

```
1 ' Square1.sb
2 Turtle.Move(60)     ' Moves 60 pixels
3 Turtle.TurnRight()  ' Turns right 90 degrees
4 Turtle.Move(60)     ' Moves 60 pixels
5 Turtle.TurnRight()  ' Turns right 90 degrees
6 Turtle.Move(60)     ' Moves 60 pixels
7 Turtle.TurnRight()  ' Turns right 90 degrees
8 Turtle.Move(60)     ' Moves 60 pixels
9 Turtle.TurnRight()  ' Turns right 90 degrees
```

Listing 5-6: Making the turtle draw a square

The turtle starts facing upward. This code tells the turtle to move 60 pixels up to draw one side of the square, turn 90 degrees to the right, move 60 pixels to draw another side, turn 90 degrees to face downward, move 60 pixels to draw a third side, turn 90 degrees to face left, and move 60 pixels to complete the square. Finally, the turtle turns 90 degrees one last time so it's facing upward like it was at the beginning. Check out the result in Figure 5-9. Does your screen look the same?

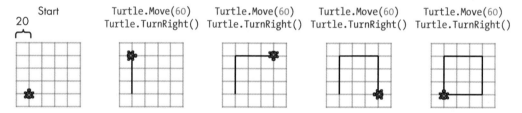

Figure 5-9: Drawing a square using move and turn commands

You repeated the Move(60) and TurnRight() methods four times. The computer doesn't mind repeating these tasks, but it's boring for you to type all that code. Wouldn't it be great if you could make the turtle draw this square using an easier approach?

Well, you can! You can make the turtle draw the same square as in Listing 5-6, just by using a few lines of code. Use a For loop, like the one in Listing 5-7.

```
1 ' Square2.sb
2 For I = 1 To 4        ' Repeats 4 times
3   Turtle.Move(60)     ' Draws one side
4   Turtle.TurnRight()  ' Turns right 90 degrees
5 EndFor
```

Listing 5-7: Making the turtle draw a square using a For loop

The For loop runs `Turtle.Move(60)` and `Turtle.TurnRight()` four times. You use a For loop when you know how many times you want to repeat some code (for more on For loops, see Chapter 13). In this example, your program starts the loop, runs the two lines of code, and then goes back to the start of the loop to run it again. It runs four times and then exits the loop. Try it out!

In this short program, you're using three new Small Basic keywords: For, To, and EndFor.

NOTE   *The keywords (For, To, and EndFor) don't have to be capitalized the way you see them in Listing 5-7, and the statements in the For loop don't have to be indented, but those are the default formats. The Editor indents the statements inside the For loop as you type to make your code easier to read.*

Figure 5-10 shows what's going on.

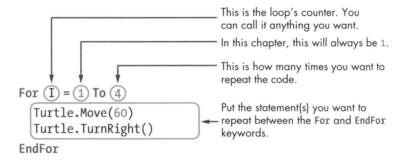

Figure 5-10: The parts of the For loop

To repeat lines of code, you simply put the statement(s) you want to repeat between the For and EndFor keywords. If you want to repeat these statements four times, write this:

```
For I = 1 To 4
```

The variable I is the *counter*. It keeps track of how many times the loop has been run and how many times it has left to go. Each time your program runs the loop, it adds one to the counter.

Remember the For loop the next time you get in trouble at school! If your teacher catches you chewing gum and asks you to write *I won't chew gum in class again* 100 times, Small Basic is there to rescue you! Write this instead:

```
For I = 1 To 100
  TextWindow.WriteLine("I won't chew gum in class again.")
EndFor
```

Try it out. No, not chewing gum in class; try out the program!

NOTE *Programmers usually use one-letter variables to name the loop's counter (such as* I, J, *or* K*), but any other name works too. It doesn't matter if you use upper- or lowercase letters—Small Basic would treat* I *and* i *as the same variable.*

TRY IT OUT 5-2

Predict the output of the following program. Then run the program to check your answer.

```
GraphicsWindow.PenColor = "Red"
GraphicsWindow.PenWidth = 3

For I = 1 To 4
  Turtle.Move(30)
  Turtle.Turn(-60)
  Turtle.Move(30)
  Turtle.Turn(120)
  Turtle.Move(30)
  Turtle.Turn(-60)
  Turtle.Move(30)
  Turtle.TurnRight()
EndFor
```

Drawing Regular Polygons

You can easily change the square-drawing program (Listing 5-7) to draw other polygons. (Don't be so square!) A *polygon* is just a simple closed figure. For some examples, look at the three polygons in Figure 5-11.

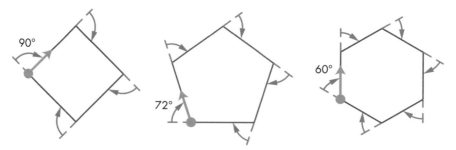

Figure 5-11: The exterior angles of three polygons

You use a general pattern to draw these shapes. To create the square in Figure 5-11, you draw four sides with a 90-degree turn angle after each side (that is, 360 degrees divided by 4). For the pentagon (the middle polygon), you draw five sides with a 72-degree turn angle after each side (360 divided by 5). For the hexagon (the polygon on the right), you draw six sides with a 60-degree turn after each side (360 divided by 6). Do you see the pattern? The angle is 360 degrees divided by the number of sides. With this in mind, you can create the polygon-drawing program in Listing 5-8.

```
1 ' Polygon.sb
2 numSides = 5        ' Set to 3 (triangle), 4 (square), 5 (pentagon)...
3
4 For I = 1 To numSides
5   Turtle.Move(60)  ' Polygon's side length
6   Turtle.Turn(360 / numSides)
7 EndFor
```

Listing 5-8: Drawing a regular polygon

To draw a different polygon, replace the whole number in the numSides variable on line 2 with another number. Figure 5-12 shows eight polygons (all with the same side length) you can draw with this program. Try it out!

Figure 5-12: The output of Polygon.sb using different values for numSides

What happens when you use a large number for the value of numSides? The polygon begins to look more like a circle! Set numSides to 36, change Move(60) on line 5 to Move(20), and see what happens.

A Star Is Born

With the knowledge you now have about the angles of different shapes, what do you think happens when you turn the turtle by multiples of 72 degrees (which is the angle you used to draw a pentagon), such as 2 × 72 = 144 degrees or 3 × 72 = 216 degrees? Run the program shown in Listing 5-9 to find out.

```
1 ' PentaStar.sb
2 For I = 1 To 5
3   Turtle.Move(150)
4   Turtle.Turn(144)  ' The turn angle is 2 * 72
5 EndFor
```

Listing 5-9: Drawing a pentagon star

If the turn angle is 144 instead of 72, the output is a star instead of a pentagon. Look at Figure 5-13 to see how this works.

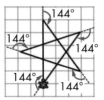

Figure 5-13: Illustrating the output of PentaStar.sb

NOTE   *If you'd like to hide the turtle after creating your masterpiece, call* `Turtle.Hide()` *at the end of your program.*

Try experimenting with different polygons and turn angles to discover the various stars you can create. Figure 5-14 shows three examples to help you get started.

Sides: 7   Sides: 8   Sides: 9
Angle: 3 × (360 ÷ 7)   Angle: 3 × (360 ÷ 8)   Angle: 4 × (360 ÷ 9)

Figure 5-14: Drawing different stars by using Listing 5-9

TRY IT OUT 5-3

Write a program that directs the turtle to draw the pentagon in Figure 5-15. (Hint: use the Angle property to set the turtle's initial direction.)

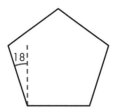

Figure 5-15: A pentagon

Creating Polygon Art Using Nested Loops

You can create beautiful shapes using polygons and stars. In this section, we'll draw a pattern created by rotating a square 12 times (see Figure 5-16).

Figure 5-16: The output of RotatedPolygon.sb

To make this art, you'll use a *nested loop*, which is when you place one loop inside another loop. Each time the outer loop runs, it also runs the inner loop. Listing 5-10 shows you how to use a nested loop to create the pretty drawing in Figure 5-16.

```
1  ' RotatedPolygon.sb
2  numSides = 4        ' Set to 3 (triangle), 4 (square)...
3  repeatCount = 12    ' How many times to rotate the polygon
4
5  For I = 1 To repeatCount
6    ' 1) Draw the desired polygon
7    For J = 1 To numSides
8      Turtle.Move(60)  ' The polygon's side length
9      Turtle.Turn(360 / numSides)
10   EndFor
11   ' 2) Turn the turtle a little
12   Turtle.Turn(360 / repeatCount)
13 EndFor
```

Listing 5-10: Drawing a pattern of rotated polygons

This program has two loops, one nested inside the other. The outer loop (line 5) uses a loop counter named I and repeats 12 times to draw 12 squares. During each round of this loop, the program performs two tasks. First, it draws a square using another For loop with a loop counter named J (line 7). Then, in line 12, it turns the turtle a little (360° ÷ 12 = 30° in this case) before it repeats the loop on line 5 to draw the next square. So fancy!

When you use nested loops, make sure you use different names for the loop counters. In Listing 5-10, we used the I variable for the outer loop and the J variable for the inner loop.

Change the numSides and repeatCount variables to experiment with different polygons and rotation counts. Figure 5-17 shows some shapes you can create by rotating a hexagon. Try changing the pen color and width to add fancy touches to your creations. The possibilities are endless!

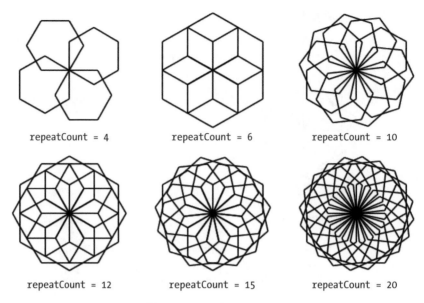

repeatCount = 4   repeatCount = 6   repeatCount = 10

repeatCount = 12   repeatCount = 15   repeatCount = 20

Figure 5-17: Patterns created by rotating a hexagon

TRY IT OUT 5-4

Predict the output of the following program. Try to imagine the result of the code before you run it. Then run the code to check your answer.

```
repeatCount = 5

For I = 1 To repeatCount
  For J = 1 To 4        ' Draws a square
    Turtle.Move(60)
    Turtle.Turn(90)
  EndFor

  For J = 1 To 3        ' Draws a triangle
    Turtle.Move(60)
    Turtle.Turn(120)
  EndFor

  Turtle.Turn(360 / repeatCount)
EndFor
```

Endless Graphics

In Listing 5-10 you created patterns by rotating a single polygon. You can also create patterns using two or more polygons of different sizes. To keep the code simple, let's draw two polygons of different sizes and rotate them.

Run the program shown in Listing 5-11 to see what patterns you can make.

```
1  ' PolygonArt.sb
2  Turtle.Speed = 10
3  numSides = 6      ' Set to 3 (triangle), 4 (square)...
4  repeatCount = 8   ' How many times to rotate
5  sideLen1 = 30     ' Side length of polygon 1
6  sideLen2 = 40     ' Side length of polygon 2
7
8  For I = 1 To repeatCount
9    For J = 1 To numSides  ' Draws the first polygon
10     Turtle.Move(sideLen1)
11     Turtle.Turn(360 / numSides)
12   EndFor
13
14   For J = 1 To numSides   ' Draws the second polygon
15     Turtle.Move(sideLen2)
16     Turtle.Turn(360 / numSides)
17   EndFor
18
19   ' Turns the turtle to prepare for the next round
20   Turtle.Turn(360 / repeatCount)
21 EndFor
```

Listing 5-11: Rotating two similar polygons

Figure 5-18 shows the output of this program. This program rotates two hexagons (the first has a side length of 30, and the second has a side length of 40) eight times. The outer loop in line 8 repeats up to the number in repeatCount. Each time the program loops, the code performs three actions:

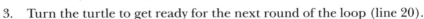

Figure 5-18: The output of PolygonArt.sb

1. Draw the first polygon using the side length in sideLen1 (lines 9–12).

2. Draw the second polygon using the side length in sideLen2 (lines 14–17).

3. Turn the turtle to get ready for the next round of the loop (line 20).

Now try using the repeatCount values in Figure 5-19 to create lots of different patterns. Try setting sideLen1 = 40 and sideLen2 = 60!

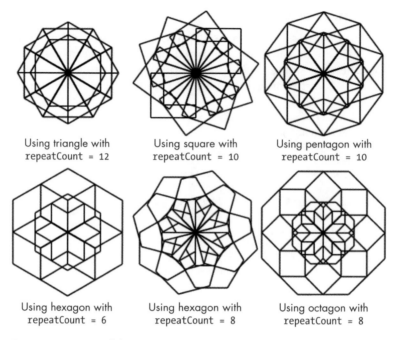

Using triangle with repeatCount = 12	Using square with repeatCount = 10	Using pentagon with repeatCount = 10
Using hexagon with repeatCount = 6	Using hexagon with repeatCount = 8	Using octagon with repeatCount = 8

Figure 5-19: Some of the patterns you can create by experimenting with PolygonArt.sb

Experiment with this program to see what other shapes you can discover!

TRY IT OUT 5-5

Change Listing 5-11 to draw three polygons (instead of two) of different sizes, and then rotate them. Save your discoveries for your next art gallery. (Or, if you don't want to become a millionaire, go to *http://tiny.cc/turtlepatterns/* and share them with the world!)

Programming Challenges

If you get stuck, check out *http://nostarch.com/smallbasic/* for the solutions and for more resources and review questions for teachers and students.

1. This code draws a circle:

```
For K = 1 To 36
  Turtle.Move(6)
  Turtle.Turn(10)
EndFor
```

Write a program to have the turtle repeat this code 12 times to create the pattern shown here:

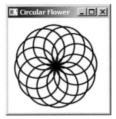

2. Write a program to draw a flowerpot like this one:

3. Re-create the following code and experiment with it:

```
For I = 1 To 20     ' Repeats 20 times
  For K = 1 To 36   ' Draws a circle
    Turtle.Move(12)
    Turtle.Turn(10)
  EndFor
  Turtle.Turn(18)   ' Gets ready for next circle
  Turtle.Move(12)   ' Moves a little bit before drawing next circle
EndFor
```

Change the Move() distance after rotating each circle to discover new patterns!

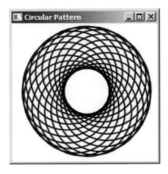

6

GETTING USER INPUT

To perform useful tasks or give you useful information, some programs need input from you. For example, in Microsoft Word you enter text, click buttons to make it look good, and enter a filename to save it. In a web browser, you click links or enter a URL or search term to find a web page. In drawing programs, you draw by clicking and dragging the mouse. When you use a program and give it information that helps it do its job, that information is called *user input*.

Programs need a way to ask users for input, process that input, and respond correctly. Programs that do this are *interactive*. In this chapter, you'll make your programs interactive by giving them the capability to accept and react to user input, which will be in the form of strings and numbers.

Talking to the Computer

Until now, all the information your programs needed was in the source code. For example, look at the program in Listing 6-1.

```
1 ' CircleArea.sb
2 radius = 5
3 area = 3.1416 * radius * radius
4 TextWindow.WriteLine("Area = " + area)
```

Listing 6-1: Finding the area of a circle

This program uses a fixed value of 5 for the radius in line 2. This is called *hard-coded* data. Hard-coded data is part of the program. If you want to change that data, you must change the source code. For example, to find the area of a circle using a different radius, you'd open the file, change the radius value in your code, save the file, and run the new code. It's a pain to do this every time you want to change the value of a variable. And if you give this code to someone who doesn't know how to program, it won't be very useful.

Your Number, Please?

Clearly, it'd be best if you could calculate the area of any circle without having to change the source code. So let's explore how to read values directly input by users. We want our program to ask the user to enter a value for the radius and then use that value in the calculation. To do this, you'll use the TextWindow method ReadNumber(). Replace line 2 in Listing 6-1 with the following statement:

```
radius = TextWindow.ReadNumber()
```

When this statement runs, a flashing cursor appears in the text window, as shown in Figure 6-1. The cursor is the program's way of saying, "It's your turn to type. I'm waiting. Don't make me come over there!"

Figure 6-1: Running the ReadNumber() method

When the user types a number and presses ENTER, the input is stored for the rest of the program to use. Whatever number the user entered is now stored in the radius variable.

NOTE *Run the program and try to enter a character other than a number. What happens? The program won't accept anything that's not a number! That's why the method is named ReadNumber().*

Introducing Yourself to Your Computer

A program can also accept user input in the form of text, or strings. Let's imagine we want to greet the player with their name. We'll store the player's name in a variable called userName but use a new TextWindow method called Read(). Run the following program, and enter your name when you see the cursor:

```
userName = TextWindow.Read()
TextWindow.Write("Hello " + userName + ". ")
TextWindow.WriteLine("It's really nice to meet you.")
```

The first statement accepts the text the user entered in the text window and stores that text in userName. The program then greets the user with their name.

So what's the difference between Read() and ReadNumber()? Read() works exactly like ReadNumber(): they both show a flashing cursor and wait for the user to type input and press ENTER. In fact, you can even use Read() to get numbers from a user. But ReadNumber() will accept *only* a number from a user, so we recommend you use it when you need your user to enter a number.

Writing Prompts for Input

A flashing cursor without instructions doesn't tell your user what kind of data to input (like a number, a name, an address, or favorite type of monkey). Unless your program is written for a magician or a mind reader like Professor X, you should provide some instructions before you allow your program to accept input from Read() or ReadNumber(). To do this, you'll display a *prompt*, which is a message that tells the user what kind of data to enter.

From Listing 6-1, replace line 2 with these two lines:

```
TextWindow.Write("Please enter a radius; then press <Enter>: ")
radius = TextWindow.ReadNumber()
```

First, we call the Write() method and pass it a message to display. In this program, the message you pass is a prompt telling your user to enter a value for the radius and then press ENTER. You end the prompt with a colon to show the user that the program's waiting for keyboard input. (You don't need the colon, but it's clearer to your user.) Use Write() instead of WriteLine() to keep the cursor on the same line as the prompt. After you call Write(), you call ReadNumber() to accept the number input by the user and store it in the variable radius.

After adding these two statements, run your program to see something like Figure 6-2.

Figure 6-2: The text window waiting for input from your user

When Small Basic runs the statement `radius = TextWindow.ReadNumber()`, it waits for the user to enter a number and press ENTER. The program won't read what the user types until they press ENTER. When the user presses ENTER, the program grabs the user input and assigns it to the `radius` variable. The program then continues with the statement after the `ReadNumber()` method.

Now that you've accepted the radius from your user, all that's left is to compute the area and display the result. Listing 6-2 shows the complete program.

```
1 ' CircleArea3.sb
2 TextWindow.Write("Please enter a radius; then press <Enter>: ")
3 radius = TextWindow.ReadNumber()
4
5 area = 3.1416 * radius * radius
6 TextWindow.WriteLine("Area = " + area)
```

Listing 6-2: Letting the user enter the radius

Let's see what the output looks like if you enter a radius of 8:

```
Please enter a radius; then press <Enter>: 8
Area = 201.0624
```

Try it out for yourself!

A Moment of Silence, Please (Pause)

At times you may need to display some instructions to your user (like explaining the rules of Hide and Go Tickle) and then wait for them to read those instructions. For example, you might display the instructions followed by "Press any key to continue . . . " and then wait for the user to press a key to show that they're ready to continue. You can do this by using the `Pause()` method.

To see this method in action, let's write a program that converts the computer into a wisdom machine. Each time the user presses a key, the computer displays a new bit of wisdom. The program is shown in Listing 6-3.

```
1 ' WisdomMachine.sb
2 TextWindow.WriteLine("WISDOM OF THE DAY")
3
4 TextWindow.WriteLine("A friend in need is a friend indeed.")
```

```
 5 TextWindow.Pause()
 6
 7 TextWindow.WriteLine("A hungry man is an angry man.")
 8 TextWindow.Pause()
 9
10 TextWindow.WriteLine("Love your enemies. They hate that.")
```

Listing 6-3: Demonstrating the Pause() method

After showing the first wise saying (line 4), the program calls Pause() to give the user time to read it (line 5). This call displays "Press any key to continue . . ." and waits for the user to press a key. When the user presses a key, the program displays the next bit of wisdom (line 7) and pauses again (line 8). The program continues to do this until the last statement is executed. Add more wise sayings to this program, and then share it with someone!

What if you want to display a statement other than "Press any key to continue . . . ," such as "Press any key to see the next line of wisdom . . ."? Well, Small Basic provides you with the PauseWithoutMessage() method for this purpose. You can write a custom prompt using Write() or WriteLine() as usual, and then call PauseWithoutMessage() to wait for the user. Try it out. Replace the calls to Pause() in lines 5 and 8 of Listing 6-3 with these statements:

```
TextWindow.WriteLine("Press any key to see the next line of wisdom...")
TextWindow.PauseWithoutMessage()
```

Your program runs the same way as before but uses a more descriptive prompt.

Working with User Input

Let's put your new knowledge to use by writing a couple of programs that read input from a user, process the input, and display the output back to the user.

Converting Fahrenheit to Celsius

Next, you'll create a program that converts a temperature from degrees Fahrenheit to degrees Celsius. The program prompts the user for the temperature in Fahrenheit and then converts it to Celsius using this formula:

$$C = (5 \div 9) \times (F - 32)$$

Run the program in Listing 6-4 several times to see how it works. To use the degree symbol, press and hold the ALT key, type **248** on your numeric keypad, and then release the ALT key.

```
1 ' Fahrenheit2Celsius.sb
2 TextWindow.Write("Enter a temperature in °F: ")
3 F = TextWindow.ReadNumber()
```

```
4 C = (5 / 9) * (F - 32)
5 C = Math.Round(C)   ' Rounds to nearest integer
6 TextWindow.WriteLine(F + " °F = " + C + " °C")
```

Listing 6-4: Converting Fahrenheit to Celsius

First, the program prompts the user to enter a temperature. When they press ENTER, their input is assigned to the variable F. Your program then converts the value stored in F to Celsius and stores the result in variable C (which is all done in line 4). Next, the program uses `Math.Round()` on line 5 to take the current value of C, round it to the nearest integer, and store the rounded value in C, which replaces the old value of C. You'll learn more about the `Round()` method in Chapter 7, but we use it here to make the program's output easier to read. Finally, your program displays the output (line 6).

TRY IT OUT 6-1

Try to guess what the following program does. Run it to check your answer:

```
TextWindow.Write("How old are you? ")
age = TextWindow.ReadNumber()
TextWindow.WriteLine("In ten years, you'll be " + (age + 10))
TextWindow.WriteLine("Wow! You'll be so old!")
```

Averaging Numbers

Let's write a program that finds the average of four numbers provided by the user. There are a couple of ways to do this; the first is to use five variables, as shown in Listing 6-5.

```
1 ' Avg1.sb
2 TextWindow.Write("Enter 4 numbers. ")
3 TextWindow.WriteLine("Press <Enter> after each one:")
4 n1 = TextWindow.ReadNumber()
5 n2 = TextWindow.ReadNumber()
6 n3 = TextWindow.ReadNumber()
7 n4 = TextWindow.ReadNumber()
8 avg = (n1 + n2 + n3 + n4) / 4
9 TextWindow.WriteLine("Average = " + avg)
```

Listing 6-5: Finding the average of four numbers

Look at the output when we enter 10, 20, 15, and 25:

```
Enter 4 numbers. Press <Enter> after each one:
10
20
```

```
15
25
Average = 17.5
```

The program prompts the user to enter four numbers and press ENTER after each number. It reads these numbers, one by one, and saves them in four variables: n1, n2, n3, and n4 (lines 4–7). It then computes the average of these numbers, saves the average in the variable avg (line 8), and displays the result (line 9).

Listing 6-6 shows a different way to write this program. Enter this program, and then run it. This time you'll use just one variable named sum.

```
1 ' Avg2.sb
2 TextWindow.Write("Enter 4 numbers. ")
3 TextWindow.WriteLine("Press <Enter> after each one:")
4 sum = TextWindow.ReadNumber()
5 sum = sum + TextWindow.ReadNumber()
6 sum = sum + TextWindow.ReadNumber()
7 sum = sum + TextWindow.ReadNumber()
8 TextWindow.WriteLine("Average = " + (sum / 4))
```

Listing 6-6: Finding the average of four numbers using an accumulator

To understand how the program works, let's say the user entered the numbers 10, 20, 15, and 25 in response to the prompt. So, in line 4, sum becomes 10. In line 5, the second number (20) is added to the first number (10) and saved to the sum variable (totaling 30). In lines 6–7, the third number (15) and fourth number (25) are added and saved to sum (totaling 70). The program then displays the average, which is sum / 4, to the user (line 8).

Because of how the sum variable keeps adding input to itself (or accumulating), it's known as an *accumulator* (also known as a *running sum*). (This might be similar to how you accumulate hairbands or Pokémon cards, but these numbers only take up computer memory and don't clutter your room.)

Reading Text

Next, let's write a simple program that makes silly sentences using the words in Shakespeare's famous quote: "To *be* or not to *be*: that is the *question*." You'll ask the user to enter two verbs and a noun, and then you'll use these entries to replace the words *be*, *be*, and *question* in Shakespeare's quote. Listing 6-7 shows the complete program.

```
1 ' Silly.sb
2 TextWindow.Write("Please enter a verb: ")
3 verb1 = TextWindow.Read()
4
5 TextWindow.Write("Please enter another verb: ")
6 verb2 = TextWindow.Read()
7
8 TextWindow.Write("Now, please enter a noun: ")
```

```
 9  noun = TextWindow.Read()
10
11  TextWindow.Write("To " + verb1)
12  TextWindow.Write(" or not to " + verb2 + ":")
13  TextWindow.Write(" that is the " + noun + ".")
14  TextWindow.WriteLine("")
```

Listing 6-7: Silly Shakespeare lines

When we ran this code, we entered *eat*, *swim*, and *cow*. This is the output:

```
Please enter a verb: eat
Please enter another verb: swim
Now, please enter a noun: cow
To eat or not to swim: that is the cow.
```

Try it out, and then come back. We'll wait. Are you back? Was your output funnier than ours? Well, go show someone!

TRY IT OUT 6-2

Write an interactive Mad Libs–style program in which you ask the user to enter the name of their favorite princess (such as Snow White), something evil, the name of a school for princesses, something yummy, a name for a short wizard, something so valuable that they'd never sell it, a verb, small creatures, and a superhero's power.

Then display the following story for the user, and replace the bracketed terms with the user's input:

"Princess [PrincessName] was traveling through the forest when suddenly the evil [SomethingEvil] jumped out at her and offered her an apple. Princess [PrincessName] refused, because her mother sent her to [NameOfSchool], where she learned that you don't take unwrapped food from strangers (it could be poisoned). So Princess [PrincessName] continued through the woods until she came upon a house made of [SomethingYummy]! Not wanting to damage private property, she kept walking. Next, Princess [PrincessName] came upon a spinning wheel where a short man named [ShortWizard'sName] tempted her to use a magic spinning wheel to make gold (in exchange for her [SomethingValuable]). But Princess [PrincessName]'s mother had already told her that an evil fairy had cast a spell on her when she was a baby and that she'd [Verb] forever if she pricked her finger on a spinning wheel. So Princess [PrincessName] kept walking and arrived safely home to a cottage with seven [SmallCreatures], where she locked herself in her room for the rest of her life because she had the power of [SuperHeroPower]."

Then make your own interactive story program with a new character (like a hero, ninja, pirate, or My Little Pony), and share it!

Programming Challenges

If you get stuck, check out *http://nostarch.com/smallbasic/* for the solutions and for more resources and review questions for teachers and students.

1. Using Small Basic, you can easily turn your computer into a number wizard! Open the file *Magician.sb* from this chapter's folder and run it. Explain how the program works.

2. Make a silly Mad Libs–style game using the phrase, "One man's trash is another man's treasure." Another version of the phrase is, "One man's loss is another man's gain." For your version, ask the user for two living creatures and two different nouns. Then have your program output in this format: "One [Creature1]'s [Noun1] is another [Creature2]'s [Noun2]."

3. Eve's mom is having a garage sale. Because Eve wants to earn some money, she sets up a table to sell lemonade, cookies, and her home-made greeting cards as the customers come up the driveway (she's a genius salesperson, so she sells a lot). Help Eve count the money her customers give her by creating a program that asks Eve to enter the number of dollars, quarters, dimes, nickels, and pennies she earned. Then have it convert them into a total dollar amount, and display that amount in dollars and cents (like $23.34). Try your program using the following amounts to make sure it works:

   a. 35 dollars, 3 quarters, 3 pennies

   b. 2 dollars, 1 quarter, 2 pennies

   c. 10 dollars, 1 nickel, 3 pennies

   d. 6 dollars, 1 quarter, 3 pennies

   e. 3 dollars, 2 quarters, 1 dime, 1 nickel, 3 pennies

   f. 1 dollar, 2 dimes, 1 nickel, 4 pennies

7

EMPOWERING PROGRAMS WITH MATH

If mathematics bores or scares you, that's okay. You'll soon realize how easy Small Basic makes it for you to write programs that do math for you. Many programs use only simple operations like addition, subtraction, multiplication, and division. For these types of problems, you need just the four basic math operators (+, -, *, and /). The asterisk (*) represents multiplication, and the slash (/) represents division.

Other programs need to use some of the math functions that you might have learned in algebra (like square root, absolute value, and trigonometric functions). Small Basic's Math object provides these functions and many others.

If you don't know what a square root or a trigonometric function is, don't panic; you still can write programs using these functions. And it's okay to skip some of the examples in this chapter, too.

To use any of the Math object methods, you'll write a statement like this:

```
ans = Math.SquareRoot(16)
```

In this example, you call the SquareRoot() method and pass 16 to it (to find the square root of 16). The output, or result of a method, is called the *return value*. In this statement, the method's return value is assigned to the ans variable (short for *answer*). In this chapter, you'll learn about the Math object's methods and how to put them to work.

Exponent Methods

The Math object has four methods related to exponents, but we'll cover just SquareRoot() and Power() in this book.

SquareRoot() and Good Old Pythagoras

In this first example, we'll find the length of the longest side, or *hypotenuse*, of a right triangle. If you call the lengths of the other two sides s1 and s2, the Pythagorean Theorem tells you that the length of the hypotenuse is the square root of the sum of each side squared. Here's the equation:

$$\sqrt{(s_1)^2 + (s_2)^2}$$

We put this formula in the program in Listing 7-1 so you don't have to think about it too much. Given the two side lengths of a right triangle, the following program uses the Pythagorean Theorem to calculate the length of the hypotenuse.

```
1 ' SquareRootDemo.sb
2 TextWindow.Write("Enter the length of side 1: ")
3 s1 = TextWindow.ReadNumber()
4
5 TextWindow.Write("Enter the length of side 2: ")
6 s2 = TextWindow.ReadNumber()
7
8 hypot = Math.SquareRoot(s1 * s1 + s2 * s2)
9 TextWindow.WriteLine("Hypotenuse = " + hypot)
```

Listing 7-1: Finding the length of a hypotenuse

This program prompts the user to enter the length of the first side (line 2) and then saves the input in s1 (line 3). It then asks for the second input and saves it in s2 (line 6). Then it computes the length of the hypotenuse (line 8) and displays the result (line 9). On line 8, notice how the square of s1 (and s2) was computed by multiplying s1 (and s2) by itself.

Here's a sample run of our program. Remember that this program works only with right triangles:

```
Enter the length of side 1: 3
Enter the length of side 2: 4
Hypotenuse = 5
```

Powerful Powers

You can use `Power()` for all sorts of calculations that involve exponents, like taking 3 to the 5th power. You might see this written in math class as 3^5, which is the same as $3 \times 3 \times 3 \times 3 \times 3$. The 3 is called the *base*, and the 5 is the *exponent*. Here's how you could perform this calculation in Small Basic:

```
answer = Math.Power(3, 5)
TextWindow.Write(answer)
```

Notice that `Power()` takes two arguments: the first is the base, and the second is the exponent. The result is saved in the `answer` variable. The second statement displays the output so you can check the answer.

Now let's look at a program that's a little more complicated. We'll use the `Power()` method to show you how money grows. If you deposit *P* dollars at a bank that gives an interest rate of *r* percent, then at the end of *n* years you'll have *A* dollars:

$$A = P \times (1 + r)^n$$

Without worrying about where this formula came from, let's write a program that computes the value of *A* for given values of *P*, *r*, and *n* (entered by the user). Enter the program in Listing 7-2.

```
1  ' PowerDemo.sb
2  TextWindow.Write("Principal (in dollars)........: ")
3  P = TextWindow.ReadNumber()
4
5  TextWindow.Write("Interest rate (decimal form)..: ")
6  r = TextWindow.ReadNumber()
7
8  TextWindow.Write("Number of years...............: ")
9  n = TextWindow.ReadNumber()
10
11 A = P * Math.Power(1 + r, n)
12
13 TextWindow.WriteLine("")
14 TextWindow.Write("After " + n + " years, ")
15 TextWindow.WriteLine("you will have $" + A)
16 TextWindow.WriteLine("That fortune is almost as big as Batman's!")
```

Listing 7-2: Calculating how your money grows

Run the program to see how much money you'll have in 20 years if you deposit $1,000 with an interest rate of 6%:

```
Principal (in dollars)........: 1000
Interest rate (decimal form)..: 0.06
Number of years...............: 20

After 20 years, you will have $3207.1354722128500
That fortune is almost as big as Batman's!
```

We admit it's rather strange to see dollars and cents written with so many decimal places. In this case, you don't need all those digits to the right of the decimal point. Next, you'll learn how to round this long answer to the nearest dollars and cents.

TRY IT OUT 7-1

The circus is looking for talent, and they think you're the one! They want to pay you $1 for balancing one cat on your head, $2 for balancing two cats on your head, $4 for balancing a third cat, and so on, doubling the money with each cat you add to the stack! Write a program to find out how much money you get when you have *n* number of cats balanced on your head, where *n* is entered by the user. Is it enough to retire and buy a cat mansion?

Rounding Methods

Sometimes you'll need to round numbers in your programs. For example, if your program finds the average number of children per household in your neighborhood, you don't want your program to display 2.25 (two and a quarter children per house). That wouldn't make any sense!

The Math object gives you three methods that round or chop numbers: Round(), Floor(), and Ceiling(). See Figure 7-1 for a quick overview of what each method does to a number.

Round(x) returns the whole number (or integer) nearest to x. Floor(x) returns the integer that's less than or equal to x, and Ceiling(x) returns the integer that's greater than or equal to x. Experiment with each of these different methods to see what results you get.

Let's use this rounding knowledge to fix the output of our interest calculator. Add the following statement after line 11 in Listing 7-2:

```
A = Math.Round(A)
```

After computing A, you round it and assign the rounded result back to A. When you run the program now with the same inputs, it will display $3207. Much better!

```
Math.Round(3.4) = 3
Math.Round(3.6) = 4
Math.Round(-3.4) = -3
Math.Round(-3.6) = -4
```

Round() behaves mostly how you'd expect it to when rounding a number. Above 0.5, it'll round up; below 0.5, it'll round down.

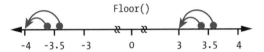

```
Math.Floor(3.4) = 3
Math.Floor(3.6) = 3
Math.Floor(-3.4) = -4
Math.Floor(-3.6) = -4
```

Floor() always rounds down, throwing away any partial fraction of a whole. Look at what happens with negative values!

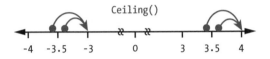

```
Math.Ceiling(3.4) = 4
Math.Ceiling(3.6) = 4
Math.Ceiling(-3.4) = -3
Math.Ceiling(-3.6) = -3
```

Ceiling() always rounds up.

Figure 7-1: The rounding methods with example arguments and return values

Traditional Rounding

Be careful when you use the Round() method if the fraction part of the number is exactly 0.5. In this case, the Round() method rounds to the nearest even integer (this is called *banker's rounding*). For example, 0.5 and −0.5 are rounded to 0, 1.5 and 2.5 are rounded to 2.0, and −1.5 and −2.5 are rounded to −2. This is different from what you learned in algebra, where the 0.5 fractions always round up to 1! Even though it's not what you're used to, banker's rounding is very common and is regularly used by bankers, which gives it its name.

But how can we make Small Basic round numbers the way you learned in school (where the 0.5 fraction is always rounded up)? We'll do some fancy footwork using the Floor() method instead of the Round() method, like this:

```
Math.Floor(x + 0.5)
```

Using this trick, x represents whatever value you want to round. So if x is 0.6, then x + 0.5 = 1.1, and Floor(1.1) = 1. Cool! That's exactly how we'd expect it to work.

But let's say x is 2.5. If we just used Math.Round(2.5), we would get 2, which isn't the result you would want if you wanted to use traditional rounding. We want to round up and get 3. Using our fancy trick, you'd get x + 0.5 = 3.0, and Floor(3.0) = 3. Now that's more like it! This gets the values you'd expect if you wanted to round a number with a .5 fraction.

Rounding to the Nearest Hundredth

Let's explore Listing 7-2 a bit more. Using Round() or Floor() on the answer gives you a whole number (dollars only). But what if you want to show the amount of money to the nearest penny? How can you make Small Basic round the answer to the nearest hundredth? Consider this statement:

```
Math.Floor(100 * x + 0.5) / 100
```

For example, if x = 2.8735, then 100 * x + 0.5 = 287.85, and the Floor() method returns 287. Dividing 287 by 100 is 2.87, which is the result we want.

You can also round to the nearest hundredth using this statement:

```
Math.Round(x * 100) / 100
```

Let's use this second technique to round the answer from Listing 7-2 to the nearest penny. Add the following statement after line 11 in Listing 7-2:

```
A = Math.Round(A * 100) / 100
```

After computing A in line 11, the program rounds it to the nearest hundredth (nearest penny) and saves the rounded answer back in A. If you run the program now using the original inputs, the output will be $3207.14. Perfect! Now we're talking money!

TRY IT OUT 7-2

Helen is having a tough time at her store. She uses a calculator to add the 6% sales tax to the purchase price. For example, if a customer's total comes to $27.46, she multiplies 27.46 by 1.06 to get 29.1076. But should she charge the customer $29.10 or $29.11? She doesn't have time to do these calculations herself! Her store keeps her much too busy!

Helen heard about your programming skills, so she's coming to you for help. She needs a program that lets her enter the total purchase amount. Then she wants the program to add the sales tax, round the result to the nearest penny, and display the answer. Create this program for Helen.

Abs(), Min(), and Max() Methods

The Math object provides methods for you to find the absolute value of a number. When you calculate the absolute value of a number, you're finding its distance from zero, which will always be a positive number. For example, the absolute value of both –1 and 1 is 1.

This code snippet shows you some examples:

```
Math.Abs(-2)        ' = 2
Math.Abs(-3.5)      ' = 3.5
Math.Abs(4)         ' = 4
```

The Abs() method takes in a number (positive or negative) and returns that number's distance from 0, or its absolute value. This return value is always a positive number. (In other words, Abs() removes the minus sign.)

For example, let's say the user of your game needs to guess a secret number (10), but the guess doesn't have to be exact. Instead, your game accepts any guess between 8 and 12. To check if the user's guess is okay, you can test the absolute difference between the user's guess (saved in the guess variable) and 10; that is Abs(guess - 10). If the result is less than or equal to 2, then your player's guess is good. You'll learn how to perform checks like this one using If statements in the next chapter.

Now let's find the minimum or maximum of two numbers. The Min() method returns the lower of two numbers, and the Max() method returns the higher number:

```
Math.Min(5, 10)        ' = 5
Math.Min(-3.5, -5.5)   ' = -5.5
Math.Max(3, 8)         ' = 8
Math.Max(-2.5, -4.7)   ' = -2.5
```

You can use these methods to limit the numbers your user can input to your program. For example, if your program expects a number that's less than 100, you can write this:

```
ans = TextWindow.ReadNumber()
ans = Math.Min(ans, 100)
TextWindow.WriteLine(ans)
```

Try it out! Run this code two times. The first time, enter a number less than 100, and the second time, enter a number greater than 100. What happens? Can you modify the code so the entered number can't go below 0?

What if you want to find the minimum of three numbers? For example, let's say you want to find the lowest score out of the three math quizzes you took last week. One way is to write this:

```
minScore = Math.Min(Math.Min(score1, score2), score3)
```

The inner Min() method finds the minimum of the score1 and score2 variables. That result and score3 are passed to the outer Min() method to determine which is lower: the first minimum (of score1 and score2) or score3. The final result is saved in the minScore variable.

The Remainder() Method

You can get the remainder from any division operation by using the Remainder() method. For example, Math.Remainder(10, 3) returns 1 because $10 \div 3 = 3$ with a remainder of 1.

You can use the Remainder() method to test whether one integer (whole number) can be divided evenly by another, smaller integer. A remainder of 0 means that the larger number's divisible by the smaller number (such as how 9 is divisible by 3). Knowing if there's a remainder has all sorts of interesting uses. For example, if you want to check whether a number is even or odd, you can examine the remainder of that number divided by 2: if the remainder is 0, the number is even; otherwise, it's odd.

To see the Remainder() method in action, let's write a program that finds the number of dollars, quarters, dimes, nickels, and pennies in a given amount of money. To find the most efficient quantity of dollars and coins, you'll need to start with the largest denomination (dollars) and work your way down the the smallest one (pennies). Listing 7-3 shows the complete program and includes example output in the comments. Read through the program, and see if you can figure out what happens when the input is 25.36.

```
 1 ' Money.sb
 2 TextWindow.Write("Enter an amount of money (such as 25.36): ")
 3 total = TextWindow.ReadNumber()          ' In dollars and cents = 25.36
 4 cents = Math.Floor(total * 100)          ' Total cents = 2536
 5 dollars = Math.Floor(cents / 100)        ' Number of dollars = 25
 6 cents = Math.Remainder(cents, 100)       ' Remaining cents = 36
 7 quarters = Math.Floor(cents / 25)        ' Number of quarters = 1
 8 cents = Math.Remainder(cents, 25)        ' Remaining cents = 11
 9 dimes = Math.Floor(cents / 10)           ' Number of dimes = 1
10 cents = Math.Remainder(cents, 10)        ' Remaining cents = 1
11 nickels = Math.Floor(cents / 5)          ' Number of nickels = 0
12 pennies = Math.Remainder(cents, 5)       ' Number of pennies = 1
13 TextWindow.Write("$" + total + " = ")
14 TextWindow.Write("$" + dollars + ", ")
15 TextWindow.Write(quarters + "Q, ")
16 TextWindow.Write(dimes + "D, ")
17 TextWindow.Write(nickels + "N, ")
18 TextWindow.Write(pennies + "P.")
19 TextWindow.WriteLine("")
```

Listing 7-3: Finding dollar and coin denominations

Let's walk through this program line by line to understand how it works. The user enters 25.36 (that is, 25 dollars and 36 cents) in response to line 2, so the total = 25.36. Line 4 computes the total cents as Floor(25.36 * 100) = 2536. This number is then divided by 100 to get 25 and saved in dollars (line 5), with a remainder of 36, which is saved in cents (line 6). Next, 36 cents is divided by 25 to get 1 quarter (line 7) and a remainder of 11 cents (line 8). The remainder of 11 cents is then divided by 10 to get 1 dime (line 9) with a remainder of 1 cent (line 10). Lines 11 and 12 compute the available nickels and the remaining pennies in the same way. The rest of the program (lines 13–19) displays the results. Figure 7-2 illustrates this program.

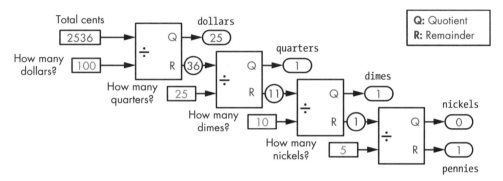

Figure 7-2: Illustrating the output of Money.sb

Let's try a different amount and look at the output:

Enter an amount of money (such as 25.36): **23.78**
$23.78 = $23, 3Q, 0D, 0N, 3P.

That's pretty handy if you're making change!

TRY IT OUT 7-4

Write a program that reads a three digit number and outputs each digit followed by its place value. For example, if the input is 368, the program should display this:

3 Hundreds
6 Tens
8 Ones

(Hint: if you divide 368 by 100, you get 3 with a remainder of 68. If you divide 68 by 10, you get 6 and a remainder of 8.)

Random Numbers

Random numbers are used in many applications, like simulations and games. They're also used for software testing (to see how a program responds to different input values) or to simulate random events (like the lottery).

The `GetRandomNumber()` method returns a random integer between one and the upper limit you pass to the method. Using this method, your program can generate random numbers that you can use in all sorts of exciting applications, for instance, to see whether a troll bops your hero on the head. Let's look at some examples.

To simulate a roll of a die, write this:

```
dice = Math.GetRandomNumber(6)
TextWindow.WriteLine("You rolled: " + dice)
```

The variable, dice, contains a number between 1 and 6 that's selected at random, similar to picking it out of a hat (but not the Hogwart's Sorting Hat). Run the program several times to see for yourself.

To simulate the flip of a coin, you can write this:

```
coinFlip = Math.GetRandomNumber(2)
TextWindow.WriteLine("Outcome: " + coinFlip)
```

The variable coinFlip is either 1 or 2. The value 1 represents heads, and the value 2 represents tails (or the other way around; it's up to you!).

To simulate rolling a pair of dice and finding their sum, you can write this code:

```
num1 = Math.GetRandomNumber(6)
num2 = Math.GetRandomNumber(6)
outcome = num1 + num2
TextWindow.Write("You got (" + num1 + "," + num2 + "). ")
TextWindow.WriteLine("The total is " + outcome)
```

Although your outcome will be a number between 2 (rolling two 1s) and 12 (rolling two 6s), don't make the mistake of writing this:

```
outcome = 1 + Math.GetRandomNumber(11)
```

Although this statement gives you a number between 2 and 12, the probability you'd get from one random number is different from adding two random numbers together.

TRY IT OUT 7-5

A bag contains 20 balls numbered from 1 to 20. Write a program that simulates drawing one ball from the bag at random.

Trigonometric Methods

Trigonometric functions are those mischievous enemies of high school students (sine, cosine, tangent, and so on). We won't explain what these are, but if you have no idea what a trigonometric function is or you've never even heard the word *trigonometry*, don't worry. Just skip ahead to Chapter 8. Otherwise, let's jump right in with an example.

Imagine that androids from the future have traveled back to our time to destroy humanity, and you're the only person who can stop their attack. You'll need to use your cannon to destroy their weapons warehouse, as shown in Figure 7-3.

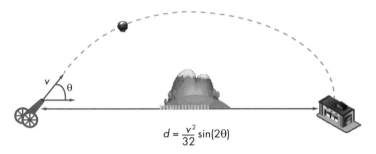

$$d = \frac{v^2}{32}\sin(2\theta)$$

Figure 7-3: Destroying the androids' warehouse

Your cannon fires with an initial speed, v, of 160 feet per second. The warehouse is 500 feet away. All you have to do is figure out the launch angle θ (the Greek letter theta). The program in Listing 7-4 prompts you to enter the desired angle, and then it computes the missile range *d* (in feet) according to the formula shown in the figure.

You need to run the program several times (using different launch angles) to find the best angle for your shot.

```
1  ' AndroidAttack.sb
2  v = 160 ' Initial speed = 160 feet/sec
3
4  TextWindow.WriteLine("Shoot the cannon to destroy the warehouse!")
5  TextWindow.Write("Enter launch angle in degrees: ")
6  angle = TextWindow.ReadNumber()
7  theta = Math.GetRadians(angle)   ' Angle in radians
8
9  d = (v * v) * Math.Sin(2 * theta) / 32
10 d = Math.Round(d)   ' Rounds to the nearest integer
11
12 TextWindow.WriteLine("Distance = " + d + " feet.")
```

Listing 7-4: Finding the launch angle

After the prompt, the program reads your input and saves it in the variable angle (line 6). Then line 7 converts the angle from degrees to radians using the GetRadians() method (the Sin() method requires its input to be given in radians).

After that, the program computes the distance using the given formula (line 9), rounds it to the nearest integer (line 10), and displays it (line 12).

Here's a sample run:

```
Shoot the cannon to destroy the warehouse!
Enter launch angle in degrees: 45
Distance = 800 feet.
```

It looks like humanity isn't quite safe yet. Enter some different angles in the program until you get it right.

In addition to the Sin() method, the Math object also provides Cos(), Tan(), ArcSin(), ArcCos(), and ArcTan(). You can read more about these methods in the Additional Resources section for this chapter at *http://www.nostarch.com/smallbasic/*.

TRY IT OUT 7-6

You want to select a 20-foot Christmas tree (for your school's festival) from a forest. One way to find the right tree is to attach a tape measure to a monkey and have it climb each tree, but let's use a little trigonometry instead. If you measure the distance, *d*, from the base of the tree and the angle, θ, as shown in Figure 7-4, you can compute the height of the tree, *h*, like this:

$$h = d \tan(θ)$$

Write a program that lets you enter *d* and θ, and computes the height of the tree.

Figure 7-4: Computing the height of a tree

Programming Challenges

If you get stuck, check out *http://nostarch.com/smallbasic/* for the solutions and for more resources and review questions for teachers and students.

1. Write a Small Basic statement for each of these algebraic expressions:

   a. $a = \pi\, r \sqrt{r^2 + h^2}$

   b. $a = x^{(y^z)}$

   c. $a = \sqrt{\dfrac{x + y}{z}}$

2. The following puzzle was written by the Egyptian scribe Ahmes in 1650 BCE.

   > "Seven houses each have seven cats. Each cat kills seven mice. Each mouse, if alive, would've eaten seven ears of grain. Each ear of grain would have produced seven bushels of wheat. How many bushels of wheat were saved by the cats?"

   Write a Small Basic program to find the answer. (Hint: use the `Power()` method.)

3. Create a program that converts a number of seconds (input by the user) to the equivalent number of hours, minutes, and seconds. For example, if the user enters 8110 seconds, the program reports 2 hours, 15 minutes, and 10 seconds.

8

MAKING DECISIONS WITH
IF STATEMENTS

Which shirt should I wear? What should I have for dinner? Where should I go? Should I wear my pants so low that my underwear shows? You ask yourself questions like these and answer them every day. Just as you make decisions, your programs can too! Of course, they won't do this on their own. Your programs only make the comparisons you want them to make, and then they either run some statements or skip them. In this chapter, you'll write programs that can make decisions.

The programs you've written so far followed a simple path where the statements execute from top to bottom. But sometimes you might need to run some statements if a condition's true or other statements if a condition's false. This is similar to how you make decisions in your life. For example, you might say, "If there's snow, then I'll go skiing" or "If I finish my work before 4:00 PM, I'll go to the movies; otherwise, I'll just go to Steve's house." In both cases, the action you take depends on a *condition*.

Small Basic uses a few different ways to control which statements run in a program: selection statements (If, If/Else, If/ElseIf), jump statements (Goto), and iteration or loop statements (For and While). In this chapter and the next, we'll explain selection and jump statements, and we'll explain loops in Chapters 13 and 14. In this chapter, you'll learn about relational operators, Boolean expressions, and how you can use If/Else statements to write some interesting programs.

The If Statement

Suppose your mom calls and tells you, "On your way home, stop at Captain Snarf's Pizza. If it's open, get us a large pizza." Her instructions don't say what to do if the pizza place is closed; you assume that you'll just go home empty-handed. Listing 8-1 represents this situation in code.

```
1 ' SnarfPizza.sb
2 TextWindow.WriteLine("Is Snarf's Pizza open?")
3 TextWindow.Write("Enter 1 (for open) or 2 (for closed): ")
4 status = TextWindow.ReadNumber()
5
6 If (status = 1) Then
7   TextWindow.WriteLine("You bought a delicious pizza!")
8 EndIf
9 TextWindow.WriteLine("Time to go home!")
```

Listing 8-1: Using If and EndIf keywords

Run this program and enter **1** in response to the prompt (to indicate that Snarf's is open). Because the condition on line 6 is true, the program displays the message on line 7, which is "You bought a delicious pizza!" The statement on line 9 (which comes after the EndIf keyword) runs whether you buy a pizza or not. Run this code again, but this time enter **2** in response to the prompt. What happens?

The statement on line 6 is an If statement. The part of the statement after the If keyword (status = 1) is the *condition*. The program checks to see whether the condition is true. In this case, it checks whether Captain Snarf's Pizza is open. The code between the Then and the EndIf keywords is the *action*—what the program does. The program does the action only if the condition's true. Programmers usually use the term *code block* to refer to the statements between the If and the EndIf keywords (between lines 6 and 8).

NOTE   *Small Basic doesn't require you to place parentheses around conditional expressions, meaning you can write the statement on line 6 like this: If status = 1 Then. But parentheses make the statement easier to read, so we'll use them in this book.*

Small Basic automatically indents If statements as you type the code. This makes the program easier to read and clearly shows when statements are part of code blocks. If your code ever gets un-indented, right-click in the Editor and select **Format Program** from the pop-up menu to indent all your code. Awesome!

The If statement is the basis of all decision making in Small Basic. Check out the illustration in Figure 8-1 to understand how it works.

The condition of an If statement is a *logical expression* (also called a *Boolean expression* or a *conditional expression*) that's either true or false. If the condition is true, the program runs the statements between the If and EndIf keywords (which is called the *body* of the If statement). But if the condition is false, the statements in the block are skipped. The program runs the statement after the EndIf keyword whether the condition is true or not.

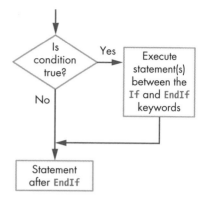

Figure 8-1: The flowchart of the If/Then/EndIf block

TIP *You can think of an If statement as a detour in the flow of a program. It's like an optional roller coaster loop.*

BOOLEANS IN THE REAL WORLD

The word Boolean is used in honor of George Boole, a 19th-century British mathematician who invented a system of logic based on just two values: 1 and 0 (or true and false). Boolean algebra eventually became the basis for modern-day computer science.

In real life, we use Boolean expressions all the time to make decisions. Computers also use them to determine which branch of a program to follow. A remote server may grant or deny access when you swipe your credit card at a department store based on whether your card was valid (true) or invalid (false). A computer in a vehicle will automatically deploy the airbags when it decides that a collision has occurred (collision = true). Your cell phone may display a warning icon when the battery is low (batteryLow = true) and remove the icon when the battery's charge is acceptable (batteryLow = false).

These are just few examples of how computers cause different actions to be taken by checking the results of Boolean conditions.

You can test all sorts of conditions using relational operators, which we'll discuss next.

Relational Operators

The condition (status = 1) in Listing 8-1 tests whether the variable status is equal to 1. We call the equal sign here a *relational operator* (or a *comparison operator*) because it tests the relationship between two values (or expressions). Small Basic supports five other relational operators that you can use in conditions. Table 8-1 shows you these relational operators.

Table 8-1: Relational Operators in Small Basic

Operator	Meaning	Mathematical symbol
=	Equal to	=
<	Less than	<
<=	Less than or equal to	≤
>	Greater than	>
>=	Greater than or equal to	≥
<>	Not equal to	≠

Let's look at a couple of short examples to see how these operators work. A lot of people want to be on Dancing with the Stars. You are hired to write an application form that potential dancers will fill out. One of the requirements is that the applicant must be at least 18 years old. How would you check this condition in your program?

Well, that's easy. You can write something like this:

```
TextWindow.Write("How old are you? ")
age = TextWindow.ReadNumber()

If (age < 18) Then
  TextWindow.WriteLine("Sorry! You're not old enough!")
EndIf
```

The If condition checks whether age is less than 18. If it is, the applicant isn't old enough, and their dream to dance with the stars is over. Nice try, tiny dancer!

Another way to check the applicant's age is like this:

```
If (age >= 18) Then
  TextWindow.WriteLine("So far so good. You may have a chance!")
EndIf
```

The If condition checks whether age is greater than or equal to 18. If it's true, the applicant passes this condition and still has a chance to dance with the stars.

But what if the applicant also needs to have exactly 9 years of dancing experience? (Don't ask why!) You can write something like this:

```
TextWindow.Write("How many years of dancing experience do you have? ")
experience = TextWindow.ReadNumber()
If (experience <> 9) Then
  TextWindow.WriteLine("Sorry! You don't have the required experience.")
EndIf
```

Note that the If condition uses the not equal (<>) operator. If an applicant enters any number other than 9, it's game over for that dancer!

TRY IT OUT 8-1

Santa wants to deliver presents more efficiently. Instead of crawling down chimneys, he'll drop the presents down the chimneys from his sleigh. He needs a program that inputs the sleigh's current height (in meters) and then computes the time it takes (in seconds) for a present to fall to the chimney. Here is the formula:

$$time = \sqrt{\frac{10 \times height}{49}}$$

The program must check that the height Santa enters is a positive number before computing the time. Run the following program two times. Enter a positive height in the first run and a negative height in the second. Explain what happens in each case.

```
TextWindow.Write("Please enter the height (meters): ")
height = TextWindow.ReadNumber()
If (height > 0) Then
  time = Math.SquareRoot(10 * height / 49)
  time = Math.Round(time * 100) / 100 ' Rounds to 2 decimal places
  TextWindow.WriteLine("Fall time = " + time + " sec. ")
EndIf
```

Complex If Conditions

Like arithmetic operators, relational operators also need two operands, one on each side. These operands can be simple, using variables and constants, or they can be complicated math expressions. For example, if you want to check that you have enough money to buy two large pizzas and pay a $5 tip, enter this:

```
If (myMoney >= (2 * pizzaPrice + 5)) Then
```

Small Basic first finds the value of 2 * pizzaPrice + 5 (using the current value of pizzaPrice). It then compares the result with the current value of myMoney to see whether the If condition is true or false.

You can also use any method that returns a value inside the If condition. For example, if you create a pizza delivery video game and want to give the player an extra life when their score gets to 100, 200, 300, and so on, you can enter this:

```
If (Math.Remainder(score, 100) = 0) Then
```

This condition checks the remainder of the current score, score, divided by 100. If the remainder is 0, the If condition is true and the player gets the extra life they earned.

TRY IT OUT 8-2

Translate each of the following statements into a logical expression, and then check whether the condition is true or false. Assume $x = 4$ and $y = 5$.

1. The sum of x and 3 is less than 8.
2. The remainder of x divided by 3 is 2.
3. The sum of x^2 and y^2 is greater than or equal to 40.
4. x is evenly divisible by 2.
5. The minimum of x and y is less than or equal to 10.

Comparing Strings

We just showed you how to use relational operators to compare numbers, but in some applications you'll need to compare strings. For example, you might need to check if a user entered the correct password for your program or if they guessed the right word in a word-guessing game.

You can use the = (equal) or <> (not equal) operators to test whether two strings are identical. Listing 8-2 asks the user to guess the secret passcode.

```
1 ' SecretCode.sb
2 TextWindow.Write("Guess the secret code! ")
3 guess = TextWindow.Read()
4 If (guess = "Pizza rules!") Then
5   TextWindow.WriteLine("You're right!")
6 EndIf
7 TextWindow.WriteLine("Goodbye!")
```

Listing 8-2: Comparing strings in Small Basic

Run this program several times, and try a few different guesses. For example, try entering **pizza rules!** (using a lowercase *p*). What happens? Run the program again, but this time enter **Pizza rules!** (with an uppercase *P*).

Did it work this time? Yep! The reason is that when you compare strings, they must be an exact match. All the capitalization, spacing, and punctuation must match.

Note that the other relational operators (<, <=, >, and >=) can't be used with strings. If you use any of these operators with non-numeric strings, the result will always be false.

The If/Else Statement

Your mom calls you back again and gives you more instructions: "One more thing! If Captain Snarf's is closed, please stop by LongLine Grocery and get a frozen pizza." Now you can use If/Else statements in Small Basic to help you!

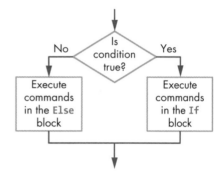

Figure 8-2: The flowchart of the If/Else statement

The If/Else statement (also called the *two-way If statement*) lets you take one action when the condition's true and another action when the condition's false. Figure 8-2 illustrates how this statement works.

If the condition is true, Small Basic runs the statements in the If block (between the If and Else keywords). If the condition is false, Small Basic runs the Else block (between the Else and EndIf keywords). So Small Basic runs the statements in only one of the two blocks (either the If block or the Else block).

You can write your mom's new instructions, as shown in Listing 8-3.

```
1  ' SnarfPizza2.sb
2  TextWindow.WriteLine("Is Snarf's Pizza open?")
3  TextWindow.Write("Enter 1 (for open) or 2 (for closed): ")
4  status = TextWindow.ReadNumber()
5
6  If (status = 1) Then
7    TextWindow.WriteLine("You bought a delicious pizza!")
8  Else
9    TextWindow.WriteLine("You got a frozen pizza!")
10 EndIf
11 TextWindow.WriteLine("Time to go home!")
```

Listing 8-3: Demonstrating the If/Else statement

If status = 1, meaning that Captain Snarf's is open, you'll buy a delicious pizza and go home. But if status is not 1 (Captain Snarf's is not open), you'll buy a frozen pizza from LongLine Grocery and go home.

Your mom's instructions assume that LongLine is always open and that you'll find what you're looking for. But what if the grocery store has run out of frozen pizzas? Stay tuned; you might receive another call from your mom to give you new instructions!

TRY IT OUT 8-3

Complete the following program to create a brainteaser quiz. This program will surprise you with its answers. Be sure to get creative with the way you present the correct answers!

```
' Asks first question
TextWindow.Write("If you take 2 apples from 3 apples, how many apples ↵
do you have? ")
ans = TextWindow.ReadNumber()
If (ans = 2) Then
  TextWindow.Write("Correct. ")
Else
  TextWindow.Write("Nope. ")
EndIf
TextWindow.WriteLine("If you take 2 apples, then you have 2 apples!")
TextWindow.WriteLine("")

' Ask more fun questions here
```

Here are some suggestions for the questions you can add:

1. How many inches of soil are in a hole 1-foot deep and 1-foot wide? (Answer: 0. Display: There is no soil in a hole!)

2. Is a ton of gold heavier than a ton of feathers? (Yes or No) (Answer: No. Display: A ton of anything weighs a ton!)

3. How many 4-cent stamps are in a dozen? (Answer: 12. Display: There are always 12 in a dozen!)

Nested If and If/Else Statements

The statements you write in the body of an If (or Else) block can be any kind of Small Basic statement, including another If or If/Else statement. Writing an If (or If/Else) statement inside another one creates a *nested If statement* (see Figure 8-3). The inner If statement can also include other If or If/Else statements, and the nesting can continue to any level you want. But be careful not to nest down too many levels, or you'll get lost in all the levels and might feel like Super Mario falling down an endless pit!

You can use nested If statements when you need to perform multiple checks on the same variable or when you need to test multiple conditions. Let's look at an example that uses a nested If/Else block to test multiple conditions.

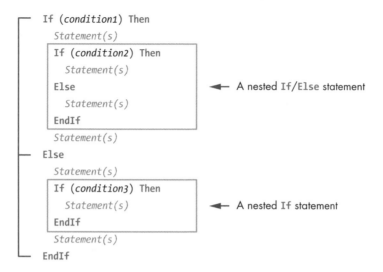

```
┌─  If (condition1) Then
│       Statement(s)
│     ┌────────────────────────────┐
│     │ If (condition2) Then        │
│     │    Statement(s)             │
│     │ Else                        │  ◄── A nested If/Else statement
│     │    Statement(s)             │
│     │ EndIf                       │
│     └────────────────────────────┘
│       Statement(s)
├─  Else
│       Statement(s)
│     ┌────────────────────────────┐
│     │ If (condition3) Then        │
│     │    Statement(s)             │  ◄── A nested If statement
│     │ EndIf                       │
│     └────────────────────────────┘
│       Statement(s)
└─  EndIf
```

Figure 8-3: Illustrating nested If and If/Else statements

After hanging up with you, your mom thought LongLine Grocery might be out of frozen pizzas. So she calls you again and says, "Listen, if Captain Snarf's is closed and LongLine doesn't have any frozen pizzas, then get a bag of frozen chicken wings." Listing 8-4 shows how to turn these instructions into code.

```
1  ' SnarfPizza3.sb
2  TextWindow.WriteLine("Is Snarf's Pizza Open?")
3  TextWindow.Write("Enter 1 (for open) or 2 (for closed): ")
4  status = TextWindow.ReadNumber()
5
6  If (status = 1) Then ' Snarf's is open
7    TextWindow.WriteLine("You bought a delicious pizza!")
8  Else ' Snarf's is closed, so you'll go to LongLine
9    TextWindow.WriteLine("Snarf's is closed. Try LongLine Grocery.")
10   hasPizza = Math.GetRandomNumber(2) ' Checks your luck
11   If (hasPizza = 1) Then
12     TextWindow.WriteLine("You got a frozen pizza!")
13   Else
14     TextWindow.WriteLine("You got a bag of frozen chicken wings!")
15   EndIf
16 EndIf
17 TextWindow.WriteLine("Time to go home!")
```

Listing 8-4: Demonstrating nested If conditions

There it is—a nested If/Else statement! If Captain Snarf's is closed, you run a nested If/Else statement to decide what to buy from the grocery store. Line 10 sets the variable hasPizza randomly to either 1 or 2. A 1 means that LongLine still has frozen pizzas, and a 2 means the grocery store has run out. Run this program several times to see what you'll pick up for dinner tonight.

But wait, your mom just realized that you might not have money, and she's calling back: "Sorry, I forgot to tell you. If you don't have enough money, just go to Steve's house and have dinner there!" Now we have to add another level of nesting. Listing 8-5 shows you how to handle this situation.

```
1  ' SnarfPizza4.sb
2  TextWindow.Write("How many dollars do you have? ")
3  myMoney = TextWindow.ReadNumber()
4
5  If (myMoney >= 25) Then ' I have enough money
6    TextWindow.WriteLine("Is Snarf's Pizza Open?")
7    TextWindow.Write("Enter 1 (for open) or 2 (for closed): ")
8    status = TextWindow.ReadNumber()
9
10   If (status = 1) Then ' Snarf's is open
11     TextWindow.WriteLine("You bought a delicious pizza!")
12   Else ' Snarf's is closed, so you'll go to LongLine
13     TextWindow.WriteLine("Snarf's is closed. Try LongLine Grocery.")
14     hasPizza = Math.GetRandomNumber(2) ' Checks your luck
15     If (hasPizza = 1) Then
16       TextWindow.WriteLine("You got a frozen pizza!")
17     Else
18       TextWindow.WriteLine("You got a bag of frozen chicken wings!")
19     EndIf
20   EndIf
21 Else ' I don't have enough money
22   TextWindow.Write("Go to Steve's house for dinner ")
23   TextWindow.WriteLine("(it's earthworm pizza night).")
24 EndIf
25 TextWindow.WriteLine("Time to go home!")
```

Listing 8-5: More levels of nesting

As you can see, you make decisions in a program in the same way that you make decisions in real life!

TRY IT OUT 8-4

Change the following program so that it starts by reading the values for x and y input by the user. Change the output messages to make the users laugh!

```
If (x > 5) Then
  If (y > 5) Then
    TextWindow.WriteLine("The skylight is falling!")
  Else
    TextWindow.WriteLine("Now it's time to play the piper!")
  EndIf
Else
  TextWindow.WriteLine("I'll huff, puff, and blow $5 on tacos!")
EndIf
```

The Goto Statement

The Goto statement also changes the flow of your program by letting you branch to a statement that appears earlier or later in your program. Look at Mark and Andy's annoying conversation in Listing 8-6.

```
1 ' GotoDemo.sb
2 Again:
3 TextWindow.Write("Mark: Pete and Repeat were in a boat. ")
4 TextWindow.WriteLine("Pete fell out, who was left?")
5 TextWindow.WriteLine("Andy: Repeat.")
6 TextWindow.WriteLine("")
7 Program.Delay(1000) ' Waits 1 sec to slow the program down
8 Goto Again
```

Listing 8-6: An endless Goto loop

The statement in line 2 is called a *label*; it's used to identify a specific line of the program. Labels end with a colon, and you can place them anywhere in a program.

This program then runs lines 3–7. When it reaches line 8, it returns to line 2 (to the Again label), and Small Basic runs lines 3–7 again. A *loop* is when you run the same block of code more than once, and this loop goes on forever (like *The Song That Never Ends* and the Barney song). Run this program to see its output (and try to get those songs out of your head; mwahaha).

The Goto statement is an *unconditional jump* (or *unconditional transfer*) statement, because the program jumps unconditionally (without asking any questions) to the location given by the Goto's label. The If/Then statement, on the other hand, is a *conditional transfer* statement, because the program changes its normal flow only when a certain condition is met.

Most programmers suggest that you don't use Goto statements because they can turn a program into *spaghetti code*—code that is so tangled and complex that no one can follow it! But sometimes a Goto statement can be very useful, and it's helpful to know when it might come in handy.

One common use of Goto is to check the data entered by a user to make sure it's correct, as shown in Listing 8-7.

```
1 ' VaildateWithGoto.sb
2 TryAgain:
3 TextWindow.Write("Enter a positive number: ")
4 num = TextWindow.ReadNumber()
5 If (num <= 0) Then
6    Goto TryAgain
7 EndIf
8 TextWindow.Write("You entered: " + num)
```

Listing 8-7: Using Goto to check the user's input

This code asks the user to enter a positive number (line 3) and reads the input into the num variable (line 4). If the user's input number isn't positive (line 5), the Goto statement sends the program back to the TryAgain label and asks the user to reenter the number. If the input number's positive, the program continues to the statement on line 8. You'll learn another way to check users' input using a While loop in Chapter 14.

TRY IT OUT 8-5

We (the authors of this book) plan to use the following program to measure our readers' satisfaction. Do you think it's fair? We do! Rewrite it and make it personal. Then have someone take your survey!

```
Again:
TextWindow.Write("How many stars do you give this book [1-5]? ")
ans = TextWindow.ReadNumber()
ans = Math.Floor(ans) ' In case the user typed a decimal
If (ans <> 5) Then
  TextWindow.Write("Invalid number! Please enter an integer. ")
  TextWindow.WriteLine("That's greater than 4 but less than 6.")
  Goto Again
EndIf
TextWindow.WriteLine("Wow! Thank you. You made our day!")
```

Programming Challenges

If you get stuck, check out *http://nostarch.com/smallbasic/* for the solutions and for more resources and review questions for teachers and students.

1. The following program creates a simple coin toss game by asking the user to toss a coin and enter either an *h* (for heads) or a *t* (for tails). Based on the user's input, the program displays a different message. Do you think the computer's playing a fair game? See if you can get a family member or friend to play this unfair coin toss game!

```
TextWindow.Write("Toss a coin. Heads(h) or Tails(t)? ")
ans = TextWindow.Read()
If (ans = "h") Then
  TextWindow.WriteLine("I won. I'm the champion!")
Else
  TextWindow.WriteLine("You lost. Cry home to Momma.")
EndIf
```

2. Captain James P. Cork is piloting the Century Hawk enterprise-class starship. He has intercepted a message from the enemy Clingoffs and needs your help cracking the code! The message has millions of sets of three numbers; each set of numbers needs to be sorted and then reentered to understand the message. Build a program that reads three numbers from the user and then displays these numbers, sorted from smallest to biggest, to Captain Cork. We wrote the sorting logic for you, but you'll need to write the user input part. Open the file *CaptainCork_Incomplete.sb* from this chapter's folder, and follow the comments to complete this application and stop the vile Clingoffs!

3. You're starting a new business called Mud in a Can. You've got mud, and people want it, so why not put it in a can? Write a program that lets your customer enter the height and radius of the can. The program should then compute the can's volume (to figure out how much mud to put in it). Have the program display an appropriate error message if the user enters a negative value for the height or the radius.

4. As the fairytale goes, Rumpelstiltskin helps a woman spin straw into gold. In return, she promises to give her firstborn child to him. When the baby is born, the woman refuses to give up the baby. Rumpelstiltskin agrees to release his claim to the child if the woman can guess his name in three days. Write a program that prompts the woman to enter her guess and then checks whether her guess is correct. Here's a sample run of the program:

```
What is my name? Paul
No! Your child will be mine! Mwahaha!
What is my name? Peter
No! Your child will be mine! Mwahaha!
What is my name? Rumpelstiltskin
Correct. You can keep the child. She's a brat anyway!
```

9

USING DECISIONS TO MAKE GAMES

Sometimes decisions are complicated. Let's say a boy and a girl want to see a movie. She wants to see an action movie, but he wants to see a comedy. She's willing to see a comedy if it has action, if it has good reviews, and if it stars an actress she likes. But the movie has to start before 10 PM and must be within a 10-mile radius of the restaurant where the couple is having dinner. Imagine what the code would look like to make a decision like that!

In this chapter, we'll continue the topic of decision-making and look at some new statements. We'll first introduce the If/ElseIf statement and show how it makes writing nested If statements easier. Then, you'll explore the logical operators And and Or, which let you do even more with your If statements. We'll also introduce the Shapes object so you get more comfortable working with graphics. And you'll put all this new information into action by building a game called Guess My Coordinates!

The If/ElseIf Ladder

It's all over the news! Franko, the alien monster, has escaped from custody. Luckily, you have your laser gun with you when you spot him attacking people in your neighborhood. You aim and shoot. Run the program in Listing 9-1 to see what happens next!

```
1 ' AlienAttack.sb
2 TextWindow.Write("A salivating alien monster approaches. ")
3 TextWindow.WriteLine("Press any key to shoot...")
4 TextWindow.PauseWithoutMessage()
5
6 damage = Math.GetRandomNumber(5) ' Randomly picks an outcome
7 If (damage = 1) Then
8   TextWindow.Write("Wow! You got him. ")
9   TextWindow.WriteLine("Now you can watch SpongeBob!")
10 ElseIf (damage = 2) Then
11   TextWindow.Write("You injured him. ")
12   TextWindow.WriteLine("He wants a Band-aid.")
13 ElseIf (damage = 3) Then
14   TextWindow.Write("Weak shot. Run for your life! ")
15   TextWindow.WriteLine("Now dance! You'll confuse him.")
16 Else
17   TextWindow.Write("You missed! He got you. ")
18   TextWindow.WriteLine("You should stick to video games.")
19 EndIf
```

Listing 9-1: Climbing the If/ElseIf ladder

The program picks a random number between 1 and 5 (line 6) and then checks that number to decide the alien's fate. Lines 7–19 are called the If/ElseIf ladder, which is commonly used to build a chain of If statements. Its general form is illustrated in Figure 9-1.

Starting from the first statement, the program runs through each test condition. As soon as it finds a true condition, it runs the statement(s) associated with that condition and moves down to the statement after the EndIf, skipping the rest of the ladder. If none of the conditions is true, the program runs the statements inside the Else clause at the end of the ladder, and then the program moves to the statement after the EndIf.

That's why the final Else statement is often called the *default case*. If you don't include the final Else statement in the ladder and all the test conditions are false, the If/ElseIf ladder does nothing, and the program continues after the EndIf keyword.

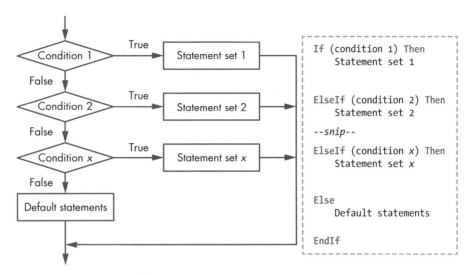

Figure 9-1: The structure of the If/ElseIf ladder

Let's look at another way to use the If/ElseIf ladder.

Letter Grades

In this example, you'll create a program that reads a test score between 0 and 100, and displays a letter grade from Table 9-1.

Table 9-1: Letter-Grade Scores

Score	Letter grade
score ≥ 90	A
80 ≤ score < 90	B
70 ≤ score < 80	C
60 ≤ score < 70	D
score < 60	F

The complete program is shown in Listing 9-2.

```
1 ' GradeLetter.sb
2 TextWindow.Write("Enter the score: ")
3 score = TextWindow.ReadNumber()
4 If (score >= 90) Then
5   grade = "A"
6 ElseIf (score >= 80) Then
7   grade = "B"
8 ElseIf (score >= 70) Then
9   grade = "C"
10 ElseIf (score >= 60) Then
11   grade = "D"
```

```
12 Else
13   grade = "F"
14 EndIf
15 TextWindow.WriteLine("The grade is " + grade)
```

Listing 9-2: Grading papers

Try running the program and inputting some numbers to see the results. Here are some output examples:

```
Enter the score: 90
The grade is A
Enter the score: 72
The grade is C
```

This program uses an If/ElseIf ladder to run tests on the entered score. Let's walk through how this program works.

The program tests whether the first condition, score >= 90, is true (line 4). If it is true, grade is set to A and the program jumps to line 15.

If it's not true, score must be less than 90, so the program checks the next condition, score >= 80, on line 6. If this condition is true (which means that score is greater than or equal to 80 but less than 90), grade is set to B and the program jumps to line 15.

If that's not true, then score must be less than 80, so the program checks the condition score >= 70 on line 8. If this condition's true (which means that score is greater than or equal to 70 but less than 80), grade is set to C and the program jumps to line 15.

If that's not true either, then score must be less than 70. In this case, the program checks the condition score >= 60 on line 10. If this condition is true (which means that score is greater than or equal to 60 but less than 70), grade is set to D and the program jumps to line 15.

Finally, if that last condition is still not true, score must be less than 60. In this case, no conditions are checked, grade is set to F, and the program jumps to line 15.

The Bug on the Ladder

When you're writing If/ElseIf ladders, the order of the conditional statements is very important. Be very careful with the order when testing your conditions. For example, go back to Listing 9-2 and replace lines 4–7 with the following code:

```
If (score >= 80) Then
  grade = "B"
ElseIf (score >= 90) Then
  grade = "A"
```

This change to the program means that you check the condition score >= 80 first instead of score >= 90. Now, if the user enters 95, the program just tests the first condition, sees that score >= 80 is true, and sets the grade to B. In this code, grade never gets set to A, no matter how high the value of score is. Nobody gets an A! When the program finds a true condition in this If/ElseIf ladder, it skips all the other statements and goes directly to EndIf.

To avoid this problem, make sure the conditions in the If/ElseIf ladder are in the correct order. You'll probably never want to check a middle value first. Also, be sure to run your program a few times to test the values and catch any problems before your users do.

TRY IT OUT 9-1

In Listing 9-2, you started by checking the condition score >= 90. You can also start by checking the last condition, score < 60, then 60 <= score < 70, then 70 <= score < 80, and so on. Rewrite the program using this reverse order of checking the grade.

Let's Get Logical

Sometimes you might want to check multiple conditions to see whether to run a statement. For example, you might adopt a dog only if the dog is big, is potty trained, and has three heads. One way to test multiple conditions is to nest If and If/Else statements like you have been doing in previous chapters. Another way is to use *logical operators* (also called *Boolean operators*). With logical operators, you can write test conditions that combine two or more logical expressions. Let's see how.

Do you remember something like $5 < x < 10$ when you learned about *inequalities* in your elementary math class? This expression describes a number, x, that is greater than 5 and less than 10. Figure 9-2 shows you how to write this expression in Small Basic.

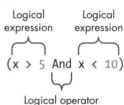

Figure 9-2: A compound condition in Small Basic

This is a *compound condition* that's made up of two logical expressions, $x > 5$ and $x < 10$, that you combine using the logical operator And. In order for this compound condition to be true, both of the expressions must be true.

Small Basic supports two logical operators: And and Or. Figure 9-3 describes how they work.

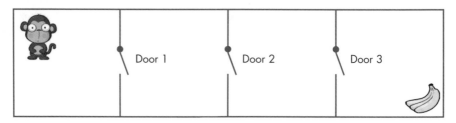

> thingie **And** thingie
>
> is true only if both thingies are true.
>
> something **Or** something
>
> is true if either or both of the somethings are true.

Figure 9-3: Explaining the logical operators And and Or

Next, we'll explain these operators a bit more.

Logical Operators in the Zoo

Look at Figure 9-4 and answer this question: how would the monkey reach the banana? That's right: Door 1 And Door 2 And Door 3 must be open. If any one of the three doors is closed, the poor monkey won't get the banana!

Figure 9-4: Performing logic with the And operator

Now look at Figure 9-5. In this case, the monkey just needs one door to be open: Door 1 Or Door 2 Or Door 3. This monkey likes its chances!

Figure 9-5: Performing logic with the Or operator

In Figure 9-6, the monkey has two options.

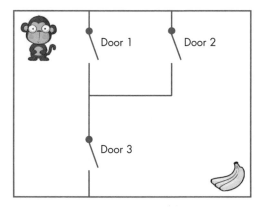

Figure 9-6: Performing logic with And and Or

If it takes the upper path, it needs both doors (Door 1 And Door 2) to be open. If it takes the lower path, it needs just Door 3 to be open. If you were programming this condition, you'd describe it like this:

```
((Door1 = open) And (Door2 = open)) Or (Door3 = open)
```

Are you ready to practice using And and Or?

The And Operator

The And operator takes two logical expressions as operands. *Operand* refers to the term that an operator acts on. Table 9-2 (called a truth table) lists the output of the And operator for all possible combinations of its two operands, X and Y.

Table 9-2: Truth Table for the And Operator

If X is	If Y is	Then (X And Y) is
"True"	"True"	"True"
"True"	"False"	"False"
"False"	"True"	"False"
"False"	"False"	"False"

If both X and Y are true, then X And Y is true too. But if one of the operands is false, then X And Y is also false.

Listing 9-3 shows two conditions (gameLevel = 1 and score > 100) combined using the And operator. The message You get 200 bonus points! is displayed when both conditions are true.

```
 1  ' AndDemo.sb
 2  TextWindow.Write("Game level: ")
 3  gameLevel = TextWindow.ReadNumber()
 4
 5  TextWindow.Write("Score.....: ")
 6  score = TextWindow.ReadNumber()
 7
 8  If ((gameLevel = 1) And (score > 100)) Then
 9    TextWindow.WriteLine("You get 200 bonus points!")
10  EndIf
```

Listing 9-3: The And operator

The statement inside the If block (line 9) is run only if gameLevel equals 1 and score is greater than 100. If either of these two conditions is false, the entire condition is found false and Small Basic won't run the WriteLine() method on line 9.

You can perform the same check by replacing lines 8–10 with the following nested If statements:

```
If (gameLevel = 1) Then
  If (score > 100) Then
    TextWindow.WriteLine("You get 200 bonus points!")
  EndIf
EndIf
```

Do you see how the And operator is a more concise way to test multiple conditions? The nested If statements require five lines of code, but using And, you can do the same thing in only three lines of code!

The Or Operator

How do you like your pizza? You might want to eat pizza only if it has four kinds of meat or if the crust is gooey. When you have multiple conditions but only one condition needs to be true, the Or operator comes into play. Take a look at the truth table for the Or operator in Table 9-3.

Table 9-3: Truth Table for the Or Operator

If X is	If Y is	Then (X Or Y) is
"True"	"True"	"True"
"True"	"False"	"True"
"False"	"True"	"True"
"False"	"False"	"False"

If either of the two operands is true, or if they're both true, the combined logical expression is true. The logical expression is false only when both operands are false.

Listing 9-4 shows an example of using the Or operator. The goal is to end the game if there's no more time to play (timeLeft = 0) or if the player has lost all their energy (energyLevel = 0).

```
1  ' OrDemo.sb
2  TextWindow.Write("Time left: ")
3  timeLeft = TextWindow.ReadNumber()
4
5  TextWindow.Write("Energy level: ")
6  energyLevel = TextWindow.ReadNumber()
7
8  If ((timeLeft = 0) Or (energyLevel = 0)) Then
9    TextWindow.WriteLine("Game Over!")
10 EndIf
```

Listing 9-4: The Or operator

If timeLeft is 0 or energyLevel is 0, Small Basic runs the command inside the If block (line 9). Run this program several times using different inputs to make sure you understand how the Or operator works.

You could use nested If statements to do the same thing. For example, you could replace lines 8–10 with the following code:

```
If (timeLeft = 0) Then
  TextWindow.WriteLine("Game Over!")
Else
  If (energyLevel = 0) Then
    TextWindow.WriteLine("Game Over!")
  EndIf
EndIf
```

However, as you can see, using nested If statements takes up seven lines of code, but using Or took only three! Using the Or operator is a more concise way to test multiple conditions.

The Cosmic Order of Evaluation

Look at the following condition. How does Small Basic evaluate this expression?

```
If (A = 1 Or B = 1 And C = 1) Then
```

As it turns out, Small Basic gives And a higher priority than Or. This means it finds B = 1 And C = 1 first, and then the result is used as the right operand for the Or expression. To change the order, you can use parentheses, like this:

```
If ((A = 1 Or B = 1) And C = 1) Then
```

This code finds A = 1 Or B = 1 first and uses the result as the left operand for the And expression. We recommend you use parentheses to avoid any confusion!

Logical operators like And *and* Or *are evaluated* after *any arithmetic operators (+, −, *, /) and relational operators (=, <, <=, >, >=, <>) in combined expressions. Among the logical operators,* And *takes priority over* Or; *use parentheses to change the order and make your code easier to read.*

It's almost time to apply all the decision-making information you've learned and build some exciting applications. But first we need to introduce a new Small Basic object, the Shapes object, which lets you build your applications using rich graphics. Let's make some pretty pictures!

TRY IT OUT 9-2

Open the file *DiceGame_Incomplete.sb* from this chapter's folder, and write the missing code to complete this game. The player enters their bet (from $1 to $10) and then throws a pair of dice. If the sum of the dice is 2 or 12, the player wins three times their bet. If the sum is 4 or 10, the player wins two times their bet. If the sum is 7 or 11, the player loses their bet. Otherwise, the player's balance doesn't change, and the player rolls the dice again.

The Shapes Object

In Chapter 3, you learned how to draw all sorts of shapes and images in the graphics window. But those shapes were *fixed*: once you drew a shape at a location, the only way to move it to a different spot was to clear the entire window and redraw that shape in the new place. If you need to move some shapes around in a program (like moving a character when the player presses a key), it's best to use the Shapes object.

The Shapes object lets you add, move, and rotate shapes in the graphics window. Run this code to draw a rectangle:

```
rectID = Shapes.AddRectangle(100, 50)
Program.Delay(1000)
Shapes.Move(rectID, 400, 200)
```

The program calls AddRectangle() to add a 100×50 rectangle and saves the identifier of the created shape in rectID. The created rectangle appears by default in the upper-left corner of the graphics window. The second statement pauses the program for 1 second so you can see the rectangle's initial position. The third statement calls Move() to move this rectangle so its upper-left corner is at (400, 200). Note how rectID is passed as the first argument to Move() to let it know the identity of the shape to move.

Think of the Shapes object as a "shape factory"—a factory that manufactures lines, triangles, rectangles, ellipses, and other shapes. When you ask it to create a new shape, it'll make the shape and return an identifier. Every time you want to do something with the shape you created, you'll pass this identifier to the Shapes object (as an argument to the method you call).

We won't cover all the methods of the Shapes object here. Instead, we'll discuss the ones you'll use in the next program. You'll learn the other methods as you progress through this book.

The two methods we'll use now are AddImage() and Move(). To understand how these methods work, open the file *ImageDemo.sb* from this chapter's folder. You'll see the code shown in Listing 9-5, which moves an image.

```
1 ' ImageDemo.sb
2 path = Program.Directory + "\Flower.png"
3 imgID = Shapes.AddImage(path)
4 Shapes.Move(imgID, 60, 20)
```

Listing 9-5: Moving an image using the Shapes object

Click the **Run** button. The output of this program is illustrated in Figure 9-7 (we added the gridlines and the numbers to show how the code works).

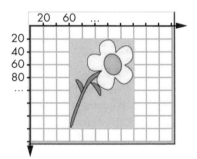

Figure 9-7: Moving the flower image

Let's assume that this program is saved to *C:\Book\Ch09\ImageDemo*. The *imageDemo* folder also contains the *Flower.png* image file. The Program.Directory property (line 2) points to the directory *C:\Book\Ch09\ ImageDemo*, which contains the executable program (the *.exe* file). Line 2 uses the + symbol to append two things to the directory: a slash (\) and the image filename (*Flower.png*). When the program runs line 2, the path variable's given the full file path (*C:\Book\Ch09\ImageDemo\Flower.png*).

Line 3 calls the AddImage() method and passes the path variable as an argument. This method loads the image from the file and returns an identifier of the loaded image; this identifier is saved in a variable named imgID. An identifier is like a tag that the Shapes object uses to keep track of the shapes it creates (for example, "Image1", "Rectangle3", "Line100", and so on). The loaded image is displayed in the upper-left corner of the graphics window.

Line 4 calls the `Move()` method to move the image. The first argument is the shape's identifier, which the program got from `AddImage()` and was saved into `imgID` (line 3). The other two arguments are the upper-left coordinates of the new position. Figure 9-7 shows the flower image with its upper-left corner at (60, 20).

The *Flower.png* image's width is 100 pixels, and its height is 140 pixels. If you want to move the image so its center's at (100, 100), you'd write this:

```
Shapes.Move(imgID, 100 - 50, 100 - 70)
```

Because you want the image's center to be at (100, 100), you need to subtract half the image's width (50) to center it horizontally and subtract half the image's height (70) to center it vertically.

This is all the information you need to learn about the `Shapes` object for you to build the application in the next section. Time to make a guessing game!

TRY IT OUT 9-3

Use code like the following to point to a small image on your computer and display it in the graphics window:

```
imgID = Shapes.AddImage("C:\Temp\icon.png")
Shapes.Move(imgID, 40, 60)
```

Update the path with the correct path for your image. Change the second statement to move your image to each of these positions: (100, 40), (10, 10), (27, 78), and then center it in the middle of the graphics window.

Create a Game: Guess My Coordinates

It's game time! In this section, you'll develop an interactive game called Guess My Coordinates that tests people's knowledge of the Cartesian coordinate system, or how well they can read an x, y graph. The game displays a star that represents a point on the Cartesian grid; Figure 9-8 shows what the interface looks like. During each round of the game, the star moves to a random location and asks the player to guess its x- and y-coordinates. The game checks the player's answers and displays a feedback message. It's like *Battleship* but more fun for math geeks!

The game uses the graphics window and the text window at the same time. The graphics window shows the grid and the star, and the text window reads the player's answers and shows the program's feedback. Now we'll walk you through the steps to create this game.

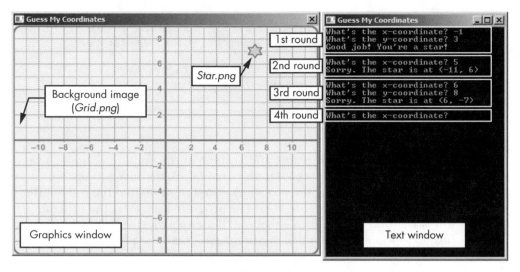

Figure 9-8: The user interface for the Guess My Coordinates game

Step 1: Open the Startup File

Start by opening the *GuessMyCoordinate_Incomplete.sb* file from this chapter's folder. This file contains only comments. You'll add all the code one step at a time.

The chapter's folder also contains the two images you'll use (*Grid.png* and *Star.png*). *Grid.png* is a 480×360 image of the Cartesian grid, and *Star.png* is a 24×24 image of a star.

NOTE *If you run into any problems, check out the finished program* (GuessMyCoordinates .sb) *included in the chapter folder to see what you did wrong.*

Step 2: Set Up the Game

Enter the code in Listing 9-6 to set up the game's user interface. This goes at the beginning of the file.

```
1 GraphicsWindow.Title = "Guess My Coordinates"
2 GraphicsWindow.CanResize = "False"
3 GraphicsWindow.Width = 480      ' Same as background image
4 GraphicsWindow.Height = 360     ' Same as background image
5 GraphicsWindow.Top = 200        ' Position on your desktop
6 GraphicsWindow.Left = 50        ' Position on your desktop
7 TextWindow.Title = "Guess My Coordinates"
8 TextWindow.Top = GraphicsWindow.Top
9 TextWindow.Left = GraphicsWindow.Left + GraphicsWindow.Width + 15
10
```

```
11  path = Program.Directory                        ' Program's directory
12  bkgnd = Shapes.AddImage(path + "\Grid.png")      ' Bkgnd (480 x 360)
13  star = Shapes.AddImage(path + "\Star.png")       ' Star image (24 x 24)
14
15  While ("True")                                   ' Runs forever
16    ' You'll add code from Listings 9-7 and 9-8 here
17  EndWhile
```

Listing 9-6: Setting up the game

Lines 1–6 set the title, size, and position of the graphics window. The window's size is set to be equal to the size of the grid image (lines 3–4). Lines 7–9 set the title of the text window and position it to the right of the graphics window (see Figure 9-8). The program then saves the program's directory (line 11) into path, which you'll use to make the full path for both images so you can draw them on the screen. Next, the program loads the two images and saves their identifiers (which are returned by the Shapes object) in these two variables: bkgnd and star (lines 12–13).

The While/EndWhile keywords on lines 15 and 17 are explained in detail in Chapter 14. For now, you just need to know that this code creates an *infinite loop* (a loop that repeats forever, like the Pete and Repeat program, *GotoDemo .sb*, you wrote in the Chapter 8). You'll add the remaining code for the application between these While/EndWhile keywords.

Test what you've written so far. You should see the two windows side by side, just like in Figure 9-8. The star image appears in the upper-left corner of the graphics window but doesn't do anything because you didn't write any code to move it yet.

Now close either the graphics window or the text window so you can add the remaining code.

Step 3: Hide the Star

During each round of the game, you'll move the star to a random position on the grid and then ask the player to guess its coordinates. Let's add the code to move the star.

Add the code in Listing 9-7 inside the While loop (line 16 back in Listing 9-6).

```
1  ' Finds the star's random position (in grid units)
2  X0 = Math.GetRandomNumber(23) - 12 ' Ranges from -11 to 11
3  Y0 = Math.GetRandomNumber(17) - 9  ' Ranges from -8 to 8
4  pt = "(" + X0 + ", " + Y0 + ")"    ' Example: (5, -3)
5
6  ' Sets to pixel units and moves the star to the random position
7  xPos = ((X0 + 12) * 20) - 12    ' Sets 12 pixels to the left
8  yPos = ((9 - Y0) * 20) - 12     ' And 12 pixels up
9  Shapes.Move(star, xPos, yPos)   ' Moves the star
```

Listing 9-7: Placing the star

In Figure 9-8, you see that the grid goes from –12 to 12 in the x-direction and from –9 to 9 in the y-direction. If you place the star at any point on the grid's boundaries, the player sees only part of it; the part of the star outside the grid gets clipped. That's why you'll restrict the star's x-coordinate to the range [–11, 11] and its y-coordinate to the range [–8, 8].

But how do you create a random number between –11 and 11? That's easy! From –11 to 11 there are 23 integers (–11, –10, . . . , 10, 11). If you call GetRandomNumber(23), you'll get a random integer between 1 and 23. If you subtract 12 from this integer, the result will be an integer between –11 (1 – 12) and 11 (23 – 12), which is what you need. Next, we'll explain the code.

You use two variables, Xo and Yo, to hold the random coordinates of the star. In line 2, the Xo variable is given a random value between –11 and 11, as explained earlier. In line 3, the Yo variable is given a random number between –8 and 8. These random values for Xo and Yo tell you which grid intersection point the star lands on. Next, the program builds a string named pt (short for point) in the form (Xo, Yo). This string shows the correct coordinates to the player if they enter the wrong answer.

Now you need to move the star to this new coordinate that you just created, (Xo, Yo). Figure 9-9 shows part of the grid and an example of where the star might be set. As you can see in the figure, each unit on the grid maps to 20 pixels in the graphics window; compare this with Figure 9-8 to understand the full scaling of the grid.

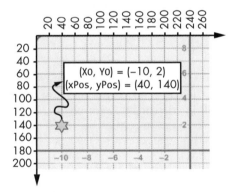

Figure 9-9: Grid coordinates for pixel positions in the graphics window

To move the star to a random position, you'll first need to translate the (Xo, Yo) grid units (what your user sees on the grid image) into (xPos, yPos) pixel units (what Small Basic sees). Let's do that now.

If the star's x-coordinate is –11, you need to draw the star at horizontal position 20 in the graphics window. If the star's x-coordinate is –10, you need to draw it at horizontal position 40, and so on. So you need a formula to map the star's x-coordinates, Xo = {–11, –10, –9, . . . , 0}, to their corresponding horizontal positions, xPos = {20, 40, 60, . . . , 240}, in the graphics window. To do this, you add 12 to x_0 to get {1, 2, 3, . . . , 12} and multiply the result by 20. Test it out! When x_0 = –11, (–11 + 12) × 20 = 20. When x_0 = –10, (–10 + 12) × 20 = 40, and so on. This is exactly what you want.

Mapping for the y-coordinate works the same way. If 8 is the star's y-coordinate, you need to draw it at vertical position 20 in the graphics window. If 7 is the star's y-coordinate, you need to draw it at vertical position 40, and so on. So you need a formula to map the star's y-coordinates, y_0 = {8, 7, 6, . . . , 0}, to their corresponding vertical positions, yPos = {20, 40, 60, . . . , 180}, in the graphics window. You do this by subtracting y_0 from 9 and multiplying the result by 20. Let's test this out! When y_0 = 8, (9 – 8) × 20 = 20. When y_0 = 7, (9 – 7) × 20 = 40, and so on, which is what you need.

You still have one minor detail to consider. Let's say the star's (x_0, y_0) coordinates are (–10, 2), as shown in Figure 9-9. You map these coordinates to pixels and find that you need to show the star at point (xPos, yPos) = (40, 140) in the graphics window. But you need that star's center to be at (40, 140). Because the star image is 24×24 pixels, the star's left position must be 28 (40 – 12), and the star's top position must be 128 (140 – 12). These are the numbers you need to pass to the Move() method. In other words, to align the star's center with the intersection of the grid lines, you have to subtract the star's width (12 pixels) from xPos and the star's height (12 pixels) from yPos.

In Listing 9-7, line 7 finds the star's xPos and line 8 finds the star's yPos in the graphics window. Line 9 then calls the Move() method to place the star at the desired position on the grid.

Step 4: Let the User Guess

Now that the star is displayed on the grid, you need to ask the player to guess its coordinates. Add the code in Listing 9-8 right after the code you added from Listing 9-7, still inside the While loop.

```
1   TextWindow.Write("What is the x-coordinate? ")
2   xAns = TextWindow.ReadNumber()
3   If (xAns = X0) Then     ' Player guessed the correct x-coordinate
4     TextWindow.Write("What is the y-coordinate? ")
5     yAns = TextWindow.ReadNumber()
6     If (yAns = Y0) Then   ' Player guessed the correct y-coordinate
7       TextWindow.WriteLine("Good job! You're a star!")
8     Else ' Player entered an incorrect y-coordinate
9       TextWindow.WriteLine("Sorry. The star is at " + pt)
10    EndIf
11  Else   ' Player entered an incorrect x-coordinate
12    TextWindow.WriteLine("Sorry. The star is at " + pt)
13  EndIf
14
15  TextWindow.WriteLine("")   ' Empties the line before a new round
```

Listing 9-8: Guessing the coordinates

This code asks the player to enter the x-coordinate of the star, and it waits for an answer (lines 1–2). Then it checks whether the x-coordinate guess is correct (line 3). If the answer is incorrect, the program moves to line 12 to display the correct coordinates of the star (see the box labeled *2nd Round* in Figure 9-8). But if the x-coordinate guess is correct, the code asks the player to enter the y-coordinate of the star and waits for an answer (lines 4–5). If the player answers correctly (line 7), the program displays Good Job! You're a star!. If not, the program moves to line 9 to display the correct coordinates.

In all these cases, the program ends up at line 15 to display an empty line, and the While loop repeats for another round of the game. The game never ends! (This is exactly how your parents feel when you're playing video games.)

The game is now complete. Try playing it now!

TRY IT OUT 9-4

Change Listing 9-8 to ask the player to enter the x- and y-coordinates, and then use the And operator to check xAns and yAns in a single If statement.

Programming Challenges

If you get stuck, check out *http://nostarch.com/smallbasic/* for the solutions and for more resources and review questions for teachers and students.

1. A love meter gives a number from 1 to 5 that indicates the warmth of your heart (a lower number is warmer). Write a program that asks the user to input their love indicator number and then displays one of these messages:

   ```
   1: Your heart is lava hot!
   2: Your heart is warm.
   3: Your heart is neutral.
   4: Your heart is cold, like the North Pole!
   5: If your heart was a movie, it would be Frozen!
   ```

2. Write a program to simulate a mouse's search for food (see the following figure). The mouse starts at room 1. From there, have the mouse go to either room 2 or room 4 (decide randomly). Pause to display this movement to the user. If the mouse goes to room 4, then for the next step it can move to room 1, room 2, or room 5 (decide randomly and then display the move). Make your simulation end when the mouse goes to room 3 (and finds the cheese) or goes to room 5, where the cat is patiently waiting for its snack. Open the file *HungryMouse_Incomplete .sb* from this chapter's folder, and follow the instructions to complete the simulation.

3. Obi-Wan Kenobi needs to know the day of the week. But R2-D2 just beeps at him. Obi-Wan counts the beeps, but he needs your help to translate that number into the day of the week. Write an If/ElseIf ladder that compares the value of the variable dayNum with 1, 2, 3, . . . , 7 and sets the value of the variable dayName to "Sunday", "Monday", "Tuesday", . . . , "Saturday" (so 1 is Sunday and 7 is Saturday). Help Obi Wan Kenobi. You're his only hope!

10

SOLVING PROBLEMS WITH SUBROUTINES

The programs you've written so far are short and easy to understand. But as you start dealing with more complex problems, you'll need to write longer programs. Understanding long programs can be a challenge, because you'll need to keep track of many different parts of the program. In this chapter, you'll learn how to organize your programs into smaller pieces.

An approach known as *structured programming* started in the mid-1960s to simplify the process of writing, understanding, and maintaining computer programs. Instead of writing a single, large program, you divide your program into smaller pieces. Each piece solves one part of the overall task, and *subroutines* implement these smaller pieces as part of a long program.

Subroutines are basic building blocks for creating large programs (see Figure 10-1). In this chapter, you'll delve into the wild world of subroutines, learn how to move data in and out of them, and use them to build large programs and fun games!

Figure 10-1: Subroutines are the building blocks of larger programs

Why Use Subroutines?

Let's say you run a construction company. Your job is to coordinate the work among your contractors and build houses. As a manager, you don't have to know all the nitty-gritty details of building a home: the plumber handles the plumbing, the roofer shingles the roof, and the electrician runs all the wires. Each contractor knows their job and is always ready to work when they receive your call.

That's very similar to how subroutines work! Each subroutine has its own name, like how the plumber's name is Mario. Each subroutine does something different, just like how the plumber and the roofer have different jobs, but all are needed to build the house. As the programmer, you're the manager, and your job is to solve problems as you build your program. You call your contractors (that is, your subroutines) and let them know when you need them to work (see Figure 10-2). You start writing the program by typing statements in the editor. When you need to perform a job that a subroutine handles, you just call that subroutine and wait. When the subroutine completes its task, you move on to the next step in your program.

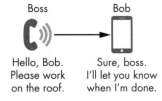

Figure 10-2: The boss (main program) calling the Bob subroutine

There's nothing new about this call-and-wait strategy; you've been doing it since Chapter 1. When you call an object's method, you're actually giving the work to that object in the Small Basic library. Subroutines are like methods, but *you* have to write all the statements in the subroutines. Subroutines help you organize your thinking process and make it easier to fix errors.

Writing Subroutines

Let's use a fun example to learn how to write a subroutine: in his travels, Gulliver had dinner with the king and queen of Lilliput (the land of tiny people). During dinner, the king explained that he was 8.5 glum-gluffs tall.

Gulliver later learned that 1 glum-gluff is about 0.75 inches. To find out how the sizes of items in Lilliput compare to sizes in our land, write the program in Listing 10-1, which converts glum-gluffs to inches.

```
1  ' GlumGluff.sb
2  TextWindow.Write("How many glum-gluffs? ")
3  glumGluffs = TextWindow.ReadNumber()
4
5  inches = 0.75 * glumGluffs              ' Converts to inches
6  inches = Math.Round(inches * 100) / 100  ' Rounds to 2 decimal places
7  TextWindow.WriteLine("That's about " + inches + " inches.")
```

Listing 10-1: Converting measurements

This program looks just like the ones you're already used to! You prompt the user to enter the glum-gluff measurement (line 2), read the input into the glumGluffs variable (line 3), convert the input number to inches (line 5), round the answer to two decimal places (line 6), and then display the result (line 7). Run the program to figure out how tall the king is in inches; remember that he's 8.5 glum-gluffs tall.

Next, let's rewrite this program and put the conversion statements (lines 5–6) in a subroutine named GlumGluffToInch(). Enter the code in Listing 10-2.

```
1  ' GlumGluff2.sb
2  TextWindow.Write("How many glum-gluffs? ")
3  glumGluffs = TextWindow.ReadNumber()
4
5  GlumGluffToInch()      ' Calls the subroutine
6  TextWindow.WriteLine("That's about " + inches + " inches.")
7
8  ' This subroutine converts from glum-gluffs to inches
9  ' Input: glumGluff; the size in glum-gluff units
10 ' Output: inches; the size in inches rounded to 2 decimal places
11 Sub GlumGluffToInch
12   inches = 0.75 * glumGluffs
13   inches = Math.Round(inches * 100) / 100
14 EndSub
```

Listing 10-2: Calling a subroutine

This code does the same thing as the code in Listing 10-1, but it uses a subroutine. A subroutine is a collection of statements that do a specific job (just like hiring Mario the plumber to build a fancy toilet). In this case, your subroutine converts glum-gluffs to inches. The statements that make up the subroutine are sandwiched between the Sub and EndSub keywords (lines 11–14). The subroutine's name comes after the Sub keyword (line 11). When you define the subroutine, don't put parentheses after its name.

But just because you define a subroutine doesn't mean your program will run it. To run a subroutine, you need to *call* (or *invoke*) it! To call a subroutine, you type its name followed by parentheses (line 5). The statement on line 5 means "run the subroutine named `GlumGluffToInch()`, and then return to the line that comes after this subroutine call" (which is line 6 in this example). It's like taking a break from cleaning your room to go watch some TV and then coming back to pick up where you left off. Figure 10-3 shows how a subroutine works in a program.

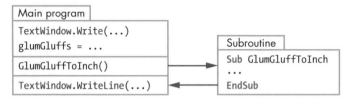

Figure 10-3: Showing how GlumGuff2.sb *calls the* `GlumGluffToInch()` *subroutine*

Here is one example of output from this program:

```
How many glum-gluffs? 8.5
That's about 6.38 inches.
```

A subroutine can access all the variables in the main program, and the main program can access all the variables in a subroutine. The variable `glumGluffs` was created and assigned a value in the main program (line 3), but it was used by the subroutine to know how many glum-gluffs it needs to convert (line 12). And the variable `inches` was created inside the subroutine (line 12), but the main program reads it and displays its value to the user (line 6).

Here are some good reasons to put the unit conversion code into a subroutine:

1. You isolate (or separate) the unit conversion details from the main program. The main program now doesn't have to worry about how the conversion is done. This makes your code easier to read and maintain.

2. If errors occur, you know where to look, which makes debugging much easier to do.

3. You don't have to write the same code over and over again! Without using subroutines, if a program needs to run the same set of statements more than once, you have to duplicate these statements in your code. But if you put those statements in a subroutine, you can call it from any point in your program (*code reuse*). You'll practice this in the next section.

NOTE *In this book, we'll start the name of a subroutine with a capital letter. We'll also write all the subroutines at the bottom of every main program. We recommend you follow the same practice in your own programs: it'll help keep you organized!*

When Gulliver asked what a glum-gluff was, he was told it was 1/20 of a mum-gluff. Write a subroutine named `MumGluffToFoot()` that converts mum-gluffs to feet. Write a program that prompts the user for a mum-gluff measurement, calls the subroutine, and then displays the result.

Subroutine Input and Output

You can think of a subroutine as a small program that provides a service to the main program. When the main program needs that service, it prepares the inputs that the subroutine needs and then calls the subroutine to start its job. The subroutine runs, saves its output(s) in some variables, and returns to the main program. When the main program continues, it looks at any new information from the subroutine and then uses that data to decide what to do next.

Small Basic doesn't let you pass arguments to subroutines between parentheses (like you do with an object's method, such as the `DrawLine()` method of `GraphicsWindow`). And it doesn't define subroutines that directly return a value (like the `Math.Round()` method does). So you need to use variables to pass data between the main program and your subroutines. Let's see how that works.

Great news! You inherited some land (Figure 10-4) from Uncle Moneybags. But you need to know the area of the land before you can sell it. The figure also shows Heron's formula, which computes the area of a triangle given the lengths of its three sides. Don't worry if you're not familiar with this formula; you don't need to fully understand something in order to use it (or most people wouldn't be allowed to use the toilet).

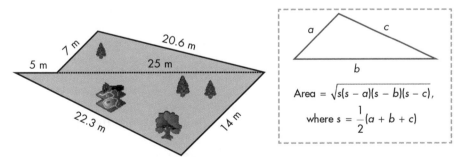

Figure 10-4: Calculating the area of the piece of land you inherited

Because the land is made up of two triangles, you can compute the area of these triangles and then add them together. Follow Listing 10-3 and note how we put the code for calculating the triangle's area (Heron's formula) in a subroutine.

```
 1  ' LandArea.sb
 2  ' Calculates the area of the first triangle
 3  side1 = 7
 4  side2 = 20.6
 5  side3 = 25
 6  TriangleArea()
 7  totalArea = area       ' Saves the result from the subroutine call
 8
 9  ' Calculates the area of the second triangle
10  side1 = 30
11  side2 = 14
12  side3 = 22.3
13  TriangleArea()
14  totalArea = totalArea + area      ' Adds the new area
15
16  totalArea = Math.Round(totalArea * 100) / 100   ' Rounds the answer
17  TextWindow.WriteLine("Area = " + totalArea + " square meters")
18
19  ' Subroutine: computes the area of a triangle given its three sides
20  ' Inputs: side1, side2, and side3; the length of the three sides
21  ' Outputs: area; the area of the triangle
22  ' Temporary variables: s; the semiperimeter
23  Sub TriangleArea
24    s = 0.5 * (side1 + side2 + side3)
25    area = Math.SquareRoot(s * (s - side1) * (s - side2) * (s - side3))
26  EndSub
```

Listing 10-3: Calling a subroutine multiple times

Here's the output of this program:

```
Area = 208.63 square meters
```

The main program sets the lengths of the three sides of the first triangle (lines 3–5) and then calls the TriangleArea() subroutine (line 6). The subroutine (lines 23–26) saves the computed area in a variable named area. After the subroutine call, the main program stores this first area in the totalArea variable (line 7). Without this, the value stored in area will be lost the next time we call the TriangleArea() subroutine. Then the main program sets the values to compute the area of the second triangle (lines 10–12) and calls the subroutine again (line 13). When the subroutine ends, the main program adds the new area to totalArea (line 14). The main program then rounds the answer (line 16) and displays it (line 17).

The TriangleArea() subroutine uses a temporary variable named s to store the *semiperimeter*, one-half of the perimeter of the current shape (line 24). Note how this variable is used to compute the area in line 25. This variable isn't intended to be used by the main program, which just cares about the area variable. But the main program knows about it (for example, it can display the variable). Because your subroutines can change variables that belong to the main program, be sure to name your variables carefully and clearly. For example, if the s variable seems confusing, rename it to semiperimeter so you'll remember what it does.

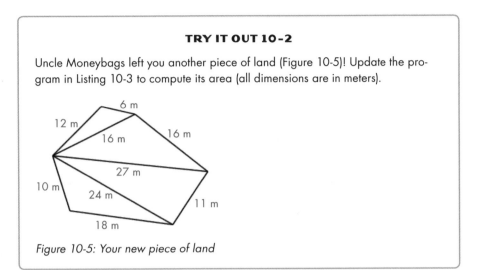

TRY IT OUT 10-2

Uncle Moneybags left you another piece of land (Figure 10-5)! Update the program in Listing 10-3 to compute its area (all dimensions are in meters).

Figure 10-5: Your new piece of land

Nesting Subroutines

If your chore is to clean the house, you might get help by making a deal with your sister to clean the windows and asking your dog to clean the floor under the table. Similarly, a subroutine might call other subroutines to help it do part of a larger job. In Figure 10-6, the main program calls a subroutine, SubA(), which then calls another subroutine, SubC(). Subroutines called from other subroutines are *nested subroutines*.

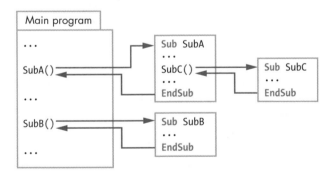

Figure 10-6: Illustrating nested subroutines

NOTE *If your program contains many subroutines, you can place these subroutines at the end of your program in any order you like. For example, it doesn't matter if you put the code for SubA() before or after SubB(). What matters is the order in which you call these subroutines, not where you place them in your code!*

To try out this concept, you'll play Pepper Dare, an exciting game of chance, against the computer. When the game starts, the player is handed 10 imaginary cards face down. One of those cards has a jalapeño pepper on it; the rest are blank. The player picks a card and hopes for a blank one. If the player picks the card with the jalapeño, the player has to eat a hot pepper and the computer wins! If the player doesn't get the pepper card, the computer takes a turn. The game ends when either the player or computer eats the pepper and runs for a drink of water. Enter the main program in Listing 10-4 into Small Basic. You'll add the subroutines in a moment.

```
1  ' PepperDare.sb
2  player = 1  ' 1 for player, 2 for computer
3  pepper = Math.GetRandomNumber(10) ' Which card has the pepper
4
5  Again:
6  Pick()       ' Updates the two variables: card and name
7  If (card = pepper) Then
8    TextWindow.Write("Hot tamale, it's a pepper! ")
9    TextWindow.WriteLine(name + " wins!")
10   TextWindow.WriteLine("")
11 Else
12   TextWindow.Write("The card is blank. ")
13   TextWindow.WriteLine("You put it back in and shuffle the deck.")
14   TextWindow.WriteLine("")
15   player = 3 - player    ' Switches the player
16   Goto Again
17 EndIf
```

Listing 10-4: Setting up Pepper Dare

The game starts by setting the player variable to 1 to give you the first turn (line 2). It then randomly picks 1 of the 10 cards to be the card that has the jalapeño pepper (line 3). Then it starts a loop (lines 5–17) to take turns. In each round, the game picks one card at random for the player (or the computer) by calling the Pick() subroutine (line 6). If the picked card has a pepper on it (line 7), the game displays the winner's name (line 9), and the game ends because the program moves out of the If loop and jumps from line 10 to line 17, bypassing the Goto loop on line 16.

Otherwise, it displays The card is blank. You put it back in and shuffle the deck. (lines 12–13) to indicate that the player (or the computer) picked a blank card. The game then switches to the next player (line 15) and goes back to start a new round (line 16). This is how the statement on line 15 works: if player is 1 (you, the user), then 3 – 1 is 2 (switching to the computer's turn), and if player is 2 (the computer), then 3 – 2 is 1 (switching back to the user's turn).

Next, you'll add the Pick() subroutine in Listing 10-5 to the bottom of your program.

```
1  Sub Pick
2    If (player = 1) Then
3      name = "The computer"
```

```
 4      TextWindow.WriteLine("Your turn. Pick a card.")
 5    Else
 6      name = "The player"
 7      TextWindow.WriteLine("The computer picks a card.")
 8    EndIf
 9
10    TextWindow.Write("[Press any key...]")
11    TextWindow.PauseWithoutMessage()
12    TextWindow.WriteLine("")
13
14    card = Math.GetRandomNumber(10) ' Picks a random card
15    Animate() ' Animates the delay in picking a card
16 EndSub
```

Listing 10-5: The `Pick()` subroutine for Pepper Dare

The subroutine starts by checking the current player (either you or the computer) and then sets the name variable (lines 3 and 6). Next, it asks you to press any key to have you or the computer pick a card (lines 10–12). Then it randomly picks a card (line 14) and calls the nested Animate() subroutine to animate an arrow in the text window.

Now add the Animate() subroutine in Listing 10-6 to the bottom of your program.

```
1 Sub Animate
2    For N = 1 To card
3      TextWindow.Write("-")
4      Program.Delay(100)
5    EndFor
6    TextWindow.Write("-> ")
7 EndSub
```

Listing 10-6: Subroutine to animate the delay

Don't worry about the For loop here. You'll learn about it in depth in Chapter 13. For now, this code just slowly displays a variable-length arrow. Here's a sample run of the completed Pepper Dare program:

```
Your turn. Pick a card.
[Press any key...]
--> The card is blank. You put it back in and shuffle the deck.

The computer picks a card.
[Press any key...]
--------> The card is blank. You put it back in and shuffle the deck.

Your turn. Pick a card.
[Press any key...]
---------> Hot tamale, it's a pepper! The computer wins!
```

NOTE   *Not only can a subroutine call other subroutines, but it can also call itself (this is called* recursion*)! See the online resources to learn more.*

Create a Dragon Game

The previous example showed you how subroutines can add structure and clarity to your programs. You break your program into smaller pieces and tackle them one at a time. Although every problem is different and there's no one-size-fits-all solution, we recommend a few ways to think through any problem.

First, spend some time trying to fully understand the problem. You wouldn't dive into a pool without looking at it first, right?! (What if it was filled with pudding?) When you have a good idea of the problem you need to solve, plan a general solution. Then divide it into major tasks. As the solution planner, you decide what those tasks are. There's no right or wrong answer; with practice you'll get better at making these choices. But if you start with the general solution and break it down into smaller tasks, the logic of your program will be in good shape.

To show you this problem-solving strategy, let's make the dragon game shown in Figure 10-7.

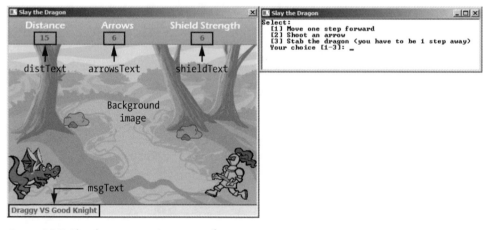

Figure 10-7: The dragon game's user interface

In this game, you control the knight, and it's your job to slay the dragon. On the screen you can see which variables we'll display to keep score and where the player makes a choice of three actions to play.

When the game starts, Good Knight is on the right, some distance from Draggy the dragon. Good Knight has a bow and some arrows, and his shield has a certain strength level (the program picks these values at random). The knight makes the first move. He can move 1 step forward, shoot an arrow at the dragon, or stab the dragon with his sword (but only if he's

1 step away). If the arrow hits the dragon, it'll slay him instantly! With the sword, the knight has a 50-50 chance of slaying the dragon (but only when he's close enough). If Good Knight slays Draggy, he'll become Knight of the Year, win his very own dance party, and get his picture on the castle wall.

Once Good Knight makes his move, Draggy breathes his flames at the knight. If he hits the knight, he'll weaken the knight's shield. When the shield loses its strength, the knight is defenseless. After this point, if the dragon's fire hits the knight, it'll burninate him! The entire city will be under the attack of the merciless, ferocious dragon. Game over!

The game uses five images that you can find in this chapter's folder: the background image (your battlefield), two images for the dragon (one image shows the dragon's fire), the knight's image, and an image of an arrow. Follow steps 1–10 to make a fun dragon game!

Step 1: Open the Startup File

Open the *Dragon_Incomplete.sb* file from the code folder for this chapter. This file contains the code in Listing 10-7 and has empty placeholders for your subroutines. You'll add the code for these subroutines one step at a time. The program's folder has all the images you need as well. It also has the complete game, *Dragon.sb*, in case you get stuck.

```
1  ' Dragon_Incomplete.sb
2  SetUp()      ' Does one-time set up
3
4  NewGame()    ' Sets the parameters for a new game
5
6  UpdateUserInterface() ' Shows values on background image
7
8  NextMove:
9  GetChoice()       ' Displays options and gets the knight's choice
10
11 ProcessChoice() ' Processes the user's choice
12
13 DragonFire()      ' Now it's the dragon's turn
14 Goto NextMove
```

Listing 10-7: High-level structure of the dragon game

First, you call the SetUp() subroutine (line 2) to draw the background image, create text shapes (for displaying the distance, number of arrows, and so on), and load the game's images (dragon, knight, and arrow). Line 4 calls NewGame() to set the parameters for a new game, including the knight's arrows, shield strength, and distance from the dragon. In line 6, you call UpdateUserInterface() to update the game's user interface (UI). Then the code goes into a loop (lines 8–14) to manage the game. Each round, you ask the knight for his next move (line 9), process his move by calling ProcessChoice() on line 11, and then give the dragon a turn (line 13). As you'll see in a moment, these subroutines will keep track of the game's status and end the game when there's a winner!

Next, you'll work on the subroutines one by one.

Step 2: Write the SetUp() Subroutine

You'll start by writing the SetUp() subroutine, which creates the scenario for
your game. Add the code in Listing 10-8 to your program.

```
1 Sub SetUp
2   GraphicsWindow.Title = "Slay the Dragon"
3   TextWindow.Title = GraphicsWindow.Title
4
5   GraphicsWindow.Width = 480
6   GraphicsWindow.Height = 380
7   GraphicsWindow.CanResize = 0
8   GraphicsWindow.FontSize = 14
9   GraphicsWindow.Left = 40
10  ' Positions the text window
11  TextWindow.Left = GraphicsWindow.Left + GraphicsWindow.Width + 20
12  TextWindow.Top = GraphicsWindow.Top
13
14  path = Program.Directory
15  GraphicsWindow.DrawImage(path + "\bkgnd.png", 0, 0)
16
17  ' Creates text objects to show distance, arrows,
18  ' shield strength, and message
19  distText = Shapes.AddText("")
20  arrowsText = Shapes.AddText("")
21  shieldText = Shapes.AddText("")
22  msgText = Shapes.AddText("Draggy VS Good Knight")
23  Shapes.Move(distText, 60, 30)
24  Shapes.Move(arrowsText, 200, 30)
25  Shapes.Move(shieldText, 370, 30)
26  Shapes.Move(msgText, 5, 362)
27
28  ' Loads the images for the knight, dragon, and arrow
29  knightImg = Shapes.AddImage(path + "\knight.png")
30  dragon1Img = Shapes.AddImage(path + "\dragon1.png")
31  dragon2Img = Shapes.AddImage(path + "\dragon2.png")
32  arrowImg = Shapes.AddImage(path + "\arrow.png")
33  Shapes.Move(dragon1Img, 0, 250)
34  Shapes.Move(dragon2Img, 0, 250)
35  Shapes.Move(knightImg, 380, 250)
36
37  Shapes.HideShape(dragon2Img)
38  Shapes.HideShape(arrowImg)
39 EndSub
```

Listing 10-8: Setting up the windows and properties

This code contains all the one-time setup for your game; it's a little
long, but we'll talk you through it. You set the titles for the graphics and
text windows (lines 2–3). These are displayed in the title bars for these windows when the game is played (see Figure 10-7).

Then you set the graphics window's size (lines 5–7), font size (line 8), and position (line 9). Next, you position the text window to appear to the right of the graphics window (lines 11–12). After drawing the background image (lines 14–15), you create and position the text shapes that you'll use to show all the numbers on the game's UI (lines 19–26). Then you load and position the images for the knight, dragon, and arrow (lines 29–35). Finally, you hide the images for the firing dragon and the arrow because they aren't needed at this time (lines 37–38): you'll show these images when Draggy breathes fire and Good Knight shoots the arrow.

When we built this program, we figured out where to place the text and images (with the numbers we're using) on the background's image by using a trial-and-error method (we guessed and tweaked it until we got it right). You'll likely need to do that when designing your own UIs for your awesome future games.

Step 3: Add a Bit of Chance

Next, you need to add some luck to the game. Each time we run the game, we want Good Knight to get a different number of arrows, be a random distance away from the dragon, and have a different shield strength. To do this, add the NewGame() subroutine in Listing 10-9 to your program.

```
1 Sub NewGame
2   dist = 9 + Math.GetRandomNumber(10)  ' 10 to 19
3   arrows = Math.Floor(0.4 * dist)       ' 4 to 8
4   shield = Math.Floor(0.4 * dist)       ' 4 to 8
5   moveStep = 280 / dist                 ' Knight's move in pixels
6 EndSub
```

Listing 10-9: Setting up a new game

In line 2, you add 9 to a random number between 1 and 10, which sets the distance, dist, between 10 and 19. This is the number of steps Good Knight has to take to get to Draggy. Next, you set the number of arrows as 40 percent of the distance (line 3). The farther the knight is from the dragon, the more arrows he'll have. In line 4, you set the strength of the knight's shield—again, as a fraction of his distance.

Let's think about the moveStep line a little. The width of the background image is 480 pixels. The width of the dragon is 100 pixels, and the width of the knight is 100 pixels. When we place the dragon and the knight on the background, the distance from the dragon's right edge to the knight's left edge is 280 pixels. So every time Good Knight moves forward, we'll move his image to the left by 280 / dist pixels.

TIP   *You can change the fraction in lines 3 and 4 from 0.4 to a different value to make the game easier or harder. After you complete the game, try changing the fraction and play the game a couple of times!*

Step 4: Let the Player Know What's Going On

After you set the game's parameters, you'll need to show them to the user. Add the UpdateUserInterface() subroutine in Listing 10-10.

```
1 Sub UpdateUserInterface
2   Shapes.SetText(distText, dist)
3   Shapes.SetText(arrowsText, arrows)
4   Shapes.SetText(shieldText, shield)
5 EndSub
```

Listing 10-10: Subroutine that updates the text

This subroutine is pretty basic (and small!). You just use the SetText() method of the Shapes object and pass the identifier of the text shape and the number you want to display. Recall that we saved these identifiers when we created these text shapes in the SetUp() subroutine (lines 19–21 in Listing 10-8).

Step 5: Get the Player in the Game with GetChoice()

If you run the game now, you should see all the images and numbers in place, but nothing will happen yet. You need to start taking the knight's orders, so it's time to add the GetChoice() subroutine in Listing 10-11.

```
1 Sub GetChoice
2   AskAgain:
3   TextWindow.WriteLine("Select:")
4   TextWindow.WriteLine("  [1] Move 1 step forward")
5   TextWindow.WriteLine("  [2] Shoot an arrow")
6   TextWindow.WriteLine("  [3] Stab the dragon (you have to be 1 step away)")
7   TextWindow.Write("  Your choice [1-3]: ")
8
9   choice = TextWindow.ReadNumber()
10  If((choice <> 1) And (choice <> 2) And (choice <> 3)) Then
11    Goto AskAgain
12  EndIf
13
14  If ((choice = 2) And (arrows = 0)) Then
15    Shapes.SetText(msgText, "You ran out of arrows! Borrow some from Link.")
16    Goto AskAgain
17  EndIf
18
19  If ((choice = 3) And (dist > 1)) Then
20    Shapes.SetText(msgText, "You're too far to use your sword. Too bad ↵
      you can't train dragons.")
21    Goto AskAgain
22  EndIf
23
```

```
24    Shapes.SetText(msgText, "")
25    TextWindow.WriteLine("")
26 EndSub
```

Listing 10-11: Getting the user's choice and displaying any errors

You start by displaying the options to the user (lines 3–7). You read the user's choice for Good Knight (line 9) and make sure it's valid. If your user enters any number other than 1, 2, or 3, you ask them to enter a number again (lines 10–12). If the user chooses to shoot an arrow but doesn't have any arrows, you tell them they're out of arrows and ask them again (lines 14–17). If they want to stab the dragon but are too far away, you tell them they're too far away and ask them to choose again (lines 19–22). Otherwise, the choice the user makes is acceptable. You clear the message text in line 24, add an empty line to the text window in line 25 to prepare for the next prompt, and return to the main program (line 26).

Step 6: Process the Player's Choice

Now that the user has made their choice, you need to examine the choice variable to decide what to do next. Add the ProcessChoice() subroutine in Listing 10-12 to your program.

```
1 Sub ProcessChoice
2   If (choice = 1) Then        ' Move-forward subroutine
3     MoveKnight()
4   ElseIf (choice = 2) Then ' Shoot-arrow subroutine
5     ShootArrow()
6   Else ' Stab subroutine
7     StabDragon()
8   EndIf
9 EndSub
```

Listing 10-12: Jumping to the choice's subroutine

You use an If/Else ladder on the choice variable and call a different subroutine for each choice. Next, you'll write these three subroutines!

Step 7: Add Motion with MoveKnight()

Add the MoveKnight() subroutine in Listing 10-13 to breathe some life into Good Knight and get him moving.

```
1 Sub MoveKnight
2   dist = dist - 1
3   Shapes.SetText(distText, dist)
4
5   Shapes.Move(knightImg, 100 + dist * moveStep, 250)
```

```
 6
 7   If (dist = 0) Then    ' Checks whether the knight touched the dragon
 8     Shapes.SetText(msgText, "The dragon swallowed you! You taste like chicken.")
 9     GameOver()
10   EndIf
11 EndSub
```

Listing 10-13: The subroutine that moves Good Knight

You start by reducing the knight's distance from the dragon by 1 step
(line 2), and then you show that new distance on the game's UI (line 3).
You then move the knight's image to the left (line 5).

To understand how this works, let's assume that the knight's initial distance from the dragon, dist, is 10, which makes moveStep = 28, as illustrated in
Figure 10-7. When the knight is 10 steps away from the dragon, the upper-left
corner of the knight's image is at (100 + (10 × 28), 250). When the knight is
9 steps away from the dragon, the upper-left corner of the knight's image is
at (100 + (9 × 28), 250), and when he's 8 steps away, the image's upper-left
corner is at (100 + (8 × 28), 250), and so on. To move the knight, you set the
image's horizontal position to 100 plus the current distance, dist, times the
moveStep, and you set the image's vertical position to 250 (see Figure 10-8).

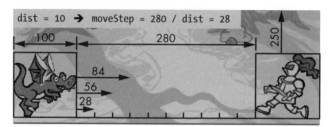

Figure 10-8: Illustrating the knight's motion

After moving the knight, you check whether he touched the dragon
(line 7). If he did, you tell Good Knight how great the dragon thinks he
tastes and call the GameOver() subroutine. This subroutine is in Listing 10-14;
add it to your program now.

```
1 Sub GameOver
2   TextWindow.Pause()
3   Program.End()
4 EndSub
```

Listing 10-14: Running the GameOver() subroutine

This subroutine calls Pause() to give your user a chance to read the message (line 2). When the user presses any key, the Pause() method ends, and
you call the End() method to exit your program (line 3).

Step 8: Shoot Arrows with ShootArrow()

Add the ShootArrow() subroutine in Listing 10-15 to make the Good Knight a master archer who puts Hawkeye to shame.

```
1  Sub ShootArrow
2    arrows = arrows - 1
3    Shapes.SetText(arrowsText, arrows)
4
5    range = Math.GetRandomNumber(dist)
6
7    ' Animates the arrow
8    pos1X = 100 + dist * moveStep
9    pos2X = 100 + (dist - range) * moveStep
10   Shapes.Move(arrowImg, pos1X, 280)
11   Shapes.ShowShape(arrowImg)
12   Shapes.Animate(arrowImg, pos2X, 280, 2000)
13   Program.Delay(2000)
14   Shapes.HideShape(arrowImg)
15
16   If (range = dist) Then     ' You hit the dragon right on
17     Shapes.SetText(msgText, "Perfect shot. The dragon's dead! You kiss the ↵
       princess's frog.")
18     GameOver()
19   Else
20     Shapes.SetText(msgText, "Your arrow missed! Robin Hood is giving lessons.")
21     Program.Delay(2000)     ' To read the message
22   EndIf
23 EndSub
```

Listing 10-15: Shooting the arrow

You start by using one arrow (line 2) and show the remaining arrows on the UI (line 3). You then set the arrow's range randomly to a number between 1 and the distance to the dragon (line 5). The closer the knight is to the dragon, the better his chances are that he'll hit his target. The next block of code (lines 8–14) animates the arrow. The horizontal start position, pos1X, is the same as the knight's position (line 8), and the end position, pos2X, is based on the selected range (line 9). You then move the arrow to its start position (line 10), show it (line 11), animate it to its final position (line 12), wait for it to reach its target (line 13), and then hide it (line 14). You can change the value 2000 in lines 12 and 13 to make the animation shorter or longer.

Once the animation is complete, you check whether the arrow hit the dragon (line 16). If it did, the game is over (lines 17–18) and the dance party is yours! Otherwise, you tell Good Knight that his arrow missed (line 20), delay the program for your user to read the message (line 21), and return to the ProcessChoice() subroutine, which returns to the main program to give the dragon his turn.

Step 9: Swing the Sword with StabDragon()

Now, add the last subroutine for the knight in Listing 10-16.

```
1 Sub StabDragon
2   If (Math.GetRandomNumber(2) = 1) Then
3     Shapes.SetText(msgText, "You killed the dragon! You marry the princess ↵
      and 7 dwarves.")
4     GameOver()
5   Else
6     Shapes.SetText(msgText, "Your sword missed! Good one, Lance-a-Little!")
7     Program.Delay(2000) ' To read the message
8   EndIf
9 EndSub
```

Listing 10-16: Stabbing the dragon

You randomly pick the number 1 or 2. If the number is 1 (line 2), the knight hits the dragon and the game ends (lines 3–4). If the knight misses, you tell the knight that he missed (line 6), delay the program for your user to read the message (line 7), and return to the ProcessChoice() subroutine.

Step 10: Breathe Fire

If the knight didn't kill Draggy and end the game, the main program calls DragonFire() to give the dragon a fair fight. Add Listing 10-17 to your program.

```
1 Sub DragonFire
2   Shapes.SetText(msgText, "The dragon ignited his fire. The Pokemon run.")
3   Shapes.HideShape(dragon1Img)
4   Shapes.ShowShape(dragon2Img)
5   Program.Delay(1000)
6   Shapes.HideShape(dragon2Img)
7   Shapes.ShowShape(dragon1Img)
8
9   If (Math.GetRandomNumber(2) = 1) Then ' Knight is hit
10    If (shield = 0) Then                ' Shield is damaged
11      Shapes.SetText(msgText, "The dragon's fire BURNINATED you!")
12      GameOver()
13    Else
14      shield = shield - 1
15      Shapes.SetText(shieldText, shield)
16      Shapes.SetText(msgText, "You're hit! Your shield became weaker. Use ↵
        the force!")
17    EndIf
18  Else
19    Shapes.SetText(msgText, "The fire missed you! Aunt Mildred could've used ↵
      your luck.")
20  EndIf
21 EndSub
```

Listing 10-17: The dragon breathing fire on Good Knight

Lines 3–7 animate the dragon's fire. You hide the normal dragon image (line 3) and show the one spitting fire (line 4). You wait 1 second (line 5) and switch the images back (lines 6–7). After that, the dragon has a 50-50 chance to hit the knight with his fire. You pick a random number that's either a 1 or a 2. A value of 1 means the dragon has hit the knight (line 9). In this case, you check the shield's strength (line 10); if it's 0, the game is over (lines 11–12). But if it isn't 0, you reduce the shield's strength by 1 (line 14), display the new value (line 15), tell the knight that he was hit (line 16), and return to the main program. If the random number is 2 (line 18), you tell the knight that the dragon's fire missed him (line 19) and return to the main program.

Your game is done! Play it several times and enjoy your creation!

TRY IT OUT 10-4

The dragon game is fun, but it isn't perfect. When you play the game several times, you'll notice some issues that you either don't like or can improve. It's now your game; make any changes you think will make the game better. You can even change the messages and the graphics. Head to http://tiny.cc/dragongame/ to share your game in the gallery and see what others did!

Programming Challenges

If you get stuck, check out *http://nostarch.com/smallbasic/* for the solutions and for more resources and review questions for teachers and students.

1. The folder for this challenge has images for the head, eyes, mouth, and body of an alien creature (see the following figure).

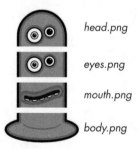

head.png

eyes.png

mouth.png

body.png

Write a program that prompts a user to enter the number of eyes (2, 4, or 6) and the number of mouths (1 or 2) of the alien. Then have your main program call DrawHead(), DrawEyes(), DrawMouths(), and DrawBody() to draw the alien! For example, here's an alien with six eyes and two mouths:

2. In this challenge, you'll develop the game Ghost Hunt (see the following figure). Open the file *GhostHunt_Incomplete.sb* from this chapter's folder (which has all the images you need for this game). A ghost is hiding in 1 of the 12 rooms. To find the ghost, the user picks a room. If the user finds the ghost in that room, they win! Otherwise, the ghost tries to find the user (by selecting a room number at random). If the ghost finds the user, the game ends. Otherwise, the ghost moves to a different room, and the user tries again.

11

EVENT-DRIVEN PROGRAMMING

So far, the programs you've written have been mostly *sequential* because they have followed the lines of code in order, from top to bottom. Some statements might have made a comparison or called a subroutine to take a detour, but overall the order of statements has been mostly linear.

In some ways, this is comparable to how you go about your daily routine: you wake up, make your bed, take a shower, eat your breakfast, watch TV, comb your hair, and so on. But what if the phone rings during your routine? If you're expecting a call from a friend to confirm that night's party, you'd better take it! Even though you're doing something at that moment, you're also listening for the phone. The minute you hear the ring (the event), you drop everything and take the call (let's just hope it isn't your aunt calling to see if you finished reading *Little House on the Freeway*).

Similarly, many computer programs (especially games) use *event-driven programming*, which means they listen and respond to events raised by the operating system (see Figure 11-1). Think of an *event* as a signal that's raised in response to an action, like moving or clicking the mouse, clicking a button, typing on the keyboard, having a timer expire, and so on. Some objects in the Small Basic library can see these events and tell you when they happen. Programmers say that an object *raised* an event. You can write some exciting applications and games by handling these events (like a super fun explosion farming game). These games typically wait patiently for the player to move the mouse or press some keys, and then they take action.

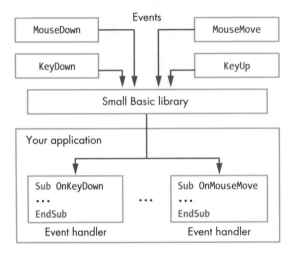

Figure 11-1: The event-driven programming model

In Figure 11-1, the events are at the top. When a user triggers an action (like pressing a key), the Small Basic library knows about it. If you want to know when an event happens, you can ask Small Basic to inform you when an event occurs so you can write programs that react to certain events.

The Small Basic library has three objects that handle events (see Figure 11-2): GraphicsWindow, Timer, and Controls. You'll study the events of GraphicsWindow and Timer objects in this chapter, and you'll tackle the events of the Controls object in the next chapter.

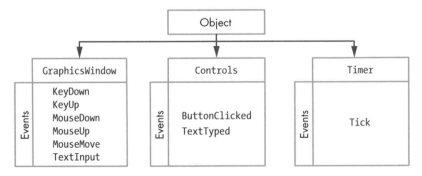

Figure 11-2: The available events in Small Basic

GraphicsWindow Events

Let's start by exploring the events in GraphicsWindow. When a user interacts with your application, GraphicsWindow knows when keys are pressed, which keys are pressed, and if the user clicks or moves the mouse. Although GraphicsWindow knows about these events, it doesn't automatically do anything when the events happen. You need to instruct GraphicsWindow to tell you when these events happen so you can use them. Next, you'll learn how to use the information Small Basic knows about the user to create interesting, interactive applications.

Create Patterns with the MouseDown Event

Let's make a simple application that draws a randomly colored circle every time the user clicks the graphics window. Enter the code in Listing 11-1.

```
1 ' Circles.sb
2 GraphicsWindow.MouseDown = OnMouseDown
3
4 Sub OnMouseDown
5   GraphicsWindow.PenColor = GraphicsWindow.GetRandomColor()
6   X0 = GraphicsWindow.MouseX - 10
7   Y0 = GraphicsWindow.MouseY - 10
8   GraphicsWindow.DrawEllipse(X0, Y0, 20, 20)
9 EndSub
```

Listing 11-1: Drawing circles with a click of the mouse

Run the program. A sample output is shown in Figure 11-3. When you click inside the graphics window, you draw a circle with a random color. Make a fun pattern, show it to someone else, and try to convince them that Pablo Picasso painted it!

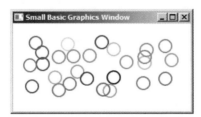

Figure 11-3: Sample output of Circles.sb

Let's look at the code in Listing 11-1 to see how Small Basic handles event-driven programming. Figure 11-4 shows an important line in this program: line 2.

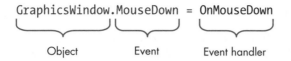

GraphicsWindow.MouseDown = OnMouseDown

Object   Event   Event handler

Figure 11-4: The event-handler registration statement

The statement in line 2 tells the GraphicsWindow object that when the MouseDown event happens, it should run the OnMouseDown() subroutine. This subroutine is also known as an *event handler*, because its purpose is to handle, or process, an event. Although you can name this subroutine anything you want, it's common to use the format On*EventName*, which is why we named the handler OnMouseDown. The statement on line 2 is known as *registering* an event handler. In this example, Small Basic calls the OnMouseDown() subroutine every time the user clicks inside the graphics window.

When the user clicks inside the graphics window, the x and y mouse positions (relative to the window's upper-left corner) are saved in the MouseX and MouseY properties of GraphicsWindow. Because the program draws a circle with a diameter of 20 centered around the mouse click, it subtracts 10 from MouseX and MouseY (to mark the circle's upper-left position) and saves the result in the X0 and Y0 variables (lines 6–7). The subroutine then draws a circle with a diameter of 20 that's centered at the mouse-click position (line 8).

TRY IT OUT 11-1

Change the code in Listing 11-1 to draw triangles and squares instead of a circle. If you need help, refer back to Chapter 3 to review GraphicsWindow's drawing methods.

Fire Missiles with the KeyDown Event

Many computer games are played using the keyboard. For example, the player might use the arrow keys to move the main character, the spacebar to shoot a missile, F1 to get help, P to pick the character's nose, and ESC to exit the game. If you want to make a game that uses the keyboard for input, you need to add the KeyDown event to your program to let you know which key the user presses and when.

To understand the KeyDown event, let's write a simple application that displays the name of each key a user presses. Enter the program in Listing 11-2.

```
1 ' KeyDown.sb
2 yPos = 10
3 GraphicsWindow.KeyDown = OnKeyDown
```

```
4
5  Sub OnKeyDown
6    GraphicsWindow.DrawText(10, yPos, GraphicsWindow.LastKey)
7    yPos = yPos + 15
8  EndSub
```

Listing 11-2: Displaying each key a user presses

A sample run, with some comments, is shown in Figure 11-5.

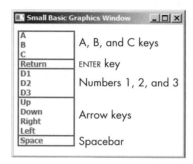

Figure 11-5: A sample run of KeyDown.sb

The yPos variable sets the vertical position where you'll display the name of the key the user presses. It starts at 10 and increases by 15 after it shows the name of the last pressed key (line 7).

You register the KeyDown event handler on line 3. Whenever a user presses a key, the program runs the OnKeyDown() subroutine. The subroutine displays the name of the pressed key (line 6) and increases yPos by 15 (line 7) to get ready to display the name of the next key on the next line. The GraphicsWindow.LastKey property on line 6 provides the name of the pressed key (as a string). This read-only property tells you the last key a user pressed.

The importance of this example is that it shows you the names that Small Basic assigns to the different keyboard keys. If you want to create an application that responds to these keys, you need to know what Small Basic calls them. Here are some other details you should know:

1. The names of the letter keys (A–Z) are always uppercase. For example, if you type the letter "a", LastKey will register it as an uppercase "A" regardless of whether caps lock is on or if you're holding down the SHIFT key.

2. The name of a number key (0–9) uses the form "D*digit*". For example, the name of the 5 key is "D5".

3. The four arrow keys are named "Up", "Down", "Right", and "Left".

4. The ENTER (or RETURN) key is named "Return", and the spacebar is named "Space".

5. The KeyDown event is raised continuously (about every 35 milliseconds) as long as a key is pressed. This is different from the MouseDown event, which is raised only once (when the left mouse button is clicked).

Knowing the names of the keys is important if you want to test for certain keypresses in your programs.

TRY IT OUT 11-2

Enter and run the following code. Press some keys on the keyboard and watch for their names in the text window. Press and hold a key for a while to see what happens. (Make sure the graphics window is the active window when you type.)

```
TextWindow.Show()
GraphicsWindow.Show()
GraphicsWindow.KeyDown = OnKeyDown

Sub OnKeyDown
  TextWindow.WriteLine(GraphicsWindow.LastKey)
EndSub
```

What did you notice when you tried this example?

Make a Typewriter Using the TextInput Event

The TextInput event is very similar to the KeyDown event, but it's raised only when the user presses a text-related key on the keyboard. This includes letters (A–Z), digits (0–9), special characters (such as !@#$%^&), and other keys, like ENTER, the spacebar, TAB, and BACKSPACE. When the TextInput event is raised, the last character pressed on the keyboard is saved in the GraphicsWindow.LastText property.

Let's see how this event works. Enter the code in Listing 11-3 to simulate a typewriter. We know that typewriters are old school, but hey, it could be worse; we could be simulating an abacus!

```
1  ' Typewriter.sb
2  x = 0                    ' x position for displaying the last character
3  y = 0                    ' y position for displaying the last character
4  GraphicsWindow.Title = "Typewriter"
5  GraphicsWindow.FontName = "Courier New"
6  GraphicsWindow.TextInput = OnTextInput
7
8  Sub OnTextInput
9    Sound.PlayClick()      ' Plays a typewriter sound effect
10   If (GraphicsWindow.LastKey = "Return") Then
11     x = 0                ' Moves to next line
12     y = y + 15
```

```
13    Else
14      GraphicsWindow.DrawText(x, y, GraphicsWindow.LastText)
15      x = x + 8          ' Advances x position for the next character
16      If (x > GraphicsWindow.Width) Then ' If more than right margin
17        x = 0            ' Moves to the next line
18        y = y + 15
19      EndIf
20    EndIf
21 EndSub
```

Listing 11-3: Making a typewriter sound with each keypress

Look at the sample output in Figure 11-6.

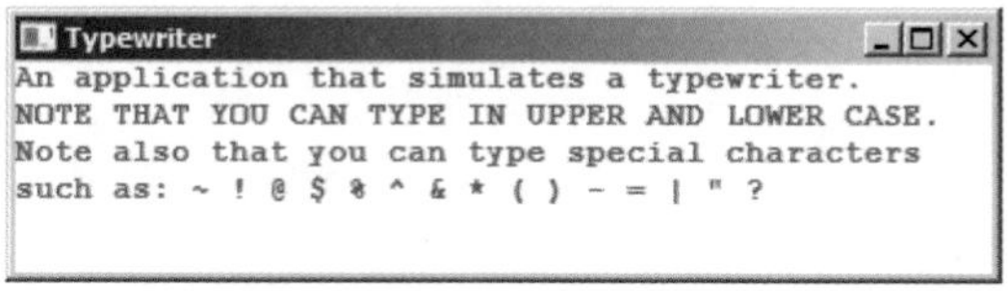

Figure 11-6: Sample output of Typewriter.sb

Lines 2 and 3 set the cursor at the corner of the graphics window. Line 4 gives the window a title, line 5 sets the font style, and line 6 registers the event handler. Line 9 plays the click sound, and lines 10–12 advance the line if the user presses ENTER. Line 14 writes the character entered by the user, line 15 moves the cursor to the next spot, and lines 16–18 move the cursor to the next line when the cursor gets to the right edge.

NOTE   *When you experiment with this application, you'll notice that the TextInput event looks at the states of the different keyboard keys before setting the value of the LastText property. For example, if you press the A key while holding down SHIFT, the LastText property reports an uppercase "A"; if you don't hold down SHIFT, it reports a lowercase "a".*

TRY IT OUT 11-3

Update Listing 11-3 to display each character in a random color. See Listing 11-1 for ideas on how to randomly change the color.

Draw Pictures with the MouseMove Event

To understand how to use the MouseMove event, you'll write an application that lets a user draw with the mouse. The user clicks the left mouse button in the graphics window and then drags the mouse to draw. The complete program is shown in Listing 11-4.

```
1  ' Scribble.sb
2  GraphicsWindow.MouseMove = OnMouseMove
3
4  Sub OnMouseMove
5    x = GraphicsWindow.MouseX    ' Current x position of mouse
6    y = GraphicsWindow.MouseY    ' Current y position of mouse
7
8    If (Mouse.IsLeftButtonDown) Then
9      GraphicsWindow.DrawLine(prevX, prevY, x, y)
10   EndIf
11
12   prevX = x                    ' Updates the last (previous) position
13   prevY = y
14 EndSub
```

Listing 11-4: Drawing a line as the user moves the mouse

A sample output of *Scribble.sb* is in Figure 11-7.

Figure 11-7: Sample output of Scribble.sb

The OnMouseMove() subroutine draws a line from the last mouse position, which you save in the variables prevX and prevY in lines 12 and 13, to the new mouse position, which you get from GraphicsWindow's MouseX and MouseY properties. Because you want the user to draw only when the left mouse button is down, the OnMouseMove() subroutine checks the state of the left mouse button using the Mouse.IsLeftButtonDown property (line 8). This property indicates whether the left mouse button is being held down. If this value is true, the subroutine draws a line segment (line 9); if the value isn't true, it doesn't draw the line.

TRY IT OUT 11-4

Change Listing 11-4 to use the TextInput event to set the pen's color (R for red, G for green, B for black, and so on).

Useful Tips

Before moving on, we'll give you some tips for dealing with events and event handlers. You can handle multiple events using the same subroutine. For example, look at these statements:

```
GraphicsWindow.MouseDown = OnMouseEvent
GraphicsWindow.MouseMove = OnMouseEvent
```

These statements cause the MouseDown and MouseMove events to call the OnMouseEvent() subroutine. This feature can come in handy for complex games that use many events, so keep this feature in mind.

You can change the event-handler subroutine after you register it. For example, let's say you registered the OnMouseDown() subroutine to handle the MouseDown event using this statement:

```
GraphicsWindow.MouseDown = OnMouseDown
```

If you later decide to stop responding to the MouseDown event (for example, because the game is over), you can write this statement:

```
GraphicsWindow.MouseDown = DoNothing
```

Now DoNothing is the new handler for the MouseDown event. If you don't write any statements in your DoNothing() subroutine, your programs won't do anything in response to the MouseDown event.

A MouseDown event is usually followed by a MouseUp event, but don't always count on that MouseUp event happening. If you click the left mouse button in the graphics window and then move the cursor outside the graphics window before you release the button, your application receives only a MouseDown event notification. This is important to remember if you write an application that needs to pair the two events (such as if you click to grab a ball and release to throw it).

In the next section, you'll put into practice what you've learned so far by creating a complete game. You'll also learn about the Timer object and its Tick event. Get ready for an exciting adventure in computer gaming!

Create a Gold Rush Game

Let's create a simple game in which a player uses the arrow keys to move a turtle to collect as many bags of gold as possible (see Figure 11-8). The bag of gold appears at random locations on the grid. If the player doesn't grab the bag in 2 seconds, it moves elsewhere. Let's see how fast you can get the turtle to move!

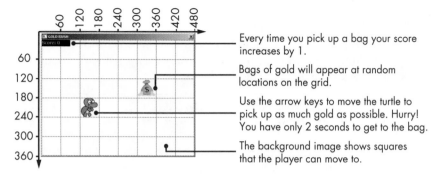

Every time you pick up a bag your score increases by 1.

Bags of gold will appear at random locations on the grid.

Use the arrow keys to move the turtle to pick up as much gold as possible. Hurry! You have only 2 seconds to get to the bag.

The background image shows squares that the player can move to.

Figure 11-8: Help the turtle grab as many bags of gold as possible.

NOTE *The grid is part of the background image, but we added the x- and y-coordinates in Figure 11-8 to help you understand the numbers used in the code. Refer to this figure to picture how the turtle and the bag of gold move.*

Step 1: Open the Startup File

Open the file *GoldRush_Incomplete.sb* from this chapter's folder. The folder also has the three images you'll need for this game. Follow the next four steps to walk through the application's code. The startup file contains the program's main code, as shown in Listing 11-5. It prepares the game's user interface, registers the event handlers, and initializes the game's variables. The file also contains empty placeholders (not shown in Listing 11-5) for all the subroutines you'll add.

```
 1  ' GoldRush_Incomplete.sb
 2  GraphicsWindow.Title = "GOLD RUSH"
 3  GraphicsWindow.CanResize = "False"
 4  GraphicsWindow.Width = 480
 5  GraphicsWindow.Height = 360
 6
 7  path = Program.Directory
 8  grid = Shapes.AddImage(path + "\Grid.png")
 9  player = Shapes.AddImage(path + "\Turtle.png")
10  gold = Shapes.AddImage(path + "\Gold.png")
11
12  ' Places the player (turtle) near the middle
13  XP = 4                  ' x position (from 0 to 7)
14  YP = 3                  ' y position (from 0 to 5)
15  Shapes.Move(player, XP * 60, YP * 60)
16
17  ' Creates the score text shape (over a black rectangle)
18  GraphicsWindow.BrushColor = "Black"
19  Shapes.AddRectangle(90, 20)
20  GraphicsWindow.FontSize = 14
```

```
21 GraphicsWindow.BrushColor = "Red"
22 scoreID = Shapes.AddText("Score: 0") ' For now
23
24 ' Registers two event handlers
25 GraphicsWindow.KeyDown = OnKeyDown
26 Timer.Tick = OnTick
27
28 ' Initializes variables
29 Timer.Interval = 2000 ' Ticks every 2 sec
30 score = 0           ' Keeps track of player's score
31 bagCount = 0        ' Counts how many bags so far
```

Listing 11-5: Setting up the Gold Rush game

Lines 3–5 set the size of the graphics window to match the size of the background image (*grid.png*). Lines 8–10 use the Shapes object to load the three images (the background grid, the turtle, and the bag of gold) and save the returned identifiers. You'll need the identifiers to move the turtle and the bag of gold later. Lines 13–15 place the turtle near the middle of the grid. Note that each square on the grid is 60×60 pixels.

Lines 18–22 create the text shape you'll use to display the player's score. The score is displayed in red on a black background in the upper-left corner of the screen (see Figure 11-8). Lines 25–26 register two event handlers. The OnKeyDown handler checks the arrow keys and then moves the turtle as the player controls it. The OnTick handler handles the Timer object's Tick event to limit the player's time to reach each bag. Line 29 sets the timer interval to 2 seconds (2,000 milliseconds), telling the Timer object to raise a Tick event every 2 seconds. Then the code initializes the two variables score and bagCount to 0: score keeps track of the player's score (line 30), and bagCount keeps track of how many bags have appeared so far (line 31).

Run the code; you should see the turtle in the middle of the grid, the bag of gold in the upper-left square of the grid, and the score text showing 0.

Step 2: Move the Turtle

To move the turtle when the player presses the arrow keys, add the code in Listing 11-6 to the bottom of your file.

```
1  Sub OnKeyDown
2    key = GraphicsWindow.LastKey
3    If ((key = "Up") And (YP > 0)) Then
4      YP = YP - 1
5    ElseIf ((key = "Down") And (YP < 5)) Then
6      YP = YP + 1
7    ElseIf ((key = "Left") And (XP > 0)) Then
8      XP = XP - 1
9    ElseIf ((key = "Right") And (XP < 7)) Then
10     XP = XP + 1
11   EndIf
```

```
12  Shapes.Move(player, XP * 60, YP * 60)
13  CheckTouch()              ' Checks if the player touched the bag
14  EndSub
```

Listing 11-6: Moving the turtle as the player presses the arrow keys

The grid has eight horizontal and six vertical squares. Squares in the horizontal direction are numbered 0 to 7, and squares in the vertical direction are numbered 0 to 5. That means the XP variable (the player's x position) takes any value between 0 and 7, and the YP variable (the player's y position) takes any value between 0 and 5. The OnKeyDown() subroutine uses an If/ElseIf ladder to check whether the pressed key is one of the four arrow keys. If one of the arrow keys is pressed while the turtle is in the graphics window, the subroutine adjusts XP or YP according to the pressed arrow key.

For example, lines 3 and 4 check if the player pressed the up arrow, and if the turtle hasn't reached the top edge yet, the turtle moves up one square. You can find the exact location on the grid (in pixels) by multiplying the square's number by 60 (because each square is 60 pixels), which is what line 12 does. The code then calls the CheckTouch() subroutine to check if the player touched the bag of gold.

Run the application again to check the code you just added. You should be able to move the turtle over the square grid using the arrow keys on the keyboard. It's alive!

Step 3: Move the Bag of Gold

Now you'll add the OnTick handler to create a time limit and the code for moving the bag of gold to a new spot. Add the subroutine in Listing 11-7 to the bottom of your program.

```
1 Sub OnTick    ' Timer expires
2    NewRound()
3 EndSub
```

Listing 11-7: The OnTick() subroutine

As mentioned earlier, the bag of gold appears at a random location and gives the player 2 seconds to grab it. If the timer expires, the player loses because they didn't grab the bag in time. In this case, the OnTick handler calls the NewRound() subroutine (line 2) to start another round of the game.

The NewRound() subroutine is shown in Listing 11-8. Add it to the bottom of your program.

```
1 Sub NewRound
2    bagCount = bagCount + 1
3    If (bagCount <= 20) Then
```

```
 4      XG = Math.GetRandomNumber(8) - 1    ' From 0 to 7
 5      YG = Math.GetRandomNumber(6) - 1    ' From 0 to 5
 6      Shapes.Move(gold, XG * 60, YG * 60)
 7      CheckTouch()
 8    Else
 9      Shapes.Remove(gold)                      ' Deletes the gold bag shape
10      GraphicsWindow.KeyDown = OnGameOver ' Do nothing
11      Timer.Tick = OnGameOver                 ' Do nothing
12    EndIf
13 EndSub
```

Listing 11-8: Starting a new round when the timer expires

The NewRound() subroutine starts by increasing bagCount by 1 (line 2); bagCount just counts how many bags have appeared so far. The plan is to show a total of 20 bags to the player. If 20 total bags have not been shown (line 3), the subroutine selects a random position for the bag (lines 4–5) and then moves the bag to that location in the graphics window (line 6). We use the variables XG and YG (for the x- and y-positions of the bag of gold) in the CheckTouch() subroutine. After moving the bag, the code calls CheckTouch() to see if the bag was placed right on top of the player (line 7)—how lucky!

If bagCount is more than 20 (line 8), we delete the gold bag shape (line 9) and register the OnGameOver handler, which is a subroutine with no statements, for both the KeyDown and the Tick events to end the game. Then when the player presses the arrow keys or when the timer expires after bag 20 has appeared, nothing happens. Of course, this might surprise the user. There are other ways to end the game, but we'll leave this to your imagination if you want to change it later.

The next subroutine you need to add is the OnGameOver() subroutine shown in Listing 11-9.

```
1 Sub OnGameOver
2 EndSub
```

Listing 11-9: The OnGameOver() subroutine

If you run the game at this point, the bag of gold should move to random positions on the grid every 2 seconds. You can still move the turtle with the arrows. After 20 bags have appeared, the bag of gold disappears, and the arrow keys will no longer move the turtle.

As you test this game, you might decide to give the user more time to pick up the bags or to remove the lucky feature where a bag could appear right on top of the player. Play around with this code until you think your game is fun to play.

Step 4: Update the User's Score

To complete the game, add the CheckTouch() subroutine in Listing 11-10 to check whether the player successfully picked up a bag of gold and, if so, increase their score.

```
1 Sub CheckTouch
2   If ((XP = XG) And (YP = YG)) Then
3     score = score + 1      ' Gives the player one point
4     Shapes.SetText(scoreID, "Score: " + score)
5     Sound.PlayClick()      ' Adds sound effect
6     Timer.Pause()          ' Resets the timer
7     Timer.Resume()         ' Starts the timer
8     NewRound()             ' Starts a new round
9   EndIf
10 EndSub
```

Listing 11-10: Checking whether the turtle gets to the money

If the player's x- and y-positions are the same as the bag, the turtle grabs the bag (line 2). Happy turtle! If the lucky turtle gets the bag of gold, we increase the score (line 3), show it (line 4), and use the Sound object to play a short click (line 5) for a nice audio effect.

We also need to reset the timer to 2 seconds for the new round. We do this by pausing the timer (line 6) and then resuming it (line 7). Then we call NewRound() to set another bag in a random spot after this historic triumph. Can your turtle do it again?

This completes the game, and you should be able to enjoy your creation after all this hard work. What's your top score? (Tip: hold down the arrow key to move across squares faster.) Share it with your friends (just click Publish in the Toolbar) to see if they can beat your score. Have fun!

TRY IT OUT 11-5

Think of some ways to enhance the game, and try out your ideas. Here are some ideas you could try:

- End the game with a bigger bang! Display a message or show some interesting graphics.

- Add a second bag of gold.

- Make the time limit shorter each time the user grabs the bag.

  Head to *http://tiny.cc/turtlegame/* to share your turtle game updates.

Programming Challenges

If you get stuck, check out *http://nostarch.com/smallbasic/* for the solutions and for more resources and review questions for teachers and students.

1. He-Man is hanging out with his friends playing *Twilight* trivia and needs a buzzer for when his friends get a question wrong. Make a program that draws a big X in the graphics window and plays a sound when He-Man clicks the left mouse button. The next click should erase the X. Make sure He-Man can repeat this as often as he wants (it's a long trivia game).

2. Make a program that stamps a turtle-face image where the mouse was clicked each time the user clicks the mouse. Get *turtleface.jpg* from this chapter's folder. (Hint: start with the code in Listing 11-1, and use the GraphicsWindow.DrawImage() method to draw your image.)

3. Open the *Maze_Incomplete.sb* file from this chapter's folder. The goal is to exit the maze in the shortest possible time, but this maze has no exit yet. Figure out how to add a maze exit condition. When the player exits the maze, display the time it took to solve the maze.

12

BUILDING GRAPHICAL USER INTERFACES

Every device has a set of *interfaces*. For example, an interface could be the buttons on a microwave or in an elevator, the knobs on a dishwasher, or even the soda pop dispenser at your favorite burger joint. Computer programs have interfaces as well. Back in the day, programs had only text menus, but now we use different ways to interact with computers, such as the icons on your desktop.

Although you've written some very useful programs in this book, they don't look like the programs you're used to, such as a word processor, a paint program, a web browser, video games, and so on.

Today, most programs use a *graphical user interface*, or *GUI* (pronounced "gooey," but don't worry, it's not sticky). GUIs can have menus, buttons, text boxes, and more.

One example is the Calculator program shown in Figure 12-1. When a user clicks one of the number buttons in the program, that number appears in the box at the top of the window. And when the user clicks the = button, the program computes the result of the math operation and displays it.

In this chapter, you'll learn about the Controls object, which lets you create graphical interfaces for your programs and games.

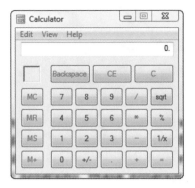

Figure 12-1: The Calculator program's user interface

Design a User Interface with the Controls Object

Let's start with a simple program that lets users enter their first and last name, and then the program greets them by name with a friendly message. Figure 12-2 shows you *FirstGUIApp.sb*, the GUI you'll create. The gridlines and coordinate points in the figure aren't part of the output, but they're included to illustrate the x- and y-coordinates of the interface's different components.

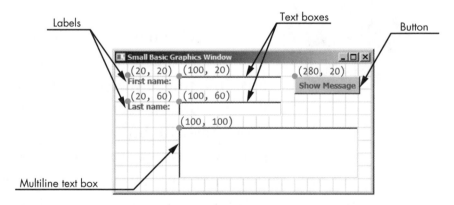

Figure 12-2: The FirstGUIApp.sb *user interface*

Step 1: The Design Phase

In this program, a user enters their first and last name in the text boxes and then clicks the Show Message button. If their first name is Alpaca and their last name is Bag, the program shows a message like the following (in the multiline text box).

Start Small Basic and enter the following two lines:

```
GraphicsWindow.DrawText(20, 20, "First name:")  ' Label
fnText = Controls.AddTextBox(100, 20)           ' First name text box
```

The first statement draws the text *First name:* at position (20, 20). In the second statement, the `Controls` object creates a text box with its upper-left corner at (100, 20). The box's identifier is saved in the variable `fnText` (first-name text box). You'll need this identifier later when you want to know what the user entered in this text box.

Click **Run**, and you'll see the *First name:* label and a text box placed to its right. The size of the text box is about 160×20 (the default size).

Next, add the following two lines to create the *Last name:* label and its associated text box:

```
GraphicsWindow.DrawText(20, 60, "Last name:")  ' Label
lnText = Controls.AddTextBox(100, 60)          ' Last name text box
```

Here, the box's identifier is saved in `lnText` (last-name text box). Click **Run** again, and you should see the text boxes and their labels perfectly aligned in the graphics window.

Now you'll create the Show Message button by calling the `Controls` object's `AddButton()` method:

```
showBtn = Controls.AddButton("Show Message", 280, 20) ' Button
```

The first argument of `AddButton()` is the button's caption, `"Show Message"`. The second and the third arguments tell the `Controls` object where the upper-left corner of the button should go. The button's identifier is saved in `showBtn` (show button). Click **Run** to see what you've just created. By default, the button's width will be as wide as its label. Try lengthening or shortening the button's label, and run the program again to see what happens.

Next, you need to add the last GUI element—the box that shows the output message. Because you can greet the user with a long message if you want to, let's use a multiline text box. The multiline text box has horizontal and vertical scroll bars that appear automatically if needed, like Harry Potter's Room of Requirement. To create a multiline text box, call the `AddMultiLineTextBox()` method:

```
msgText = Controls.AddMultiLineTextBox(100, 100) ' Message text box
```

Again, the two arguments specify the upper-left position of the box. The box's identifier is saved in `msgText` (message text box); you'll need it later to set the box's text. Click **Run**, and you'll see a multiline text box located at (100, 100). By default, the size of this box is about 200×80. Let's make this box wider by calling the SetSize() method. Add this line of code just after creating the multiline text box:

```
Controls.SetSize(msgText, 280, 80)    ' Makes width = 280 and height = 80
```

The first argument is the identifier of the control you want to resize, in this case msgText. The second argument (280) is the width, and the third (80) is the height. If you run the code now, you'll see an interface similar to the one shown earlier in Figure 12-2. Note that the upper-left corner of the message text box didn't change when you called SetSize().

Step 2: Program Interactivity

You've created all the controls you need and positioned them where you wanted them. Next, you'll make these controls interactive. You need to write some code that responds to the button's click. When a user clicks the button, the program needs to read the contents of the first name and the last name text boxes and then display the greeting in the multiline text box. Add lines 13–21, as shown in Listing 12-1, to complete the program (you've already written lines 2–11 to create the GUI elements).

```
 1 ' FirstGUIApp.sb
 2 GraphicsWindow.DrawText(20, 20, "First name:")  ' Label
 3 fnText = Controls.AddTextBox(100, 20)            ' First name text box
 4
 5 GraphicsWindow.DrawText(20, 60, "Last name:")  ' Label
 6 lnText = Controls.AddTextBox(100, 60)            ' Last name text box
 7
 8 showBtn = Controls.AddButton("Show Message", 280, 20)  ' Button
 9
10 msgText = Controls.AddMultiLineTextBox(100, 100)       ' Message text box
11 Controls.SetSize(msgText, 280, 80)      ' Makes width = 280 and height = 80
12
13 Controls.ButtonClicked = OnButtonClicked  ' Handler for button click
14
15 Sub OnButtonClicked
16   firstName = Controls.GetTextBoxText(fnText)  ' First name text box
17   lastName = Controls.GetTextBoxText(lnText)   ' Last name text box
18   fullName = firstName + " " + lastName        ' Constructs full name
19   message = "Hello there, " + fullName + "!"    ' Greeting message
20   Controls.SetTextBoxText(msgText, message)
21 EndSub
```

Listing 12-1: Creating a simple GUI program

Line 13 registers a handler for the ButtonClicked event. This line tells the Controls object to call the OnButtonClicked() subroutine whenever the user clicks the Show Message button.

In the OnButtonClicked() subroutine, GetTextBoxText() is called first to get the text that's entered into the first-name text box and save it into the firstName variable (line 16). This method takes one argument—the identifier of the text box whose text is needed. GetTextBoxText() is called again, but with a different argument, to get the text that's entered into the last-name text box and save it into lastName (line 17). Then the fullName variable is set by concatenating firstName and lastName with a space between them (line 18). At line 19 you create your greeting message and save it in the message variable. Finally, you call SetTextBoxText() to set the text of the message text box. The first argument is the control's identifier whose text is to be set, and the second argument is the new text (line 20). Run the program, enter some text in the text boxes, and then click the button to see how the program works.

In the next section, you'll learn how to make GUI programs that have more than one button. Now you can push Small Basic's buttons!

TRY IT OUT 12-1

Using the code in Listing 12-1, take the first name and last name from the user, and then update the code to display a silly short story that includes the user's name.

Make a Colorful Drawing Program

If you create a program with several buttons, the ButtonClicked event handler gets called when a user clicks any of these buttons. To find out which button was clicked, you can use the Controls.LastClickedButton property to get the clicked button's identifier; it's like asking your friend to tell you who noticed your brand-new shoes.

To show you how to use the ButtonClicked event when a program has more than one button, let's add to the *Scribble.sb* program you made in Chapter 11 (see Listing 11-4 on page 156). The user can select the pen's color by clicking a button. Check out the program's GUI in Figure 12-3.

Try out the updated program, *Scribble2.sb*, shown in Listing 12-2. You might notice that this program uses the same OnMouseMove event handler as the one in Listing 11-4.

Figure 12-3: Sample output of Scribble2.sb

```
1 ' Scribble2.sb
2 btnR = Controls.AddButton("Red", 10, 30)
3 btnG = Controls.AddButton("Green", 10, 65)
4 btnB = Controls.AddButton("Blue", 10, 100)
5 Controls.SetSize(btnR, 60, 30)
6 Controls.SetSize(btnG, 60, 30)
7 Controls.SetSize(btnB, 60, 30)
8
```

```
 9  GraphicsWindow.MouseMove = OnMouseMove
10  Controls.ButtonClicked = OnButtonClicked
11
12  Sub OnButtonClicked            ' Changes the pen color
13    If (Controls.LastClickedButton = btnR) Then
14      GraphicsWindow.PenColor = "Red"
15    ElseIf (Controls.LastClickedButton = btnG) Then
16      GraphicsWindow.PenColor = "Green"
17    Else
18      GraphicsWindow.PenColor = "Blue"
19    EndIf
20  EndSub
21
22  Sub OnMouseMove
23    x = GraphicsWindow.MouseX     ' Current x position of mouse
24    y = GraphicsWindow.MouseY     ' Current y position of mouse
25
26    If (Mouse.IsLeftButtonDown) Then
27      GraphicsWindow.DrawLine(prevX, prevY, x, y)
28    EndIf
29
30    prevX = x ' Updates the last (previous) position
31    prevY = y
32  EndSub
```

Listing 12-2: Clicking the buttons to change the pen color

Lines 2–4 create the three color selection buttons. The coordinates of the upper-left corner of the three buttons are (10, 30), (10, 65), and (10, 100). The statements in lines 5–7 set the size of each button to 60 × 30 (width = 60 and height = 30). Lines 9–10 register the handlers for the MouseMove and ButtonClicked events.

The program calls the OnButtonClicked() subroutine (line 12) when a user clicks any of the three buttons. To know which one was clicked, the subroutine uses an If/ElseIf ladder to compare the LastClickedButton property with the identifiers of the three buttons (lines 13–19). After identifying the clicked button, the subroutine sets the PenColor property (of GraphicsWindow) to the selected color. The OnMouseMove() subroutine is the same as the one in the previous version of the program, and it is defined on lines 22–32.

TIP *You can also write the OnButtonClicked() subroutine like this:*

```
Sub OnButtonClicked
  btnID = Controls.LastClickedButton
  GraphicsWindow.PenColor = Controls.GetButtonCaption(btnID)
EndSub
```

Instead of hardcoding the color of the clicked button, you get the color from the clicked button's caption using the GetButtonCaption() method.

Explore Circuits with Code

In this section, you'll create a program that demonstrates an electrical series circuit. (Your skills are shocking!) The circuit includes a battery, three resistors, and a switch connected in series. A user can change the battery's voltage and the values of the three resistors by entering their values in the text boxes. When the user enters a new value in any of the text boxes, the Controls object raises the TextTyped event. In response to this event, the program automatically calculates (and displays) the current that flows through the circuit and the voltages across each of the three resistors (see Figure 12-4).

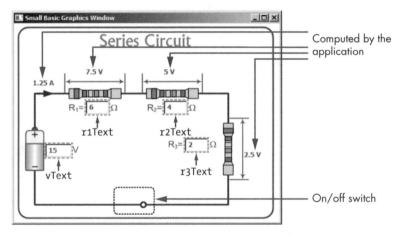

Figure 12-4: A program that shows you the operation of a series circuit

Here are the equations that describe the science behind the program:

Total resistance $R_{tot} = R_1 + R_2 + R_3$

Current through the circuit $I = V \div R_{tot}$, where V is the battery voltage

Voltage across R_1 $V_1 = I \times R_1$

Voltage across R_2 $V_2 = I \times R_2$

Voltage across R_3 $V_3 = I \times R_3$

Let's look at the computations. You calculate the total resistance (R_{tot}) by adding the values of the three resistors together. Next, you calculate the current (I) that flows in the circuit by dividing the battery voltage (V) by the total resistance. Then you calculate the voltage across each resistor by multiplying the current by the value of that resistor. (Try reading this paragraph aloud to your friends as if it's super easy. It will blow their minds!)

The following steps guide you through creating this program. So buckle your seat belt, hold on tight, and get set to rocket into the exciting world of computer simulations.

Step 1: Open the Startup File

To start creating this circuit simulator, open *SeriesCircuit_Incomplete.sb* from this chapter's folder. The file contains comments that tell you where to add your code and empty placeholders for the subroutines you'll write.

The folder for this chapter also includes the two background images you'll need: *bkgndOff.bmp* and *bkgndOn.bmp* (see Figure 12-5; we added the image names for clarity). The two images are the same except for the state of the switch: the switch is in the open position in *bkgndOff.bmp* but is closed in *bkgndOn.bmp*.

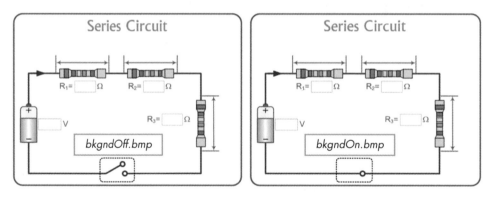

Figure 12-5: The two background images of SeriesCircuit.sb

When you start writing the code for this program, you'll see many hard-coded numbers. These numbers represent the coordinate points for the text boxes and labels and for checking the switch's boundaries. To help you understand where these numbers come from, refer to Figure 12-6. In this figure, we added coordinate axes and gridlines on top of the background image, and we marked the coordinates of all the points you'll use in the program.

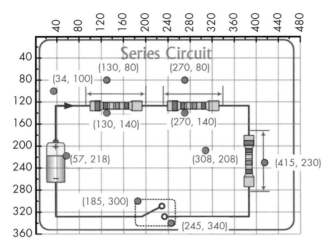

Figure 12-6: Illustrating the magic numbers used in SeriesCircuit.sb

Step 2: Add the Main Code

As in the previous examples, you'll start by designing the user interface. You'll write the code to load the background images, create and position the GUI elements (the text boxes), and then register the event handlers. Add the main part of the program, which is shown in Listing 12-3.

```
1  ' SeriesCircuit_Incomplete.sb
2  offImg = ImageList.LoadImage(Program.Directory + "\bkgndOff.bmp")
3  onImg = ImageList.LoadImage(Program.Directory + "\bkgndOn.bmp")
4  bkgndImg = offImg    ' Starts with the switch-off image
5
6  GraphicsWindow.Width = ImageList.GetWidthOfImage(offImg)
7  GraphicsWindow.Height = ImageList.GetHeightOfImage(offImg)
8  GraphicsWindow.DrawImage(bkgndImg, 0, 0)
9
10 r1Text = Controls.AddTextBox(130, 140)   ' R1 text box
11 r2Text = Controls.AddTextBox(270, 140)   ' R2 text box
12 r3Text = Controls.AddTextBox(308, 208)   ' R3 text box
13 vText = Controls.AddTextBox(57, 218)     ' Voltage text box
14 Controls.SetSize(r1Text, 42, 25)         ' Resizes the text boxes
15 Controls.SetSize(r2Text, 42, 25)
16 Controls.SetSize(r3Text, 42, 25)
17 Controls.SetSize(vText, 48, 25)
18 Controls.SetTextBoxText(vText, 10)       ' Sets the initial values
19 Controls.SetTextBoxText(r1Text, 4)
20 Controls.SetTextBoxText(r2Text, 4)
21 Controls.SetTextBoxText(r3Text, 2)
22
23 GraphicsWindow.MouseDown = OnMouseDown
24 Controls.TextTyped = OnTextTyped
```

Listing 12-3: Setting up the GUI

You start by loading the two background images and saving their identifiers in the `offImg` and `onImg` variables (line 2–3). The `bkgndImg` variable holds the current background image, which changes when a user clicks the switch. When the program starts, the switch is open, so the program sets `bkgndImg = offImg` (line 4). Lines 6–7 adjust the width and height of the graphics window to match the size of the background image, and line 8 draws the background image (`offImg` in this case) in the graphics window.

Lines 10–17 create the four text boxes (for the three resistors and the battery voltage) and resize them so they're exactly on top of their positions in the background image. In lines 18–21, you set default values for these text boxes. In line 23, you register a handler for the `MouseDown` event, because you'll want to know when a user clicks the switch. Line 24 registers a handler for the `TextTyped` event, because you'll calculate and display the values of I, V1, V2, and V3 automatically when the user enters a new value in any of the four text boxes.

Step 3: Toggle the Switch

When a user clicks the switch, you need to change the background image to toggle the switch. Add the `OnMouseDown()` subroutine in Listing 12-4.

```
1 Sub OnMouseDown ' Switches the background image
2   x = GraphicsWindow.MouseX
3   y = GraphicsWindow.MouseY
4   If ((x > 185) And (x < 245) And (y > 300) And (y < 340)) Then
5     If (bkgndImg = offImg) Then
6       bkgndImg = onImg
7     Else
8       bkgndImg = offImg
9     EndIf
10    UpdateUserInterface()
11  EndIf
12 EndSub
```

Listing 12-4: Changing the background image

The subroutine starts by getting the x- and y-coordinates of the point where the mouse was clicked and setting them to the variables x and y (lines 2–3). Line 4 then checks if this point lies within the rectangular region of the switch; if the mouse was inside the boundaries of the switch, the subroutine toggles the current value of the `bkgndImg` variable (from on to off or from off to on) at lines 5–9 and then calls the `UpdateUserInterface()` subroutine to switch the background image and update the calculated values (line 10). As you'll see in a moment, if the user opens the switch, the program shows only the `offImg` background image; the values of I, V1, V2, and V3 won't show because no current's flowing through the circuit when the switch is open.

Step 4: Respond to Changes

Add the OnTextTyped() subroutine in Listing 12-5. This subroutine is called when the user enters a new value in any of the four text boxes. As you can see, this subroutine just calls UpdateUserInterface(), which updates the UI to show the current values of V, R1, R2, and R3 as well as the state of the switch.

```
1 Sub OnTextTyped
2   UpdateUserInterface()
3 EndSub
```

Listing 12-5: The OnTextTyped() subroutine

Step 5: Update the Program's Interface

Now add the UpdateUserInterface() subroutine in Listing 12-6.

```
1 Sub UpdateUserInterface      ' Puts new values on the background
2   GraphicsWindow.DrawImage(bkgndImg, 0, 0)
3   If (bkgndImg = onImg) Then
4     R1 = Controls.GetTextBoxText(r1Text)
5     R2 = Controls.GetTextBoxText(r2Text)
6     R3 = Controls.GetTextBoxText(r3Text)
7     V = Controls.GetTextBoxText(vText)
8     Rtot = R1 + R2 + R3
9     If (Rtot > 0) Then
10      I = V / Rtot
11      V1 = Math.Round(I * R1 * 100) / 100
12      V2 = Math.Round(I * R2 * 100) / 100
13      V3 = Math.Round(I * R3 * 100) / 100
14      I = Math.Round(I * 100) / 100
15      GraphicsWindow.DrawText(130, 80, V1 + " V")
16      GraphicsWindow.DrawText(270, 80, V2 + " V")
17      GraphicsWindow.DrawText(415, 230, V3 + " V")
18      GraphicsWindow.DrawText(34, 100, I + " A")
19    EndIf
20  EndIf
21 EndSub
```

Listing 12-6: Updating the text boxes

The UpdateUserInterface() subroutine starts by redrawing the selected background image. If the switch is in the off position, the If statement on line 3 is false and the subroutine ends; the UI doesn't show any of the computed values (because no current is flowing through the circuit). But if the switch is on (which means the current background image is set to onImg), the subroutine moves on to compute the values of I, V1, V2, and V3. It starts by collecting the content of the four text boxes (lines 4–7). It then computes the total resistance by adding the values R1, R2, and R3 together (line 8). If the total resistance is greater than 0 (line 9), the subroutine computes the current (I) that flows through the circuit (line 10) and the values of V1, V2, and V3, rounding each value to the nearest hundredth (lines 11–14). The subroutine then shows the computed values at the correct locations on top of the background image (lines 15–18).

Most of the work in this program was designing the GUI (drawing the background images and positioning the text boxes on top of the background image). Then you had to write the code for handling the events, performing the calculations, and displaying the results. Congratulations; you just made a virtual electrical circuit!

In the next section, you'll write a GUI program that explains another object in the Small Basic library, the Flickr object.

TRY IT OUT 12-3

Think of ways to change this simulation to something else. Use different background images, like architectural blueprints, a pizza, or a Google Maps photo of your neighborhood. Then update the placement of the text boxes and the logic/math of what's entered to match your new theme. Head to *http://tiny.cc/sharesimulation/* to show off your program and to see what others have created.

Program Your Own Image Viewer

In this section, you'll create an image viewer called *ImageViewer.sb* that displays images from Flickr (a photo-sharing website) based on search input from a user. Small Basic gives you an object, appropriately named Flickr, which gets images from the Flickr website: *http://www.flickr.com/*. Figure 12-7 shows the GUI for this program.

Figure 12-7: Sample output of ImageViewer.sb

You'll need Small Basic version 1.1 or later to use the `Flickr` *object.*

The *ImageViewer.sb* program includes a text box into which the user enters the search tag and a button (labeled Next). When the user clicks the button, the program uses the `Flickr` object to get (and display) an image that matches the user's search tag. The program is shown in Listing 12-7.

```
1  ' ImageViewer.sb
2  GraphicsWindow.DrawText(10, 14, "Search for an image:")
3  tagText = Controls.AddTextBox(140, 10)
4  Controls.SetSize(tagText, 160, 26)
5  Controls.AddButton("Next", 305, 10)
6
7  Controls.ButtonClicked = OnButtonClicked
8
9  Sub OnButtonClicked
10   tag = Controls.GetTextBoxText(tagText)
11   If (tag <> "") Then
12     img = ImageList.LoadImage(Flickr.GetRandomPicture(tag))
13     If (img = "") Then
14       GraphicsWindow.ShowMessage("No images found.", "Sorry.")
15     Else
16       GraphicsWindow.Width = ImageList.GetWidthOfImage(img)
17       GraphicsWindow.Height = ImageList.GetHeightOfImage(img) + 40
18       GraphicsWindow.DrawImage(img, 0, 40)
19     EndIf
20   EndIf
21 EndSub
```

Listing 12-7: Loading images from Flickr

The program starts by designing the GUI (lines 2–5) and registering the `ButtonClicked` event handler (line 7). When the button is clicked, the `OnButtonClicked()` subroutine gets the search text from the text box and saves it in the `tag` variable (line 10). If tag isn't empty (line 11), the code searches Flickr using the given `tag` text for a random picture and then grabs the URL (line 12) by using `Flickr.GetRandomPicture()`.

That URL is passed to `ImageList.LoadImage()`, which loads an image from a file or the Internet and saves it into the `img` variable (line 12). If `img` is empty, which means Flickr didn't find an image with the user's tag, you let the user know in a message box (line 14). If Flickr found an image, you resize the graphics window to the dimensions of the loaded image (lines 16–17) and draw the image directly below the text box and the button (line 18).

Programming Challenges

If you get stuck, check out *http://nostarch.com/smallbasic/* for the solutions and for more resources and review questions for teachers and students.

1. In this program, you'll create a hidden treasure game. Open the file *HiddenTreasure_Incomplete.sb* from this chapter's folder. When you run the program, you'll see the following interface.

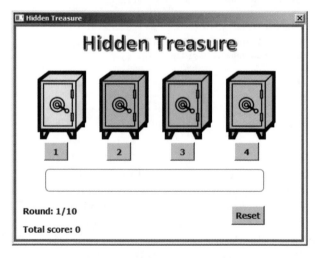

The purpose of the game is to guess the location of a hidden treasure. The player makes a guess by pressing one of the four buttons. If they guess correctly, they gain $10. Otherwise, they lose $5. The game ends after 10 rounds. Follow the comments shown in the program's source code to write the missing code and complete the program.

2. In this exercise, you'll create a program that computes the total cost of attending a special show at Sea World. Open the file *SeaWorld_Incomplete.sb* from this chapter's folder. When you run the program, you'll see the following user interface. The user enters the number of adult, senior, student, and VIP tickets they want to buy and then clicks the Compute button to calculate the total charge. Complete the program to display the total charge when the user clicks Compute.

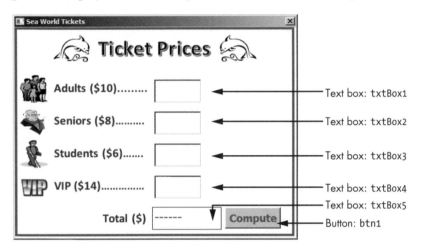

13

REPEATING FOR LOOPS

Have you ever noticed that no matter how many times you take out the trash, clean dirty dishes, and do laundry, you always have to do it again? What if you only had to do each task once, and then you created a robot version of yourself to do it every time after that? That would be amazing!

In the Small Basic universe, automating repetitive tasks is a breeze. You only have to write code for a repetitive task once, and then you can use a loop to repeat that task as many times as you need.

Small Basic uses two types of loop statements: For *loops* and While *loops*. In this chapter, you'll learn about For loops, explore nested For loops in depth, and create some programs that take advantage of your computer's passion for repetition. You'll learn how to use For loops in a wide range of practical applications. Let's get loopy!

The For Loop

Let's say you want to make a program that displays the multiplication table for nine: 1 × 9, 2 × 9, 3 × 9, through 10 × 9. Your first attempt might look like this:

```
TextWindow.WriteLine(" 1 x 9 = " + (1 * 9))
TextWindow.WriteLine(" 2 x 9 = " + (2 * 9))
TextWindow.WriteLine(" 3 x 9 = " + (3 * 9))
TextWindow.WriteLine(" 4 x 9 = " + (3 * 9))
TextWindow.WriteLine(" 5 x 9 = " + (3 * 9))
TextWindow.WriteLine(" 6 x 9 = " + (3 * 9))
TextWindow.WriteLine(" 7 x 9 = " + (3 * 9))
TextWindow.WriteLine(" 8 x 9 = " + (3 * 9))
TextWindow.WriteLine(" 9 x 9 = " + (3 * 9))
TextWindow.WriteLine("10 x 9 = " + (10 * 9))
```

Phew! Look at that wall-o-code! Although Small Basic lets you easily copy and paste selected statements, this program repeats a lot of code. What if you want to display the multiplication table up to 100 or 1000? Clearly, this isn't the best way to write your program. Here's a version of this program that uses a For loop to get the same result:

```
For N = 1 To 10
  TextWindow.WriteLine(N + " x 9 = " + (N * 9))
EndFor
```

Run this program and check out what happens. Wasn't that easier than writing out every line? Now you've seen the power of loops!

The loop runs the same statement but with a different value of N each time. First, the code sets the value of N to 1, which is the value we want to start creating the multiplication table from. Next, it runs all the statements between the For and the EndFor keywords. In this case, it runs the WriteLine() method, replacing N with its current value. This is called an *iteration* of the loop.

Then it sets N to 2. The value of N is compared with the ending value (or *terminal value*) of the loop, which is 10 in this case. If N is less than 10, the statements in the body of the For loop run again, completing another iteration of the loop. Note that the For loop automatically increases N by 1 during each iteration. This process continues, using N = 3, then N = 4, all the way to N = 10.

After the program runs the tenth iteration, it moves to the statement after the EndFor keyword (if there is one), and the loop is complete.

Now that you've seen a basic For loop in action, look at the syntax in Figure 13-1.

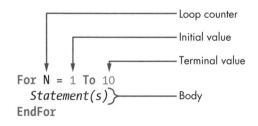

Figure 13-1: Syntax of a basic For loop

Each For loop starts with the keyword For. The statements contained between the For and EndFor keywords are called the *body* of the For loop. The variable, N, is the *loop control variable* (or *loop counter*). It controls the number of times the loop runs, and it's treated like any other variable in the program. The 1 To 10 part of the statement determines how many times the loop runs.

It's important to note that the condition to check whether or not the loop runs is tested at the top of the loop. For example, the following code sets N to 1 and then compares it to a terminal value of –10. Because 1 is greater than –10, the code won't run even once:

```
For N = 1 To -10
  TextWindow.WriteLine(N)    ' This won't be executed
EndFor
```

Let's look at some fun examples that show you how to use a For loop.

TRY IT OUT 13-1

Think about some other repetitive tasks that you could automate with a loop. Describe a program you'd build with a For loop.

Magical Moving Text

In this example, you'll create a program that moves a word or sentence across the text window from left to right. Figure 13-2 shows that with each iteration, the word displayed in the last iteration disappears, so the text appears to be animated, moving across the screen to the right.

CursorLeft	0	1	2	3	4	5	6	7	8	9	10	...
Iteration 1		M	o	v	i	n	g					
Iteration 2			M	o	v	i	n	g				
Iteration 3				M	o	v	i	n	g			
Iteration 4					M	o	v	i	n	g		

Figure 13-2: Using the Write() method to move a word across the text window

Recall that in Chapter 2 you used the CursorLeft property to display text in different places inside the text window. In this example, you'll set CursorLeft to 0 and use the Write() method to write the word. After a short delay, you'll change CursorLeft to 1 and write the word again. You'll then change CursorLeft to 2, then 3, and so on. Using a For loop, you'll automate this process to make it look like the word is moving across the text window. Enter the program in Listing 13-1.

```
1  ' MovingWord.sb
2  For N = 0 To 40
3    TextWindow.CursorLeft = N
4    TextWindow.Write(" Moving")  ' Erases the previous line
5    Program.Delay(250)            ' Delays so you can read it
6  EndFor
7  TextWindow.WriteLine("")
```

Listing 13-1: Moving a word across the text window

The program starts a loop that runs from N = 0 To 40 (line 2). During each iteration, it sets the CursorLeft property equal to the loop counter N (line 3) and then uses the Write() method to write the word (line 4). The space before the text Moving helps to erase the previous word. The Program.Delay(250) call at line 5 causes the program to wait for 250 milliseconds before it starts the next iteration of the loop. When the loop ends, the program writes an empty line (line 7).

Let's move on to another example.

TIP *Although it isn't required, indenting the statements in the body of a For loop makes your code easier to read.*

TRY IT OUT 13-2

Change Listing 13-1 to animate your own message to your friends or family members and share it with them. Mine is "I Like Tacos!"

Adding 'em Up

In programming, loops are used in different ways. One important use of loops is called an *accumulator loop*, which accumulates (or adds up) a value during each iteration of the loop. Accumulator loops are commonly used to keep count of values in programs.

Let's say you need to find the sum of all integers from 1 to 10: 1 + 2 + 3 + . . . + 10. That's what the program in Listing 13-2 does.

```
1  ' Sum.sb
2  sum = 0
3  For N = 1 To 10
4    sum = sum + N     ' Adds the new value of N to the sum
5  EndFor
6  TextWindow.WriteLine("sum = " + sum)
```

Listing 13-2: Using a For loop to add numbers

The program uses a variable named sum to hold the running total (this variable is usually called an *accumulator*). The program starts by initializing sum to 0 (line 2). Then a For loop with a loop counter named N runs from 1 to 10 (line 3). During each iteration, the program adds the value of N to the accumulator by using the statement at line 4. This statement adds the current value of N to the current value of sum and stores the result back into sum. After the first iteration, sum is 1 (0 + 1); after the second iteration, sum is 3 (1 + 2); after the third iteration, sum is 6 (3 + 3); and so on. When the loop ends, the program displays the value of the sum variable on line 6: sum = 55.

TRY IT OUT 13-3

When the great mathematician Carl Gauss first went to school, his teacher asked the class to find the sum of all the numbers between 1 and 100, that is, 1 + 2 + 3 + 4 + . . . + 100. Gauss took one look at the problem and immediately put his answer on the teacher's desk. The teacher was amazed—Gauss was right! Write a program to find the answer that Gauss worked out in his head. Of course, Gauss didn't use Small Basic, but he did find a shortcut. Can you figure out his secret method?

Formatting Your Output

The way you display the output of a program is often just as important as the information you display. If the output is difficult to read, people won't be able to understand what the information means. A well-laid-out display is an essential part of your program design, but getting the formatting right can be tedious. To make it easier, you can use For loops. For example, let's use a For loop to write a program that outputs the squares of 1 to 5 in a table format (see Figure 13-3).

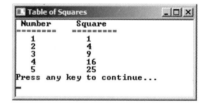

Figure 13-3: The output of SquareTable.sb

Enter and run the program in Listing 13-3.

```
1  ' SquareTable.sb
2  TextWindow.Title = "Table of Squares"
3  TextWindow.WriteLine(" Number      Square")
4  TextWindow.WriteLine("========    =========")
5
6  For N = 1 To 5
7      TextWindow.CursorLeft = 3      ' Moves to middle of col 1
8      TextWindow.Write(N)            ' Writes the number
```

```
 9    TextWindow.CursorLeft = 14   ' Moves to next column
10    TextWindow.WriteLine(N * N) ' Writes its square
11 EndFor
```

Listing 13-3: Using a For loop to display tabular data

Lines 3–4 write the headers for the two table columns. The loop at line 6 writes the five numbers and their squares. The TextWindow.CursorLeft property sets the desired position under each column (lines 7 and 9). Each time the code loops, it displays the correct value in its proper spot.

TRY IT OUT 13-4

The famous song *Twelve Days of Christmas* goes like this: "On the first day of Christmas my true love gave to me a partridge in a pear tree. On the second day of Christmas my true love gave to me two turtle doves and a partridge in a pear tree. On the third day of..." and so on for 12 days. On the twelfth day, the singer received 12 + 11 + . . . + 2 + 1 gifts. Write a program that shows the total gifts received on each of the 12 days. Include two columns in your output: the day number and the total gifts received on that day.

Drawing All Kinds of Lines

You can use For loops to change all kinds of values, including visual displays. Listing 13-4 draws 10 lines of increasing width in the graphics window.

```
1 ' Lines.sb
2 GraphicsWindow.Title = "Lines"
3 GraphicsWindow.PenColor = "Blue"
4 For N = 1 To 10
5   GraphicsWindow.PenWidth = N
6   y = N * 15     ' Vertical position of the line
7   GraphicsWindow.DrawLine(0, y, 200, y)
8 EndFor
```

Listing 13-4: Increasing the line width with each iteration

After setting the window's title and the pen's color (lines 2–3), the program starts a For loop with a loop counter named N that runs from 1 to 10 (line 4). In each iteration, the program sets the pen's width to the current value of N (line 5), sets the vertical position of the line (line 6), and then draws a line that is 200 pixels long (line 7). The output is shown in Figure 13-4.

Figure 13-4: The output of Lines.sb

Changing the Step Size

The previous section showed you the syntax of the For loop that automatically increases the loop counter by one after each iteration. But For loops have a general form that lets you control the Step size of the loop's control variable to increase it or decrease it by however much you want. Here's the general form of the For loop:

```
For N = A To B Step C
  Statement(s)
EndFor
```

It works like the simplified loop you saw earlier. But instead of incrementing the loop counter N by one, you can decide how much to change N. You do this by setting the amount in the Step size, C, which can be a positive or negative number or any Small Basic expression. Let's look at some examples that show you how to use this general form of the For loop.

Counting Down by Twos

In this example, the program counts from a starting value (10 in this case) down to 0, subtracting 2 at a time so the program writes the numbers 10, 8, 6, 4, 2, 0 in the text window. Enter and run the program in Listing 13-5.

```
1  ' CountDown.sb
2  For N = 10 To 0 Step -2    ' Uses a negative step size
3    TextWindow.WriteLine(N)
4  EndFor
```

Listing 13-5: Counting down with Step

A negative value was used for the Step size (line 2) to reduce the value of the loop counter by 2 after each iteration.

Here's the output:

```
10
8
6
4
2
0
```

Making a Fractional Step

The Step size doesn't have to be an integer value. You can also use a decimal value, as shown in Listing 13-6.

```
1  ' DecimalStep.sb
2  GraphicsWindow.FontSize = 10
3  GraphicsWindow.BrushColor = "Black"
4
5  yPos = 0
6  For angle = 0 To (2 * Math.PI) Step 0.3
7    xPos = 100 * (1 + Math.Sin(angle))
8    GraphicsWindow.DrawText(xPos, yPos, "Hello")
9    yPos = yPos + 8
10 EndFor
```

Listing 13-6: Making a design with text

The loop counter in this example is an angle (in radians) that uses the values from 0 to 2π in increments of 0.3 (line 6). In each iteration, the sine of the angle is computed, and the answer is used to set the horizontal position of the cursor (line 7). The word Hello is then displayed at that position (line 8), and the variable yPos is adjusted to set the vertical position for the next output text (line 9). Experimenting with different Step sizes can create some very cool stuff, like the wavy design shown in Figure 13-5.

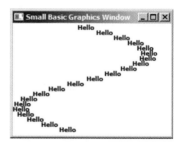

Figure 13-5: The output of DecimalStep.sb

TRY IT OUT 13-6

Write a program that finds the sum of all odd numbers from 5 to 25.

Nested Loops

The statements in the body of a For loop can be any Small Basic statement, including another For loop. *Nesting* is when you put one For loop inside another For loop (no birds are involved). Using nested loops allows you to create iterations in two or more dimensions. This technique is important, and you can use it to solve a wide range of programming problems.

To understand the idea of nested For loops, you'll examine a program that causes your computer to "jump" four times and "clap" three times after each jump. Because the program needs to count two actions (jumps and claps), it needs to use two loops, as shown in Listing 13-7. The counter for the outer loop, j, runs from 1 to 4. The counter for the inner loop, c, runs from 1 to 3.

```
1  ' NestedLoops.sb
2  For j = 1 To 4      ' The jump counter
3    TextWindow.Write("Jump " + j + ": ")
4    For c = 1 To 3    ' The clap counter
5      TextWindow.Write("Clap " + c + " ")
6    EndFor
7    TextWindow.WriteLine("")
8  EndFor
```

Listing 13-7: Nesting For loops

In the first iteration of the outer loop (where j = 1), the inner loop repeats three times (for the three values of c); each time, it writes the word Clap followed by a space, the current value of c, and another space (line 5). When you nest For loops like this, the inner loop goes through all its iterations for each iteration of the outer loop. So the first iteration of the outer loop makes the program display Jump 1: Clap 1 Clap 2 Clap 3. When the inner loop ends, the program outputs an empty line (line 7) to move the cursor to the beginning of the next line, and the second iteration of the outer loop starts with j = 2. The inner loop runs again for c = 1, 2, and 3. This causes the program to display Jump 2: Clap 1 Clap 2 Clap 3. This continues, so the program displays Jump 3: Clap 1 Clap 2 Clap 3 and then Jump 4: Clap 1 Clap 2 Clap 3. Then the program ends. Perhaps your computer wants to be a cheerleader!

Figure 13-6 helps to explain how the program works. The outer circle represents each time the outer loop runs: for example, at the top of the outer circle, when j = 1 in the outer loop, the inner loop runs three times, where c = 1, c = 2, and c = 3. Follow the outer loop and think through each inner loop. Continue until you get all the way around the outer circle.

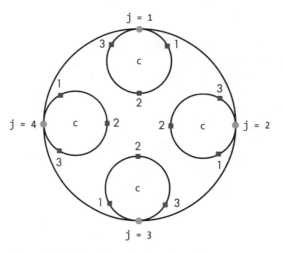

Figure 13-6: How NestedLoops.sb works

The output should look like this:

```
Jump 1: Clap 1 Clap 2 Clap 3
Jump 2: Clap 1 Clap 2 Clap 3
Jump 3: Clap 1 Clap 2 Clap 3
Jump 4: Clap 1 Clap 2 Clap 3
```

Now let's look at other problems where nested For loops come in handy!

Tessellating for Fun

In this example, an application covers the graphics window by stamping a small image over it. The complete program is shown in Listing 13-8.

```
1 ' Stamp.sb
2 GraphicsWindow.Title = "Stamp"
3
4 path = Program.Directory
5 img = ImageList.LoadImage(path + "\Trophy.ico")
6
7 width = ImageList.GetWidthOfImage(img)     ' Width of image
8 height = ImageList.GetHeightOfImage(img)   ' Height of image
9
10 GraphicsWindow.Width = 8 * width     ' 8 columns
11 GraphicsWindow.Height = 3 * height   ' 3 rows
12
13 For row = 0 To 2        ' 3 rows
14   For col = 0 To 7      ' 8 columns
15     GraphicsWindow.DrawImage(img, col * width, row * height)
16   EndFor
17 EndFor
```

Listing 13-8: Stamping a pattern across the graphics window

Copy the *Trophy.ico* file from this chapter's folder to your application's folder, and then run this program to see the result. Your screen should look like Figure 13-7. Way to go, champ!

Figure 13-7: The output of Stamp.sb

The program loads an image file (*Trophy.ico*) from your application's folder and saves the image's identifier in a variable named img (line 5). This is done by calling the ImageList object's LoadImage() method. The program then uses the ImageList object's methods to tell you the width and height of the loaded image in pixels (lines 7–8). The image's identifier (the img variable) is passed as an argument to the called methods. In lines 10–11, the program resizes the graphics window to hold eight horizontal and three vertical copies of the image. The program then uses a nested loop to stamp the image at different positions in the graphics window. The outer loop runs for three rows, and the inner loop runs for eight columns, for a total of 24 (3 × 8) iterations (lines 13–14). In each iteration, the x- and y-positions of the image are computed based on the dimensions of the image, and the image is drawn at that location (line 15). Now your trophy collection is bigger than Michael Jordan's is!

TRY IT OUT 13-7

Update Listing 13-8 to stamp a different image instead of a trophy. Then show your friends and family!

Multiple Nesting Levels

You can have more than two levels of nesting. Listing 13-9 displays all possible combinations of quarters, dimes, and nickels that add up to 50 cents.

```
1  ' CoinsAdder.sb
2  TextWindow.WriteLine("Quarters    Dimes     Nickels")
3  TextWindow.WriteLine("--------    -----     -------")
4
5  For Q = 0 To 2        ' Quarters
6    For D = 0 To 5      ' Dimes
7      For N = 0 To 10   ' Nickels
8        If (Q * 25 + D * 10 + N * 5 = 50) Then
9          TextWindow.Write(Q)
10         TextWindow.CursorLeft = 13
11         TextWindow.Write(D)
12         TextWindow.CursorLeft = 24
13         TextWindow.WriteLine(N)
14       EndIf
```

```
15      EndFor
16    EndFor
17 EndFor
```

Listing 13-9: Listing the combinations of coins that add up to 50 cents

The first loop initially keeps track of quarters by setting Q = 0. The second loop runs six times and counts all the dimes: For D = 0 To 5. For each pass of the second loop, the third loop runs 11 times, keeping track of the nickels: For N = 0 To 10. That means the If condition in line 8 is checked 198 times ($3 \times 6 \times 11$)! If the coin values total 50, that combination is displayed (lines 9–13). While looping through, the code uses the CursorLeft property to line up the columns and rows properly. Here's the output:

Quarters	Dimes	Nickels
0	0	10
0	1	8
0	2	6
0	3	4
0	4	2
0	5	0
1	0	5
1	1	3
1	2	1
2	0	0

TRY IT OUT 13-8

Write a program that finds all the sets of three integers that are less than 20 and can be the sides of a right triangle.

Programming Challenges

If you get stuck, check out *http://nostarch.com/smallbasic/* for the solutions and for more resources and review questions for teachers and students.

1. Write a For loop that displays this output:

```
I had 1 slices of pizza.
I had 2 slices of pizza.
I had 3 slices of pizza.
...
I had 10 slices of pizza.
```

2. Although the pizza in the previous exercise is very yummy, it's not grammatically correct, because the program outputs 1 slices of pizza. Fix the program so that its output is grammatically correct (and you won't embarrass your English teacher). (Hint: use an If statement inside the For loop.)

3. We built a game for you to quiz Alice on her multiplication so she'll be ready for the queen's questions. The program generates 10 random multiplication questions and asks Alice to enter the answer for each question. Alice earns one point for each correct answer. If she enters a wrong answer, show her the correct answer. The program ends by showing her total score. Re-create the program, run it, and explain how it works:

```
score = 0
For N = 1 To 10    ' Asks 10 questions
  n1 = Math.GetRandomNumber(10)
  n2 = Math.GetRandomNumber(10)

  TextWindow.Write(n1 + " x " + n2 + "? ")
  ans = TextWindow.ReadNumber()

  If (ans = n1 * n2) Then    ' Increases the score
    score = score + 1
  Else                       ' Shows the correct answer
    TextWindow.WriteLine("Incorrect --> " + (n1 * n2))
  EndIf
EndFor
TextWindow.WriteLine("Your score is: " + score + "/10")
```

4. Write a program that draws the following image. (Hint: use a For loop to draw the line pattern for each of the four corners.)

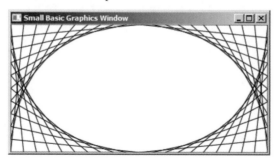

14

CREATING CONDITIONAL WHILE LOOPS

In Chapter 13, we showed you how to use the For loop to repeat code a certain number of times. For loops are ideal to use when you know exactly how many times you want to repeat code. While is another Small Basic keyword that lets you create loops. It's useful when you don't know how many times you want to repeat a loop in advance, because While loops keep running code as long as a condition is true.

A While loop condition is similar to how your parents keep telling you to clean your room until it's spotless or how you keep eating Thanksgiving turkey until you're stuffed! When the loop's condition becomes false, the loop ends, and the program moves on.

In this chapter, you'll learn how to write While loops and use them to verify user input and make games. While loops are a powerful programming concept; once you master them, you'll be able to make all kinds of cool applications.

When to Use While Loops

Let's say you want to make a number-guessing game that selects a random number between 1 and 100 and prompts a player to guess it. If the player's guess is wrong, the game tells them whether their guess was higher or lower than the secret number, and then it asks them to guess again. The game keeps asking the player to guess the number until they get it right.

A For loop isn't the best choice to use here, because you don't know how many times it will take a player to guess the secret number. Maybe the player will get it right on the first try, or it might take 100 tries! While loops are perfect in cases like this one.

In the next section, you'll learn the While loop's syntax and use it to create your own number-guessing game.

Writing a While Loop

Try out the code in Listing 14-1.

```
1  ' GuessMyNumber.sb
2  num = Math.GetRandomNumber(100)  ' From 1 to 100
3  ans = 0                ' Any value that isn't equal to num
4  While (ans <> num)     ' Repeats as long as the guess is wrong
5    TextWindow.Write("Enter your guess [1-100]: ")
6    ans = TextWindow.ReadNumber()
7    If (ans = num) Then  ' Player guessed correctly
8      TextWindow.WriteLine("Good job! You get sprinkles!")
9    ElseIf (ans > num) Then
10     TextWindow.WriteLine("Too High. Lower your standards.")
11   Else
12     TextWindow.WriteLine("Too Low. Aim for the stars!")
13   EndIf
14 EndWhile
```

Listing 14-1: Number-guessing game

The program randomly selects a number from 1 to 100 and assigns it to num (line 2). Then a variable called ans, which will hold the player's guess, is created and set to 0 (line 3). We set this initial value to 0 because we need it to be different from the correct answer. Let's take a closer look at the first line of the While loop (line 4):

```
While (ans <> num)
```

This piece of code simply says, "As long as ans is not equal to num, run the statement(s) between the While and the EndWhile keywords."

First, the test condition (ans <> num) is evaluated. If it's true, the program runs the statements in the loop's body and keeps repeating until the condition becomes false. When the test condition becomes false, the loop ends, and the program moves to the next statement after the EndWhile keyword. The flowchart in Figure 14-1 illustrates how the While loop works.

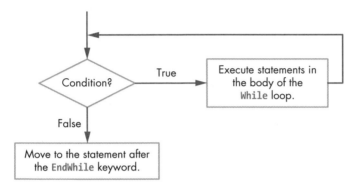

Figure 14-1: Flowchart of the While loop

In the number-guessing game, when the program runs line 4 for the first time, the condition (ans <> num) is true (because we know that num can't be 0), and the loop runs the statements in its body (lines 5–13). During each iteration of the loop, the player is prompted to enter a guess (line 5), which is saved into the variable ans (line 6). The code then compares the player's guess with the secret number. If the player guessed correctly (line 7), the code displays Good Job! You get sprinkles! and moves to the statement after EndIf. In this example, it finds EndWhile, which takes your program back to check the condition of the While loop. Because ans is now equal to num, the test condition is false and the While loop terminates, ending the program (because there are no statements after EndWhile).

If the player's guess was incorrect, the code checks whether the guess was higher than the secret number (line 9). If it's higher, the program displays Too High. Lower your standards. Then the loop goes for another round. If the player's guess is lower than the secret number (the Else statement on line 11), the program displays Too Low. Aim for the stars! (line 12) and starts another round.

Here is an example of a rather lucky user playing the game:

```
Enter your guess [1-100]: 50
Too High. Lower your standards.
Enter your guess [1-100]: 25
Too Low. Aim for the stars!
Enter your guess [1-100]: 37
Good Job! You get sprinkles!
```

Play this game several times to see how it works!

Although it's not required by Small Basic, we'll make programs easier to read by using parentheses around the While *loop's condition and indenting the body of a* While *loop.*

In the next section, we'll show you how to use a While loop to check data entered by a user.

TRY IT OUT 14-1

How much wood could a woodchuck chuck if a woodchuck could chuck wood? Open the *Woodchuck.sb* file from this chapter's folder, and run it to answer this age-old question. Then figure out some ways to improve the program.

Validating Your Inputs

When you write a program that reads data from a user, you should always check the input data before continuing with your program. This is called *validation*. In this section, we'll show you how to use While loops to ensure that your user enters the correct input to your program.

Let's say you need the user to enter a number between 1 and 5 (including 1 or 5). If they enter a number less than 1 or greater than 5, you need to prompt them to re-enter a number. Listing 14-2 shows you how to use a While loop to achieve this.

```
1 ' InputValidation.sb
2 num = -1    ' Invalid value (to force a pass through the loop)
3
4 While ((num < 1) Or (num > 5))
5   TextWindow.Write("Enter a number between 1 and 5: ")
6   num = TextWindow.ReadNumber()
7 EndWhile
8 TextWindow.WriteLine("You entered: " + num)
```

Listing 14-2: Using a While loop to check the input number

Line 2 sets the variable num (which will hold the number entered by the user) to –1. This makes the condition of the While loop (line 4) true, so the loop's body runs at least once. Although the loop in this example runs fine without the initialization statement on line 2 (because the variable num will be seen as 0), we recommend that you always initialize your variables and not rely on their default values. This will help you prevent future mistakes.

The program prompts the user for a number and assigns their input to the num variable (lines 5–6). Then the loop runs again. If num is less than 1 or greater than 5 (the user entered an invalid number), the loop's body runs again, prompting the user to re-enter the number. If num is between 1 and 5 (inclusive), the loop ends, and the program moves to line 8 to display the number.

Make sure you initialize any variable before you use it in a While loop's test condition. If you don't, your program might skip over the loop entirely!

Now you know how to verify user input using a While loop.

TRY IT OUT 14-2

Write a program that asks a user whether they think SpongeBob could become Santa, and then prompt them to enter Y (for yes) or N (for no). They can also enter y or n. Write a While loop that only accepts Y, y, N, or n as valid inputs. Then tell the user what they did wrong each time.

Infinite Loops

If a While loop's condition doesn't become false, the loop runs forever, creating an *infinite loop*. Sometimes this can cause a problem, but sometimes infinite loops are useful, such as when you want to make a game run forever.

But how do you create an infinite loop in Small Basic? There are a few ways to do this, but here is a common shortcut that many Small Basic programmers use:

```
While ("True")
  TextWindow.WriteLine("Loop forever!")
EndWhile
```

In this code, the loop's condition is always true; the loop never stops, and it displays Loop forever! forever. To see this in action, you'll program a simple game that quizzes kids on their addition skills. The complete code is shown in Listing 14-3. Run this program to see how it works.

```
1  ' AddTutor.sb
2  While ("True")
3    num1 = Math.GetRandomNumber(10)  ' Sets num1 between 1 and 10
4    num2 = Math.GetRandomNumber(10)  ' Sets num2 between 1 and 10
5    correctAns = num1 + num2         ' Adds both numbers
6    TextWindow.Write("What is " + num1 + " + " + num2 + "? ")
7    ans = TextWindow.ReadNumber()    ' User enters an answer
8    If (ans = correctAns) Then       ' Checks if the answer is correct
9      TextWindow.WriteLine("This is correct.")
10   Else                            ' Gives the correct answer
11     TextWindow.WriteLine("Sorry. The answer is " + correctAns)
12   EndIf
13 EndWhile
```

Listing 14-3: A program that quizzes a user with addition problems

In lines 3 and 4, num1 and num2 are set to random numbers between 1 and 10. Line 5 adds them together to set the correct answer. Line 6 asks the user for the correct answer. Line 7 gets the user's answer. Line 8 checks whether the answer is true, and if it is, line 9 tells them they're right. Otherwise, line 11 tells them the correct answer. The game runs forever. When the user wants to quit, they can close the application by clicking the X icon in the upper-right corner of the application's window.

TIP *You can use a Goto statement inside a While loop to jump to a label outside the loop in order to break out of the loop.*

Now it's time to put what you've learned in this chapter to work by designing a complete game. Head to the fridge to get plenty of brain food before reading on!

TRY IT OUT 14-3

Change the *AddTutor.sb* program so it won't give the correct answer to the player when they get it wrong. Instead, have the program tell the player that their answer is incorrect and let them try again.

Create a Rock-Paper-Scissors Game

In this section, you'll create a rock-paper-scissors game in which a user plays against the computer. Figure 14-2 shows the user interface for this game. The three buttons represent rock, paper, and scissors. The player chooses one by clicking it. Then the computer randomly picks an action. The rules that determine the winner are paper beats rock, rock beats scissors, and scissors beats paper.

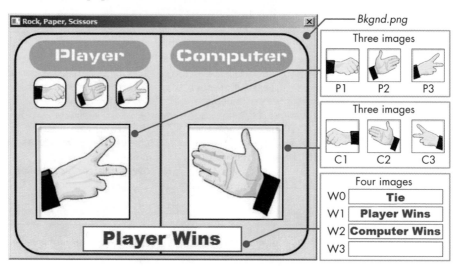

Figure 14-2: The user interface for the rock-paper-scissors game

Images *P1*, *P2*, and *P3* show the player's selection, and images *C1*, *C2*, and *C3* show the computer's choice. Images *W0*, *W1*, *W2*, and *W3* show the result of each round of the game. Everything else you see in Figure 14-2 is part of the background image, including the rock, paper, and scissors images that represent the three buttons.

Step 1: Open the Startup File

Open the file *RockPaper_Incomplete.sb* from this chapter's folder and follow along. The folder includes all the images you need for this game. The startup file, shown in Listing 14-4, contains the main part of the game. It also contains empty placeholders for all the subroutines you need to add.

```
1  ' RockPaper_Incomplete.sb
2  GraphicsWindow.Title = "Rock, Paper, Scissors"
3  GraphicsWindow.CanResize = "False"
4  GraphicsWindow.Width = 480
5  GraphicsWindow.Height = 360
6
7  path = Program.Directory
8  GraphicsWindow.DrawImage(path + "\Bkgnd.png", 0, 0)
9  choice1 = 0                    ' 0 = Unknown; 1 = Rock; 2 = Paper; 3 = Scissors
10 GraphicsWindow.MouseDown = OnMouseDown
11
12 While ("True")                      ' Loops forever
13   If (choice1 <> 0) Then            ' If player made a choice
14     blankImg = path + "\W3.png"     ' Clears last result
15     GraphicsWindow.DrawImage(blankImg, 115, 310)
16     choice2 = Math.GetRandomNumber(3) ' 1 to 3
17     SwitchImages()                  ' Shows player and computer choices
18     ShowWinner()                    ' Shows image for the result
19     choice1 = 0                     ' Ready for another round
20   EndIf
21   Program.Delay(10)                 ' Waits a little, then checks again
22 EndWhile
```

Listing 14-4: Setting up the window and choice

If you run the program now, all you'll see is the background image because you haven't created any of the subroutines yet. You'll get there, but first let's check out the setup and main loop of the game. First, the size of the graphics window is set, and the background image is drawn (lines 2–8). The variable choice1 holds the player's choice: 0 means unknown, 1 means rock, 2 means paper, and 3 means scissors. To start, we set choice1 to 0, because the player hasn't made a choice yet (line 9). Then we register a handler for the MouseDown event to be able to find out when the player clicks one of the three buttons (line 10). Then the game's main loop starts (lines 12–22).

The loop continuously checks the value of choice1. As you'll see in a moment, this variable is changed by the OnMouseDown() subroutine when the player makes a choice. If choice1 is 0, the loop waits for 10 milliseconds (line 21) and checks again. Using a loop makes the program wait for choice1 to become a value other than 0 (this is called *polling*; it's similar to asking "Are we there yet?" during a long trip). When choice1 becomes a value other than 0 (line 13), the body of the If block is executed (lines 14–19). We draw image W3 to show a blank result (lines 14–15). Next, we set the computer's choice, choice2, to a random value between 1 and 3 (line 16). Then we call SwitchImages() to show the images that correspond to choice1 and choice2 (line 17). Then we call ShowWinner() to show the result of this round of the game (line 18). Finally, we set choice1 back to 0 to tell the OnMouseDown() subroutine that the main loop is ready for another round of the game (line 19).

Next, you'll add each subroutine one at a time.

Step 2: Add the MouseDown Handler

Now let's handle the MouseDown event to figure out the player's choice. Add the OnMouseDown() subroutine in Listing 14-5 to the bottom of the program.

```
1 Sub OnMouseDown
2   If (choice1 = 0) Then            ' Ready for another round
3     y = GraphicsWindow.MouseY      ' Vertical click position
4     If ((y > 80) And (y < 120)) Then  ' Within range
5       x = GraphicsWindow.MouseX       ' Horizontal click
6       If ((x > 40) And (x < 80)) Then       ' Rock
7         choice1 = 1
8       ElseIf ((x > 110) And (x < 150)) Then ' Paper
9         choice1 = 2
10      ElseIf ((x > 175) And (x < 215)) Then ' Scissors
11        choice1 = 3
12      EndIf
13    EndIf
14  EndIf
15 EndSub
```

Listing 14-5: Checking the choice the user clicked

Small Basic calls this subroutine when the player clicks anywhere in the graphics window. First, the subroutine checks the value of choice1 (line 2). If choice1 is 0, the subroutine checks where the player clicked to see whether they clicked one of the three buttons. If choice1 is not 0, that means the main loop is still processing the player's last choice, so the subroutine just ignores the mouse click. This way your game won't get confused if the player clicks all over the place.

To see whether the player clicks one of the three image buttons, the subroutine checks the vertical position of the click (line 4). If it's within the range of the images, the subroutine checks the horizontal position (line 6). The If/ElseIf ladder then compares the horizontal position with the left and right edges of each image and sets choice1 accordingly (lines 6–12).

If you want to find out the exact positions of the three image buttons, add this code to your program:

```
GraphicsWindow.MouseMove = OnMouseMove
Sub OnMouseMove
  mx = GraphicsWindow.MouseX
  my = GraphicsWindow.MouseY
  TextWindow.WriteLine(mx + ", " + my)
EndSub
```

Move the mouse over the background image to see the coordinates displayed in the text window. Don't forget to delete this code before you share your game with your friends!

Step 3: Switch the Images

When the player makes a choice, you need to show the computer's pick so they know the computer isn't cheating. To create some excitement, you'll animate the images before showing the final choices. Add the SwitchImages() subroutine in Listing 14-6.

```
1 Sub SwitchImages
2   For M = 1 To 10   ' Flips images 10 times
3     N = 1 + Math.Remainder(M, 3)      ' N = 1,2,3,1,2,3...
4     img1 = path + "\P" + N + ".png"   ' {\P1, \P2, or \P3}.png
5     img2 = path + "\C" + N + ".png"   ' {\C1, \C2, or \C3}.png
6     GraphicsWindow.DrawImage(img1,  40, 150) ' Draws img1
7     GraphicsWindow.DrawImage(img2, 280, 150) ' Draws img2
8     Program.Delay(100)                ' Waits a short time
9   EndFor
10
11  ' Shows the actual choices of the player and the computer
12  img1 = path + "\P" + choice1 + ".png"
13  img2 = path + "\C" + choice2 + ".png"
14  GraphicsWindow.DrawImage(img1,  40, 150)
15  GraphicsWindow.DrawImage(img2, 280, 150)
16 EndSub
```

Listing 14-6: Switching images for a visual effect

SwitchImages() starts by switching the images for the player and the computer 10 times very quickly for a fun visual effect (lines 2–9). Then the code shows the images that correspond to choice1 and choice2 by appending a number to the letters P and C, which represent the names of the images.

Run the code to test it. When you click any of the three image buttons, the player and the computer selections will change 10 times before landing on the images that correspond to the actual choices. (Don't flip images too quickly, or you'll get a headache!)

Step 4: Announce the Winner

The last part of the game, the ShowWinner() subroutine, checks the result and displays the winner. Add the ShowWinner() subroutine in Listing 14-7.

```
1 Sub ShowWinner
2   ' W0: Tie; W1: Player1; W2: Computer
3   If ((choice1 = 1) And (choice2 = 2)) Then      ' Paper (2) beats rock (1)
4     img = "\W2.png"
5   ElseIf ((choice1 = 1) And (choice2 = 3)) Then ' Rock (1) beats scissors (3)
6     img = "\W1.png"
7   ElseIf ((choice1 = 2) And (choice2 = 1)) Then ' Paper (2) beats rock (1)
8     img = "\W1.png"
9   ElseIf ((choice1 = 2) And (choice2 = 3)) Then ' Scissors (3) beats paper (2)
10    img = "\W2.png"
11  ElseIf ((choice1 = 3) And (choice2 = 1)) Then ' Rock (1) beats scissors (3)
12    img = "\W2.png"
13  ElseIf ((choice1 = 3) And (choice2 = 2)) Then ' Scissors (3) beats paper (2)
14    img = "\W1.png"
15  Else
16    img = "\W0.png"
17  EndIf
18
19  GraphicsWindow.DrawImage(path + img, 115, 310)
20 EndSub
```

Listing 14-7: Checking who won to display the right image

This subroutine compares the values of choice1 and choice2 using an If/ElseIf ladder and decides which image (img) to display (lines 3–17). Remember that choice 1 means rock, 2 means paper, and 3 means scissors. Then, line 19 draws the selected image.

TRY IT OUT 14-4

See if you can turn the rock-paper-scissors game into a two-player game!

Programming Challenges

If you get stuck, check out *http://nostarch.com/smallbasic/* for the solutions and for more resources and review questions for teachers and students.

1. Open the file *Race_Incomplete.sb* from this chapter's folder. This application simulates a race between two players. When you run the program, you'll see the following interface. Follow the comments provided in the application's source code to write the missing code and complete the application.

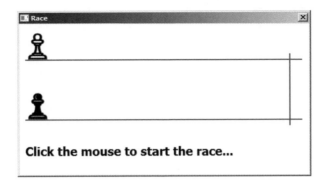

2. Open the file *SimpleSlot.sb* from this chapter's folder. This program simulates a simple slot machine, as shown in the following figure. When you click the mouse, the game displays three objects at random. If all three objects are alike, you win $20. If two are alike, you win $5; otherwise, you lose $1. After playing the game, study the code and explain how the program works.

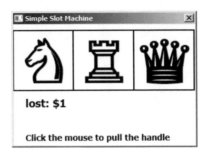

3. Open the file *Space.sb* from this chapter's folder. In this game, you shoot at a UFO flying across the top of the screen (see the following figure). Use the left and right arrow keys to move, and press the spacebar to shoot. You have only 100 shots, and the game tracks your score. Think of some ways to improve the game and add them.

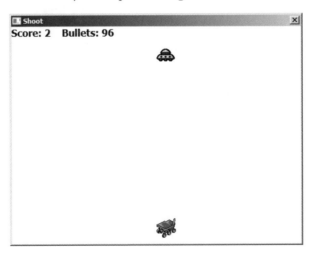

15

GROUPING DATA IN ONE-DIMENSIONAL ARRAYS

So far you've worked with variables to store single pieces of information, and you've created some pretty awesome programs. But you can create even more amazing programs by storing lots of information in a single variable! In Small Basic, you do that by using an array.

An *array* is a built-in data type that lets you work with groups of data. For example, you wouldn't build a separate closet for every pair of shoes you own (unless you're a giant who loves shoe shopping); you'd put them all in one closet. Well, arrays let you store many pieces of data together to make it easier to work with them all at once. You can think of the closet as a one-dimensional array that contains a row of shoe boxes.

Small Basic has two types of arrays: indexed arrays and associative arrays. The pieces of data in an *indexed array* are referenced using an integer index, such as score[1], name[3], and so on. This is like putting a numbered label on each shoe box in your closet. But the elements of an *associative array* are referenced using a string index, such as price["apple"] or address["John"]. This chapter explores indexed arrays. We'll cover associative arrays, also called *hashes* or *maps*, in the next chapter.

Getting Started with Indexed Arrays

Let's say you want to write a program that takes four test scores from a user and then displays them along with their average value. Based on what you've learned so far, you might write a program like the one in Listing 15-1.

```
1 ' Average1.sb
2 TextWindow.Write("Enter 4 scores. ")
3 TextWindow.WriteLine("Press <Enter> after each score.")
4 s1 = TextWindow.ReadNumber()    ' Reads the 1st score
5 s2 = TextWindow.ReadNumber()    ' Reads the 2nd score
6 s3 = TextWindow.ReadNumber()    ' Reads the 3rd score
7 s4 = TextWindow.ReadNumber()    ' Reads the 4th score
8 avg = (s1 + s2 + s3 + s4) / 4   ' Calculates the average
9 TextWindow.Write("Numbers: " + s1 + ", " + s2 + ", ")
10 TextWindow.WriteLine(s3 + ", " + s4)
11 TextWindow.WriteLine("Average: " + avg)
```

Listing 15-1: Storing scores in separate variables

This program prompts the user to enter four scores (lines 2–3). It reads these scores and saves them in the four variables s1, s2, s3, and s4 (lines 4–7). Then it computes the average (line 8), displays the four numbers on a single line (lines 9–10), and displays the computed average (line 11).

Now imagine that you want a user to input 100 scores instead of 4. Defining 100 variables and copying almost the same statement 100 times would take a long time. Well, Small Basic's array stores a collection of values. Using an array, you don't have to create each variable separately. You can put all the values into one *array variable*. For example, you can read 10 scores a user enters and store them in one array using this loop:

```
For N = 1 To 10
  score[N] = TextWindow.ReadNumber()
EndFor
TextWindow.WriteLine(score)
```

Instead of creating 10 variables, like s1, s2, and so on to s10, you create one array variable called score. To refer to each piece of data in the score array, you use the syntax score[N], where N is a variable that will take on the values 1 through 10. Writing score[N] is like writing score[1], score[2], . . . , score[10], and the For loop increments N for you.

Run this code. After you enter 10 different numbers, Small Basic displays the score array, and you can see all 10 values stored in it (we'll show you a better way to display an array later in this chapter).

One way to think of an array is as a collection of variables that share the same name. For example, the average rainfall in the 10 largest US cities could be saved in `rainLevel[1]` through `rainLevel[10]`, and the daily sales for the 100 McDonalds in your area could be saved in `sales[1]` through `sales[100]`. Think of all the Happy Meals!

Arrays can help you organize your data in a way that makes the data much easier to change and use. The name of an array follows the same rules and guidelines you use for naming variables.

Array Basics

Each piece of information in an array is called an *element*. To access an element in an array, you use this syntax:

arrayName[*index*]

The *arrayName* variable is the array's name, and *index* is an identifier, either a number or a string, that identifies an element in the array (see Figure 15-1). This syntax is known as an *indexed variable*, or a *subscripted variable*. The index, which is placed between square brackets, uniquely identifies one element in the array.

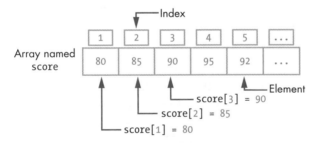

Figure 15-1: Graphical representation of a one-dimensional array

You can treat an indexed variable just like a regular variable by using the proper syntax. For example, the following statements initialize and display the first three elements of the score array in Figure 15-1:

```
score[1] = 80
score[2] = 85
score[3] = 90
TextWindow.WriteLine(score[1] + ", " + score[2] + ", " + score[3])
```

If you run this code, you'll see this output:

```
80, 85, 90
```

If you wanted to change the first score, you could write this statement:

```
score[1] = score[1] + 5
```

This line of code adds five to the first score at index 1. If you displayed the value of score now, you'd see that score[1] = 85. You could use the next statement to multiply the two elements at indices 1 and 2:

```
score[1] = score[1] * score[2]
```

If score[1] is 80 and score[2] is 85, they are multiplied to get 6,800, which is saved back into score[1]. High score!

Initializing Arrays

Before using an array in your program, you need to fill it up (or initialize it) with some data. In Small Basic, you can do this in two ways: by direct (element-by-element) initialization or string initialization.

Let's say you want to create an array that holds four scores (not the Abe Lincoln type). Here's the direct way to do this:

```
score[1] = 80
score[2] = 85
score[3] = 90
score[4] = 95
```

You can also use a *string initializer*, which allows you to set the four values in just one line like this:

```
score = "1=80;2=85;3=90;4=95;"
```

This string initializer has four tokens (or fields), which are terminated by semicolons. Each token is in this form (and no, you can't exchange these tokens for prizes):

```
index=value;
```

In this example, the first token is 1=80, the second is 2=85, the third is 3=90, and the fourth is 4=95. The number before the equal sign is the element's index, and the value after the equal sign is the value stored in that element. Note that there are no spaces before or after the equal sign. Figure 15-2 shows you how this string initializer works.

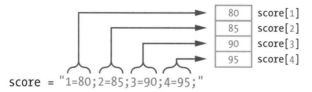

Figure 15-2: The syntax of an array's string initializer

The string initializer lets you fill an array in one statement, but its syntax is a bit complex, and you could accidentally introduce errors in your code. Until you become more comfortable with arrays, we recommend that you stick to the basic element-by-element initialization technique in your programs. But if you do use the string initializer and run into problems, try reinitializing your array one element at a time. We'll use both initialization types in this book, to save space and to get you more familiar with them.

NOTE   *Small Basic lets you choose any numbers you want for indices. It even lets you use negative and decimal numbers, and it doesn't require the indices to be consecutive. But in this book we'll always use integer indices starting from 1 for the first array element.*

Arrays and For loops are often used together. When the size of an array is known, you can use a For loop to cycle through and perform operations on every element in that array. The next examples show you how to use For loops to perform operations on arrays.

TRY IT OUT 15-1

Suppose that the elements in array S and variables A and B have the values in Figure 15-3. What is S[A], S[B], S[A * B - 2], S[A + B], and S[A] - 2 * S[B]?

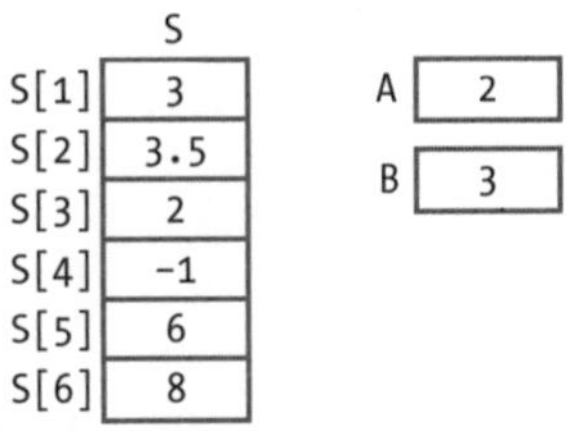

	S
S[1]	3
S[2]	3.5
S[3]	2
S[4]	-1
S[5]	6
S[6]	8

A	2

B	3

Figure 15-3: Values in S array and variables A and B

Filling Arrays with a For Loop

Many times you'll need to fill the elements of an array with a constant value, a random value, a value calculated from a formula, or a value entered by a user. Let's look at each scenario!

Constant Initialization

The following code snippet shows how to initialize the first 10 elements of a tasty array (named scoobySnack) with a constant value of 0.

```
For N = 1 To 10
  scoobySnack[N] = 0
EndFor
```

The For loop repeats 10 times. In the first iteration, the value of N is 1, so the loop sets scoobySnack[1] = 0. In the second iteration, the value of N is 2, so the loop sets scoobySnack[2] = 0, and so on. This creates an array with 10 elements, all of which are 0.

Random Initialization

You can also fill the elements of the scoobySnack array with random numbers, like this:

```
For N = 1 To 10
  scoobySnack[N] = Math.GetRandomNumber(5)
EndFor
```

The For loop iterates 10 times. In the Nth iteration, the element at index N, scoobySnack[N], is assigned a random number between 1 and 5. Try displaying the value of scoobySnack to see what random numbers you get! Add the following statement after you set scoobySnack[N] inside the For loop:

```
TextWindow.WriteLine(scoobySnack[N])
```

Formula Initialization

You can also initialize the elements of an array using a formula. In this example, you'll set the Nth element of the scoobySnack array to N * 8; this code will store the multiplication table of eight in your array:

```
For N = 1 To 10
  scoobySnack[N] = N * 8
EndFor
```

Add the code that displays the value of scoobySnack to see the results!

User Initialization

What if you want to initialize the elements of your array using values entered by a user? The following program prompts the user to enter five numbers and press ENTER after each number. The program then starts a For loop to read the five numbers and store them in thunderCat[1], thunderCat[2], . . . , thunderCat[5].

```
TextWindow.WriteLine("Enter 5 numbers. Press Enter after each one.")
For N = 1 To 5
  thunderCat[N] = TextWindow.ReadNumber()
EndFor
```

This technique is very useful for storing lots of data from a user. What other collections of data might you ask for? How about breakfastMenu, favoriteGames, bestPasswords, funnyJokes, or frozenNames?

TRY IT OUT 15-2

Write a program that fills an array called skeletor with even integers from 20 to 40 (for example, skeletor[1] = 20, skeletor[2] = 22, . . .).

Displaying Arrays

Let's say we have an array named age that holds the ages of three brothers, like this:

```
age[1] = 14
age[2] = 15
age[3] = 16
```

You can display the contents of this array in two ways. The first and easiest way is to pass the array's name to the WriteLine() method, like this:

```
TextWindow.WriteLine(age)
```

Here's the output of this statement:

```
1=14;2=15;3=16;
```

This statement displays the elements of the array on a single line separated by semicolons. Each token in this string shows the index and the value of the array's element at that index. Can you see now where the array's string initializer syntax came from?

If you want to display the array in an easier-to-read format, you can use a For loop to display each element of the array in its own row:

```
For N = 1 To 3
  TextWindow.WriteLine("age[" + N + "] = " +  age[N])
EndFor
```

Here's the output of this loop:

```
age[1] = 14
age[2] = 15
age[3] = 16
```

If you're working with a short array, it's fine to display it on a single line. But if you're working with a lot of data, it's best to display the array in a format that's easy to read.

TRY IT OUT 15-3

Write a program that fills an array called burps with five random numbers between 80 and 100 and then displays the array. Try displaying the array by passing the array's name to TextWindow.WriteLine() and then by using a For loop. Which looks nicer?

Processing Arrays

Many programs involve processing the elements of an array, such as adding them and finding their average, minimum, maximum, and so on. You'll learn how to do these tasks in this section.

Finding the Sum

A superhero named Super Here-O wants to know how much money he rescued from 10 robbers in his town. The following program lets Super Here-O enter the amounts he rescued into an array named moneyReturned. The program finds the sum of all the elements of this array:

```
sum = 0
TextWindow.WriteLine("Enter the 10 amounts that were returned:")
For N = 1 To 10
  moneyReturned[N] = TextWindow.ReadNumber()
  sum = sum + moneyReturned[N]
EndFor
For N = 1 To 10
  TextWindow.Write("$" + moneyReturned[N])
  TextWindow.WriteLine(" rescued from robber " + N)
EndFor
TextWindow.WriteLine("$" + sum + " was rescued by Super Here-O!")
```

To find the sum, you start by initializing the sum variable to 0. You then run a For loop to read each element of the moneyReturned array and add it to the sum variable. When the loop terminates, you start another loop to show

how much money was rescued from each robber, and then you display the total amount returned. Run the program to find out whether it's enough money to buy a new superhero spandex suit!

Finding the Maximum Element

Say you're competing with nine of your good friends to see who has the most friends on Facebook. Use the following code snippet to find the largest value in an array named friends:

```
friends = "1=10;2=30;3=5;4=10;5=15;6=8;7=1;8=23;9=6;10=11"
max = friends[1]
For N = 2 To 10
  If (friends[N] > max) Then   ' Nth element is larger than max
    max = friends[N]           ' Update max to hold the new maximum
  EndIf
EndFor
TextWindow.WriteLine("The most friends is " + max + ".")
```

First, we filled the 10 elements of the friends array with the number of Facebook friends that you and your nine closest friends have. In this example, your first friend has 10 friends, your second friend has 30, your third friend has 5, and so on, and you (number 10 in the array) have 11 friends. Feel free to change these numbers. The program starts by assuming that the first element, friends[1], is the largest. It then enters a loop that examines the remaining elements of the array, starting at the second element. Every time it finds a number larger than the current maximum, it updates the maximum, max, to that number. When the loop terminates, the maximum value displays.

Using String Values in Arrays

Arrays aren't restricted to numbers. You can also use arrays to store strings. Let's say, for example, that you want to create an array to store the names of the books in your collection. You could initialize this array:

```
book[1] = "The Hobbit"
book[2] = "Little Women"
book[3] = "My Little Pony vs Hello Kitty"
```

NOTE   *You could also use a string initializer to initialize the book array like this (make sure the entire statement is on one line):*

```
book = "1=The Hobbit;2=Little Women;3=My Little Pony vs Hello Kitty"
```

Saving Records

You can mix different data types within a single array. You can store numbers, both whole and decimal, and strings as different elements in the same array. For example, the following array is valid (do you know this building?):

```
arr[1] = 1600
arr[2] = "Pennsylvania Avenue NW"
arr[3] = 20500
```

The first and third elements of this array are numbers. The second element is a string. These three elements could represent a home's number, its street name, and its ZIP code, respectively. This is one way to create a *record*, which is a collection of related pieces of data, in Small Basic.

Whew! Well, we've covered more than enough to solve oodles of problems. Now let's spend some time writing fun programs!

Using Indexed Arrays

The first example in this section shows you how to select random elements from an array. The second example simulates a Magic 8 Ball game in which the computer provides randomly selected answers to a player's questions. Let's get random!

Random Selection

Let's say we have a bag that contains 10 balls numbered 1 through 10, and we want to take out five random balls (see Figure 15-4). We'll write a program that randomly selects five balls and then displays their numbers.

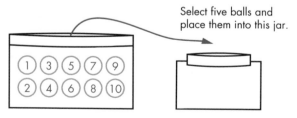

Figure 15-4: Randomly selecting five balls from a bag

To create this program, we'll use an array named `ball` to hold the numbers of the 10 balls (ball[1] = 1, ball[2] = 2, ..., ball[10] = 10). Then the program selects a random number between 1 and 10 to pick a ball. For example, if it picks number 2, it sets ball[2] = 0 to indicate that the second ball has been selected and is no longer available. Then it selects another random number. Let's say that the second number is also 2. First, the program checks ball[2]. Because it's 0, it knows that ball[2] has already been selected (you can't take the same ball out of the bag twice!), and it picks another random number. It continues this until it selects five different random numbers. The complete program is shown in Listing 15-2.

```
1  ' RandomSelect.sb
2  For N = 1 To 10    ' Puts the 10 balls in an array
3    ball[N] = N
4  EndFor
5
6  For N = 1 To 5                    ' Loops to select 5 balls
7    idx = Math.GetRandomNumber(10)  ' Gets random ball number
8    While (ball[idx] = 0)           ' Ball already selected
9      idx = Math.GetRandomNumber(10) ' Gets another number
10   EndWhile
11
12   TextWindow.Write(ball[idx] + ", ") ' Displays selected ball
13   ball[idx] = 0                    ' Marks it out (taken)
14 EndFor
15 TextWindow.WriteLine("")
```

Listing 15-2: Randomly selecting five different balls

The program starts by setting ball[1] = 1, ball[2] = 2, ..., ball[10] = 10 in a For loop (lines 2–4). It then begins a loop to select the five balls (line 6). In each iteration of the loop, it picks a random number, idx, between 1 and 10 (line 7). A While loop continually sets idx until ball[idx] is not 0 (lines 8–10). After selecting a unique ball number, the program displays the number (line 12), and then it marks that ball as selected by setting its array element to 0 (line 13) so it doesn't try to select that number again. Here's a sample run of this program:

```
5, 9, 10, 1, 2,
```

Run the program to see which numbers you get!

A Magic 8 Ball

In this example, we'll write a program that simulates a Magic 8 Ball game. A user asks a yes or no question, and the computer answers. Of course, it's just for fun, so don't use it to make important decisions like choosing your spouse or house! The complete program is shown in Listing 15-3.

```
1  ' Magic8Ball.sb
2  ans[1] = "It is certain. Like really, really certain."
```

```
 3  ans[2] = "It is decidedly so. By me. I decided."
 4  ans[3] = "Without a doubt. Maybe one doubt."
 5  ans[4] = "Yes, definitely. Isn't it obvious?"
 6  ans[5] = "Very doubtful. The doubt is very full."
 7  ans[6] = "Maybe. Depends on the horse race."
 8  ans[7] = "No. Wait, yes. Wait, no. Yes, it's no."
 9  ans[8] = "Let me consult my Magic 8 Ball... It says yes."
10  ans[9] = "Outlook not so good. Restart Outlook."
11  ans[10] = "Try again. It's funny when you shake things."
12
13  While ("True")
14    TextWindow.WriteLine("Ask me a yes-no question. Do it!")
15    ques = TextWindow.Read()
16    num = Math.GetRandomNumber(10)
17    TextWindow.WriteLine(ans[num])
18    TextWindow.WriteLine("")
19  EndWhile
```

Listing 15-3: A Magic 8 Ball simulation

The game has 10 possible answers saved in the ans array. After initializing the array (lines 2–11), the game starts an infinite loop to interact with the user. In each iteration it asks the user to enter a yes or no question. It reads the user's question (line 15), generates a random number between 1 and 10 (line 16), and uses that number to display one of the answers using ans[num] (line 17). After displaying the message, we display a blank line (line 18). For someone who doesn't know the trick, the computer might look intelligent! Ask your friends to play this game, and see what they think.

How're you feeling? Sharp as a sponge and fresh as a tack? Great, because it's game creation time!

TRY IT OUT 15-5

Modify the Magic 8 Ball game so it shows each answer only once. End the game when all the answers have been displayed.

Create the Catch Apples Game

Figure 15-5 shows a game in which apples appear in random positions at the top of the graphics window at random times and fall to the ground. The player has to move the cart using the mouse to catch the apples before they hit the ground. Each apple is worth 1 point. Don't worry about bruising the apples; they're hard core!

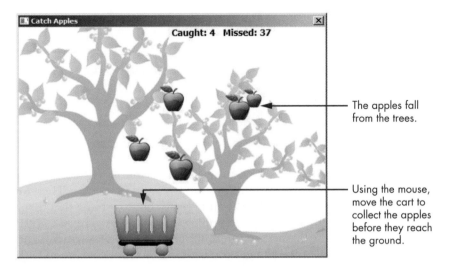

The apples fall from the trees.

Using the mouse, move the cart to collect the apples before they reach the ground.

Figure 15-5: The Catch Apples game

Follow these steps to put this great game together one piece at a time.

Step 1: Open the Startup File

Open the file *CatchApples_Incomplete.sb* in this chapter's folder. The folder also has all the images you'll need for this program. The startup file contains the main code (shown in Listing 15-4) and empty placeholders for the four subroutines that you'll write. Let's start with the main code.

```
1  ' CatchApples_Incomplete.sb
2  GraphicsWindow.Title = "Catch Apples"
3  GraphicsWindow.CanResize = "False"
4  GraphicsWindow.Width = 480
5  GraphicsWindow.Height = 360
6  GraphicsWindow.FontSize = 14
7  GraphicsWindow.BrushColor = "Black"
8
9  path = Program.Directory
10 GraphicsWindow.DrawImage(path + "\Background.png", 0, 0)
11
12 msgID = Shapes.AddText("")
13 Shapes.Move(msgID, 240, 0)
14
15 MAX_APPLES = 5      ' Change this to have more apples
16 AddApples()         ' Creates the apple array
17
18 cartImg = Shapes.AddImage(path + "\Cart.png")   ' 100x80 pixels
19
```

```
20 numMissed = 0    ' Missed apples
21 numCaught = 0    ' Caught apples
22
23 While ("True")
24   Shapes.Move(cartImg, GraphicsWindow.MouseX - 50, 280)
25   MoveApples()
26   Program.Delay(5)
27 EndWhile
```

Listing 15-4: The main code for the Catch Apples game

In lines 2–7, we set the graphic window's title; size, to match the size of the background image; font size; and font color. Then we draw the background image (line 10) and create the text shape that displays the number of caught and dropped apples (lines 12–13). The MAX_APPLES variable in line 15 is the maximum number of apples that will appear in the graphics window. Once you get the game running, experiment with this number to make the game easier or harder.

Line 16 calls the AddApples() subroutine to create the array that will hold the falling apples. Line 18 adds the cart's image and saves its identifier in cartImg; we need this identifier to move the cart.

Lines 20–21 initialize the variables numMissed (the number of missed apples) and numCaught (the number of caught apples) to 0. The code then starts the game's main loop (lines 23–27). In each iteration, we move the cart so its center lines up with the mouse's x position (line 24). Because the cart's width is 100 pixels, the cart's left position is set to MouseX - 50. The cart's y-position is fixed. We call the MoveApples() subroutine to make apples fall and check whether they touch the cart or the ground (line 25); then we wait 5 milliseconds before repeating these steps (line 26). But don't tell your dad to wait 5 milliseconds, or he might think you're sassing!

Run the game now, and move the mouse. The cart follows the mouse, but no apples appear yet. You'll add the missing subroutines next to finish the game.

Step 2: Add the Apples

Add the AddApples() subroutine in Listing 15-5.

```
1 Sub AddApples
2   For aplNum = 1 To MAX_APPLES
3     apple[aplNum] = Shapes.AddImage(path + "\Apple.png")
4     scale = (3 + Math.GetRandomNumber(5)) / 10
5     Shapes.Zoom(apple[aplNum], scale, scale)
6     SetApplePosition()
7   EndFor
8 EndSub
```

Listing 15-5: The AddApples() subroutine

The subroutine uses a For loop to create the five apples. In each iteration, we call AddImage() to load the apple's image from the game's folder and save the returned identifier in the apple array (line 3). The first apple is saved in apple[1], the second apple is saved in apple[2], and so on.

To add some variety to the apple game, we'll change the sizes of the apples. In line 4, we set the scale variable to a random value from the set {0.4, 0.5, 0.6, 0.7, 0.8}, which is calculated by (3 + Math.GetRandomNumber(5)) / 10. In line 5, we pass that value to the Zoom() method to change the apple's size. This sets the apple's size to a fraction (between 40 and 80 percent) of its original size.

Next, we'll call the SetApplePosition() subroutine to position the new apple. Let's examine what this subroutine does.

Step 3: Position the Apples

Add the SetApplePosition() subroutine in Listing 15-6.

```
1 Sub SetApplePosition
2    xPos = Math.GetRandomNumber(420)
3    yPos = -Math.GetRandomNumber(500)
4    Shapes.Move(apple[aplNum], xPos, yPos)
5 EndSub
```

Listing 15-6: The SetApplePosition() subroutine

We set the horizontal position to a random integer between 1 and 420 (line 2) and the vertical position to a negative value between –1 and –500 (line 3). The call to Move() in line 4 puts the apple (at index aplNum in the apple array) at some invisible point above the top edge of the graphics window using the two numbers xPos and yPos. This way, when the apples start falling, they appear at the top of the screen at random times; the apple that was placed at yPos = -100 appears sooner than the one placed at yPos = -500 because it has less distance to fall. As you'll see in a moment, we'll also call this subroutine when the player catches or misses an apple.

Step 4: Move the Apples

Now we're ready to make it rain apples (give the cats and dogs a break). Add the code in Listing 15-7 to the program in the placeholder for the MoveApples() subroutine.

```
1 Sub MoveApples
2    For aplNum = 1 To MAX_APPLES
3      xPos = Shapes.GetLeft(apple[aplNum])
4      yPos = Shapes.GetTop (apple[aplNum])
5      Shapes.Move(apple[aplNum], xPos, yPos + 1)
6
```

```
 7     CheckCatch()         ' Checks if the apple landed in the cart
 8     If (gotIt = 1) Then
 9       Sound.PlayClick()
10       numCaught = numCaught + 1
11       SetApplePosition()
12     ElseIf (yPos > 320) Then
13       numMissed = numMissed + 1
14       SetApplePosition()
15     EndIf
16   EndFor
17
18   msg = "Caught: " + numCaught + "    Missed: " + numMissed
19   Shapes.SetText(msgID, msg)
20 EndSub
```

Listing 15-7: The MoveApples() *subroutine*

In line 2, we start a For loop to drop five apples. We get the upper-left corner of each apple (lines 3–4), and then we move it down by 1 pixel (line 5). We then call CheckCatch() to see whether this apple was caught by the player (line 7). As you'll see in a moment, this subroutine sets the gotIt flag to 1 if the player caught the apple; otherwise, it sets gotIt to 0. It's okay if you miss an apple. You won't hurt its peelings.

When CheckCatch() returns, we check the gotIt flag. If it's 1 (line 8), that means the apple was caught by the player. In this case, we play a click sound, increment numCaught by 1, and call SetApplePosition() to reposition this apple and let it fall again (lines 9–11). On the other hand, if gotIt isn't 1, we check the apple's y-position to see whether it went below the cart's center, which means that the player missed it (line 12). In this case, we increase numMissed by 1 and call SetApplePosition() to reposition this apple and let it fall again (lines 13–14). If the apple was neither caught nor missed, then it's falling and will be processed again the next time we call MoveApples().

After moving and checking the status of the five apples, we update the message that shows the number of caught and missed apples (lines 18–19).

Step 5: Catch or Miss

The last piece to add is the CheckCatch() subroutine in Listing 15-8.

```
1 Sub CheckCatch
2   xApple = Shapes.GetLeft(apple[aplNum]) + 32 ' Center point
3   yApple = Shapes.GetTop(apple[aplNum]) + 32  ' Bottom point
4   xCart = Shapes.GetLeft(cartImg) + 50        ' Center point
5   yCart = Shapes.GetTop(cartImg) + 40         ' Around the center
6   xdiff = Math.Abs(xApple - xCart)
7   ydiff = Math.Abs(yApple - yCart)
8   gotIt = 0   ' Assumes we didn't get the apple
```

```
 9    If ((xdiff < 20) And (ydiff < 20)) Then
10      gotIt = 1 ' We got it
11    EndIf
12 EndSub
```

Listing 15-8: The CheckCatch() subroutine

This subroutine checks the distance between the center of an apple (whose index is given by aplNum) and the center of the cart. If the apple is within 20 pixels from the cart's center, the subroutine sets gotIt to 1. Otherwise, it sets gotIt to 0.

The game is now complete, and you can play it! Maybe you'll catch enough apples for an apple pie.

TRY IT OUT 15-6

Currently, the Catch Apples game runs forever. Think of a way to end the game, and then implement it. Can you think of some other ways to improve the game? Maybe you could give the player more points if they catch a big apple! What about the statement to move the cart inside the While loop? Can you move this statement to a new MouseMove event handler?

Programming Challenges

If you get stuck, check out *http://nostarch.com/smallbasic/* for the solutions and for more resources and review questions for teachers and students.

1. Write a program that simulates rolling a die. Make the program roll a die 10,000 times and keep track of how many times each number appears. A sample run of the program follows. (Hint: use an array named dice that has six elements. If you get 1 in a roll, increment dice[1]. If you get 2, increment dice[2], and so on.)

Num	Count	Probability
1	1640	0.164
2	1670	0.167
3	1638	0.1638
4	1684	0.1684
5	1680	0.168
6	1688	0.1688

2. Open the file *PinBall.sb* in this chapter's folder. This program simulates a pinball machine. As shown in the following illustration, the ball is dropped at the top of the machine. As it rolls down, it strikes fixed pins

and bounces to the left or to the right in a random fashion. At the end, the ball lands in one of the seven pockets. The program drops the ball 10,000 times and counts the number of times it lands in each pocket. Study the program and explain how it works.

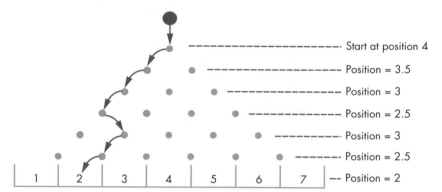

3. Open the file *FlowerAnatomy.sb* from this chapter's folder. This program presents an educational game that quizzes the player on the parts of a flower (shown next). The player enters the letters to match the labeled parts of the flower and then clicks the Check button to check the answers. The program compares the user's answers with the correct ones; then it shows you how the user did by placing a green check mark next to each correct answer and a red X next to each incorrect answer. Study the program and explain how it works.

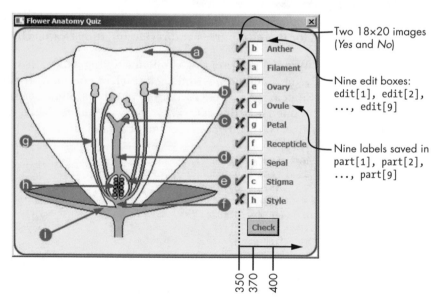

4. Open the file *USMapQuiz_Incomplete.sb* from this chapter's folder. The folder also contains the background image shown here (and the *Yes* and *No* images from the previous exercise). Complete the program to make this quiz work. Display the two-letter abbreviations for the nine states and provide nine text boxes to let the player match each state with its code.

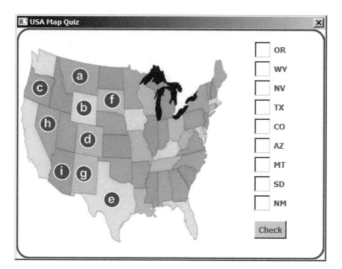

16

STORING DATA WITH ASSOCIATIVE ARRAYS

On social websites like Facebook and LinkedIn, people enter information into text boxes, such as their names, relationship statuses, and even regular updates to their friends (like, "Oh noes!! I just stepped on a bug, and I think I got bug poisoning!"). Programs that need to search or filter this data may use associative arrays to store the various parts of the text.

In addition to the indexed arrays you used in Chapter 15, Small Basic supports other types of arrays that can simplify many programming tasks. In this chapter, you'll start by learning about *associative arrays*. Then you'll learn about the Array object, use it to create some fun applications, and even turn your computer into a poet!

Associative Arrays

In the previous chapter, you learned how to use an integer index to access an array's elements. But in Small Basic, an array's index can also be a string. Arrays indexed by strings are called *associative arrays, maps,* or *dictionaries*. In this book, we'll call them associative arrays. Just like an indexed array, an associative array can store values of any type. You can use an associative array to create an association between a set of *keys* (string indices) and a set of values, which is called creating a *map* of key-value pairs.

The following code shows a simple example of an associative array in action. It's a list of states keyed by their two-letter abbreviations:

```
state["CA"] = "California"
state["MI"] = "Michigan"
state["OH"] = "Ohio"
' ... and so on
```

To display the name of a state, you simply use its corresponding key and the proper syntax. For example, to display Michigan, you can write this statement:

```
TextWindow.WriteLine(state["MI"])
```

By writing the name of the array followed by the key enclosed in square brackets, you can access the corresponding item. An associative array works like a *lookup table* that maps keys to values; if you know the key, you can find its value very quickly.

To learn how to use associative arrays, let's write a program that keeps track of the ages of your friends by name. Enter the program in Listing 16-1.

```
1 ' AssociativeArray.sb
2 age["Bert"] = 17
3 age["Ernie"] = 16
4 age["Zoe"] = 16
5 age["Elmo"] = 17
6 TextWindow.Write("Enter the name of your friend: ")
7 name = TextWindow.Read()
8 TextWindow.Write(name + " is [")
9 TextWindow.WriteLine(age[name] + "] years old.")
```

Listing 16-1: Using associative arrays

Lines 2–5 create an associative array named age with four elements in it. You can add more if you'd like, or you can change the array to store the ages of your own friends. Line 6 asks you to enter a friend's name, and line 7 reads it into the name variable. In line 9, age[name] looks up the age of that friend.

Let's look at some sample runs of this program:

```
Enter the name of your friend: Ernie
Ernie is [16] years old.

Enter the name of your friend: ernie
ernie is [16] years old.
```

Note that the key is case insensitive: it doesn't matter if you enter age["Ernie"], age["ernie"], or even age["ERNIE"]. If the array contains a key named Ernie, regardless of its case, Small Basic returns the value for that key.

Let's say you forget which friends' names you stored in the array, and you try to access the age of someone you forgot to include:

```
Enter the name of your friend: Grover
Grover is [] years old.
```

If the array doesn't contain a certain key, Small Basic returns an empty string, which is why age["Grover"] is empty.

ASSOCIATIVE ARRAYS VS. THE IF/ELSEIF LADDER

In programming, there are usually lots of different ways to approach a particular problem. Here's another way to write the program like the one in Listing 16-1:

```
TextWindow.Write("Enter the name of your friend: ")
name = TextWindow.Read()
If (name = "Bert") Then
  age = 17
ElseIf (name = "Ernie") Then
  age = 16
ElseIf (name = "Zoe") Then
  age = 16
ElseIf (name = "Elmo") Then
  age = 17
Else
  age = ""
EndIf
TextWindow.WriteLine(name + " is [" + age + "] years old.")
```

Although this program seems similar to the one in Listing 16-1, the two have one important difference: here, string comparison is case sensitive. If you enter ernie (with a lowercase e), the program displays the following output:

```
ernie is [] years old.
```

(continued)

The expression If("ernie" = "Ernie") is false. This version of the program is also harder to read and write. When you need to map between a set of keys and values, it's best to use associative arrays so you don't have to worry about case.

Putting Associative Arrays to Use

Now that you understand the basics of associative arrays, let's examine a couple of programs that show you how to use them.

Days in French

The first example translates the days of the week from English to French. This program prompts a user to enter the name of a day in English and outputs that name in French. Enter the code in Listing 16-2.

```
1 ' FrenchDays.sb
2 day["Sunday"] = "Dimanche"
3 day["Monday"] = "Lundi"
4 day["Tuesday"] = "Mardi"
5 day["Wednesday"] = "Mercredi"
6 day["Thursday"] = "Jeudi"
7 day["Friday"] = "Vendredi"
8 day["Saturday"] = "Samedi"
9
10 TextWindow.Write("Enter the name of a day: ")
11 name = TextWindow.Read()
12 TextWindow.WriteLine(name + " in French is " + day[name])
```

Listing 16-2: An English-to-French translator

The day array stores the French names for the days of the week (lines 2–8). Each key in the array is the day's name in English. The program prompts the user to enter the name of a day in English (line 10) and stores the user's input in the name variable (line 11). The program then looks up the French name using the user's input as a key, using the syntax day[name], and displays it (line 12). Here's the output from a sample run:

```
Enter the name of a day: Monday
Monday in French is Lundi
```

Do you know any other languages? Change the program to help your friends learn how to say the days of the week in a new language. Feeling sneaky? You could even make up your own secret language!

Storing Records

Business is booming, and Moe Mows, a local lawn-mowing service in your town, has hired you to write a program that displays the contact information of its customers. When the company enters a customer's name, the program needs to display the customer's home address, phone number, and email address. Enter the program in Listing 16-3.

```
1  ' MoeMows.sb
2  address["Natasha"] = "3215 Romanoff Rd"
3  phone["Natasha"] = "(321) 555 8745"
4  email["Natasha"] = "blackwidow64@shield.com"
5
6  address["Tony"] = "8251 Stark St"
7  phone["Tony"] = "(321) 555 4362"
8  email["Tony"] = "ironman63@shield.com"
9
10 TextWindow.Write("Name of customer: ")
11 name = TextWindow.Read()
12 TextWindow.WriteLine("Address...: " + address[name])
13 TextWindow.WriteLine("Phone.....: " + phone[name])
14 TextWindow.WriteLine("Email.....: " + email[name])
```

Listing 16-3: Building a simple database

The program uses three associative arrays: address, phone, and email. All three arrays use the customer's name as a key, and the arrays are used collectively to store customers' records. A *record* is a collection of related data items. In this example, each customer's record has three fields: address, phone, and email. Whether the program has two records or 1,000 records, the search is done the same way. For example, the statement address[name] in line 12 returns the value associated with the key name in the address array. We don't have to search the address array; Small Basic does this for us, for free!

Here's the output from a sample run of this program:

```
Name of customer: Tony
Address...: 8251 Stark St
Phone.....: (321) 555 4362
Email.....: ironman63@shield.com
```


TRY IT OUT 16-2

Update the program in Listing 16-3 to store the contact information of some of your friends (but not all 500 of your Facebook friends). Add another array that stores the birth date of each friend. You'll never forget a birthday again!

The Array Object

The Array object in the Small Basic library can help you find important information about the arrays in your programs. In this section, we'll explore this object in detail and look at some examples on how to use it. To explore the Array object, let's start by entering the following code:

```
name = "Bart"            ' An ordinary variable
age["Homer"] = 18        ' An associative array with two elements
age["Marge"] = 17
score[1] = 90            ' An indexed array with one element
```

This code defines an ordinary variable called name, an associative array called age that has two elements, and an indexed array called score that has one element. You'll use these arrays in the examples that follow. What can the Array object tell you? Let's find out!

Is It an Array?

Do you think Small Basic knows that name is an ordinary variable and that age and score are arrays? Run the program in Listing 16-4 to find out.

```
1  ' IsArray.sb
2  name = "Bart"
3  age["Homer"] = 18
4  age["Marge"] = 17
5  score[1] = 90
6  ans1 = Array.IsArray(name)      ' Returns "False"
7  ans2 = Array.IsArray(age)       ' Returns "True"
8  ans3 = Array.IsArray(score)     ' Returns "True"
9  TextWindow.WriteLine(ans1 + ", " + ans2 + ", " + ans3)
```

Listing 16-4: Demonstrating the IsArray() method

This code uses the `Array` object's `IsArray()` method. If the variable is an array, this method returns "True"; otherwise, it returns "False". This method shows that the variables age and score are arrays, but the name variable isn't an array. The `IsArray()` method can help you to be sure that the variables in your programs are arrays.

How Big Is an Array?

The `Array` object can also tell you how many elements are stored in your arrays. Run the program in Listing 16-5.

```
1 ' GetItemCount.sb
2 name = "Bart"
3 age["Homer"] = 18
4 age["Marge"] = 17
5 score[1] = 90
6 ans1 = Array.GetItemCount(name)       ' Returns: 0
7 ans2 = Array.GetItemCount(age)        ' Returns: 2
8 ans3 = Array.GetItemCount(score)      ' Returns: 1
9 TextWindow.WriteLine(ans1 + ", " + ans2 + ", " + ans3)
```

Listing 16-5: Demonstrating the `GetItemCount()` method

The `GetItemCount()` method returns the number of items in the specified array. Note how `GetItemCount(name)` returns 0, because name isn't an array. The other two calls return the number of elements in each array. Use `GetItemCount()` to keep track of how many items you're storing in an array. You might use this method in a game that allows the player to store items in an inventory and you want to check how many items they have picked up.

Does It Have a Particular Index?

You can also use the `Array` object to find out whether one of your arrays contains a certain index. To see how, run the program in Listing 16-6.

```
1  ' ContainsIndex.sb
2  age["Homer"] = 18
3  age["Marge"] = 17
4  score[1] = 90
5  ans1 = Array.ContainsIndex(age, 1)          ' Returns "False"
6  ans2 = Array.ContainsIndex(age, "homer")    ' Returns "True"
7  ans3 = Array.ContainsIndex(age, "Lisa")     ' Returns "False"
8  TextWindow.WriteLine(ans1 + ", " + ans2 + ", " + ans3)
9
10 ans1 = Array.ContainsIndex(score, "1")      ' Returns "True"
11 ans2 = Array.ContainsIndex(score, 1)        ' Returns "True"
12 ans3 = Array.ContainsIndex(score, 2)        ' Returns "False"
13 TextWindow.WriteLine(ans1 + ", " + ans2 + ", " + ans3)
```

Listing 16-6: Demonstrating the `ContainsIndex()` method

The ContainsIndex() method takes two arguments. The first argument is the name of the array, and the second argument is the index you're checking for. The method returns "True" or "False" depending on whether the index exists in the array.

Line 6 shows that searching for the index is case insensitive, which is why the search for the index homer returns "True". Also, searching the score array for index "1" (as a string) or index 1 (as a number) both returned "True".

If you're not sure whether an array includes a particular index, you can use the ContainsIndex() method to find out. This method is especially helpful if you're working with very long arrays.

Does It Have a Particular Value?

The Array object also offers a method that checks whether an array contains a certain value. Run the program in Listing 16-7 to discover how the ContainsValue() method works.

```
1  ' ContainsValue.sb
2  age["Homer"] = 18
3  age["Marge"] = 17
4  score[1] = 90
5  ans1 = Array.ContainsValue(age, 18)      ' Returns "True"
6  ans2 = Array.ContainsValue(age, 20)      ' Returns "False"
7  ans3 = Array.ContainsValue(score, 90)    ' Returns "True"
8  TextWindow.WriteLine(ans1 + ", " + ans2 + ", " + ans3)
```

Listing 16-7: Demonstrating the ContainsValue() method

The ContainsValue() method returns "True" or "False" depending on whether the value it checks for exists in the array.

NOTE *Unlike the ContainsIndex() method, the ContainsValue() method is case sensitive. So it's best to be consistent with your casing!*

Give Me All the Indices

Another useful method of the Array object is GetAllIndices(). This method returns an array that has all the indices of a given array. The first element of the returned array has an index of 1. To understand how this method works, run the program in Listing 16-8.

```
1  ' GetAllIndices.sb
2  age["Homer"] = 18
3  age["Marge"] = 17
4  names = Array.GetAllIndices(age)
5  TextWindow.WriteLine("Indices of the age array:")
```

```
6 For N = 1 To Array.GetItemCount(names)
7   TextWindow.WriteLine("Index" + N + " = " + names[N])
8 EndFor
```

Listing 16-8: Demonstrating the GetAllIndices() method

Line 4 calls GetAllIndices() to find all the indices of the age array. This method returns an array, which it saves in the names identifier. The code then starts a loop that runs from the first to the last element in names. Note how the code uses the GetItemCount() method to figure out this value. Here's the output of this code:

```
Indices of the age array:
Index1 = Homer
Index2 = Marge
```

Now let's put the methods you've learned to good use. Do you think your computer is intelligent enough to write poems? Well, let's see!

TRY IT OUT 16-3

Open the file *AnimalSpeed.sb* from this chapter's folder. This game quizzes the player on the top speed (in miles per hour) of different animals. The program has an associative array that looks like this:

```
speed["cheetah"] = 70
speed["antelope"] = 60
speed["lion"] = 50
' ... and so on
```

Run this game to see how it works. Which Array object methods does the game use? Explain how the game works, and then come up with some ideas to make the game more fun. Make sure you do all of this assignment. Don't be a cheetah!

Your Computer the Poet

Now let's use what we've learned about associative arrays to write a program that generates poems. This artificial poet selects words randomly from five lists (article, adjective, noun, verb, and preposition) and combines them into a fixed pattern. To give the poems a central theme, all the words in these lists are related to love and nature. Of course, we might still end up with some silly poetry, but that's just as fun!

NOTE   *The idea of this program is adapted from Daniel Watt's* Learning with Logo *(McGraw-Hill, 1983).*

Figure 16-1 shows the user interface for the application.

Figure 16-1: The user interface for Poet.sb

Every time you click the New button, the poet recites a new poem. Each poem includes three lines that follow these patterns:

- Line 1: article, adjective, noun
- Line 2: article, noun, verb, preposition, article, adjective, noun
- Line 3: adjective, adjective, noun

The following sections guide you through the creation of this program.

Step 1: Open the Startup File

Open the file *Poet_Incomplete.sb* from this chapter's folder. The file contains one subroutine named CreateLists(), which creates the five lists you'll need in this program. This subroutine was added to save you from having to type a whole bunch of words. This is what it looks like:

```
Sub CreateLists
  article = "1=a;2=the;...;5=every;"
  adjective = "1=beautiful;2=blue;...;72=young;"
  noun = "1=baby;2=bird;...;100=winter;"
  verb = "1=admires;2=amuses;...;92=whispers;"
  prepos = "1=about;2=above;...;37=without;"
EndSub
```

The ellipses (...) take the place of the missing array elements, but you can see all these elements when you open the file. Note that the article array also includes other determiners, such as one, each, and every.

Step 2: Set Up the Graphical User Interface

Add the code in Listing 16-9 to the beginning of the program file to set up the graphical user interface (GUI) and register the button's event handler.

```
1 GraphicsWindow.Title = "The Poet"
2 GraphicsWindow.CanResize = "False"
3 GraphicsWindow.Width = 480
4 GraphicsWindow.Height = 360
5 GraphicsWindow.FontBold = "False"
6 GraphicsWindow.FontItalic = "True"
7 GraphicsWindow.FontSize = 16
8
9 path = Program.Directory
10 GraphicsWindow.DrawImage(path + "\Background.png", 0, 0)
11 Controls.AddButton("New", 10, 10)
12
13 CreateLists()
14
15 artCount = Array.GetItemCount(article)
16 adjCount = Array.GetItemCount(adjective)
17 nounCount = Array.GetItemCount(noun)
18 verbCount = Array.GetItemCount(verb)
19 prepCount = Array.GetItemCount(prepos)
20
21 Controls.ButtonClicked = OnButtonClicked
22 OnButtonClicked()
```

Listing 16-9: Setting up the GUI

The program starts by initializing the graphics window (lines 1–7), drawing the background image (lines 9–10), and creating the New button (line 11). Next, it calls the CreateLists() subroutine to initialize the five indexed arrays (line 13). Then the program uses the Array object to get the number of items in each array and saves these values in lines 15–19. This way, you can append more elements to the end of these arrays without affecting the rest of the program. For example, if you wanted to add a 73rd adjective, you could add 73=callipygous; within the quotes at the end of the adjectives array line in the CreateLists() subroutine. Because line 16 in Listing 16-9 gets the count of the elements in that array, the new elements you add are automatically counted and randomly selected for the poem, just like the other elements.

Finally, the program registers a handler for the ButtonClicked event (line 21) and calls the handler subroutine to display the first poem (line 22).

Step 3: Respond to Button Clicks

Now you need to add the OnButtonClicked() subroutine, which is shown in Listing 16-10.

```
 1 Sub OnButtonClicked
 2   GraphicsWindow.DrawImage(path + "\Background.png", 0, 0)
 3
 4   MakeLine1()   ' Constructs poemLine1
 5   MakeLine2()   ' Constructs poemLine2
 6   MakeLine3()   ' Constructs poemLine3
 7
 8   GraphicsWindow.DrawText(180, 140, poemLine1)
 9   GraphicsWindow.DrawText(100, 165, poemLine2)
10   GraphicsWindow.DrawText(180, 190, poemLine3)
11 EndSub
```

Listing 16-10: The OnButtonClicked() subroutine

This subroutine redraws the background image to clear the graphics window (line 2). It then calls the three subroutines that author the three lines of the poem (lines 4–6) and draws these lines in the graphics window (lines 8–10). Next, you'll add the three missing subroutines.

Step 4: Write the Poem's First Line

The poem's first line is written in this form: article, adjective, noun. Add the subroutine in Listing 16-11, which creates the poem's first line and assigns it to the poemLine1 variable.

```
1 Sub MakeLine1
2   art1 = article[Math.GetRandomNumber(artCount)]
3   adj1 = adjective[Math.GetRandomNumber(adjCount)]
4   noun1 = noun[Math.GetRandomNumber(nounCount)]
5   poemLine1 = art1 + " " + adj1 + " " + noun1
6 EndSub
```

Listing 16-11: The MakeLine1() subroutine

The MakeLine1() subroutine selects three random words from the article, adjective, and noun arrays and stores the values in art1, adj1, and noun1 (lines 2–4). It then fills poemLine1 by appending these variables with a whitespace in between them (line 5).

Step 5: Write the Poem's Second and Third Lines

The MakeLine2() and MakeLine3() subroutines are very similar to the MakeLine1() subroutine. The second line takes this form: article, noun, verb, preposition, article, adjective, noun. The third line takes this form: adjective, adjective, noun. Create these subroutines on your own. If you get stuck, open the file *Poet.sb* to see how we wrote these subroutines. When you're done, recite your favorite poem output to your family or friends, and see if they think you wrote it!

NOTE *The Array object includes three more methods that create a different type of array:* SetValue(), GetValue(), *and* RemoveValue(). *Although these methods work well, the bracketed style of array is more universal among programming languages and is the reason this book focuses on that style.*

Programming Challenges

If you get stuck, check out *http://nostarch.com/smallbasic/* for the solutions and for more resources and review questions for teachers and students.

1. Write a program that keeps track of your friends' phone numbers. Use an associative array that uses your friends' names as keys; for example, phone["Yoda"] = "555-1138".

2. Write a program that saves book information. The key is the ISBN of the book. For each book, you need to know the title, the author, and the publication year. Use three associative arrays: title[ISBN], author[ISBN], and year[ISBN].

3. Open the file *VirtualPiano.sb* from this chapter's folder. The program implements a virtual piano using the keyboard. Explain how the program works.

17

EXPANDING TO HIGHER-DIMENSION ARRAYS

In the previous two chapters, you learned how to use one-dimensional arrays to store collections of items. In this chapter, we'll expand this concept to two dimensions and higher. Working in more than one dimension is also called working in *higher* dimensions.

In a *two-dimensional (2D)* array, you can store values in a table or a grid. For example, think about the scoreboard at a baseball game (see Figure 17-1). The left column lists the team names, and the right columns list the innings and other statistics.

Figure 17-1: Baseball scoreboard

The arrays you'll make in this chapter are similar to a scoreboard. They let you organize your data in rows and columns.

When you complete this chapter, you'll understand 2D and other higher-dimensional arrays and you'll be able to use them to build new types of applications, including a treasure-hunting game!

Two-Dimensional Arrays

A 2D array has two dimensions: rows and columns. You can think of a 2D array as a table. For example, Figure 17-2 shows a 2D array named score that stores a student's test scores in three subjects.

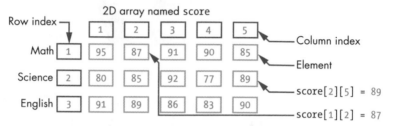

Figure 17-2: A pictorial view of a 2D array

The first row contains math test scores, the second row records the science test scores, and the next row stores English scores. This 2D arrangement of elements is also referred to as a *matrix* (the plural is *matrices*). But this matrix won't teach you slow-motion kung fu!

To access the individual elements of a matrix, you need two indices: one for the rows and the other for the columns. Here are some examples:

```
score[1][1] = 95 ' Row 1, column 1
score[1][2] = 87 ' Row 1, column 2
score[2][1] = 80 ' Row 2, column 1
score[2][3] = 92 ' Row 2, column 3
```

The variable score is a *double-scripted variable* because it requires two indices to access its elements. The first index is the row number, and the second index is the column number.

As with one-dimensional arrays, the index of each dimension can be a number or a string. Also, the values stored in the matrix can be numbers, strings, or other identifiers returned by objects in the Small Basic library. Let's look at some simple examples of 2D arrays next.

A Random Matrix

A client named MI6 wants your help to generate passwords for security locks. The program shown in Listing 17-1 creates a matrix named mat consisting of random numbers. The matrix contains three rows and four columns, which is a 3×4 (read *3 by 4*) matrix, or a 3×4 array.

```
1  ' Random2DArray.sb
2  For r = 1 To 3     ' 3 rows
3    For c = 1 To 4   ' 4 columns
4      mat[r][c] = Math.GetRandomNumber(9)
5    EndFor
6  EndFor
7
8  ' Displays the matrix to see its contents
9  For r = 1 To 3     ' 3 rows
10   For c = 1 To 4   ' 4 columns
11     TextWindow.Write(mat[r][c] + " ")
12   EndFor
13   TextWindow.WriteLine("")
14 EndFor
```

Listing 17-1: Filling a 3×4 array with random numbers

The program uses a nested For loop to fill the matrix with random numbers (lines 2–6). Nested For loops are extremely helpful when you're working with 2D arrays, because you can use one to loop through rows and the other to loop through columns. In this example, the outer loop uses a control variable r (for *rows*) and runs from 1 to 3 (line 2); the inner loop uses a control variable c (for *columns*) and runs from 1 to 4 (line 3).

The first pass of the outer loop (r = 1) causes four passes inside the inner loop (c = 1, 2, 3, and 4), which fills mat[1][1], mat[1][2], mat[1][3], and mat[1][4]. The second pass of the outer loop (r = 2) causes another four iterations of the inner loop (c = 1, 2, 3, and 4) and fills mat[2][1], mat[2][2], mat[2][3], and mat[2][4]. Likewise, the third pass of the outer loop (r = 3) fills the third row of the matrix. Figure 17-3 illustrates this process.

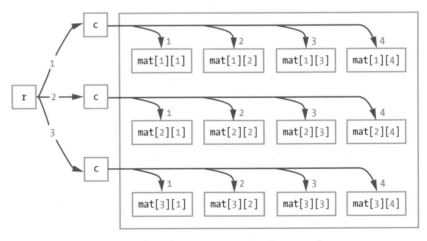

Figure 17-3: Using a nested For loop to access the elements of a matrix

Following along with this figure, when r = 1, the program takes the top c branch and fills in all four sets of the 2D array elements. When r = 2, it iterates through the middle branch four times. When r = 3, it iterates through the bottom branch.

After filling the matrix with random numbers, the program uses another nested loop to display its contents (lines 9–14) using a similar process. The outer loop runs from 1 to 3 to index the three rows (line 9), and the inner loop runs from 1 to 4 to index the four columns (line 10). Line 11 displays the element at index mat[r][c] (column c in row r), followed by a space. When the inner loop ends, it means an entire row has been displayed, and the cursor moves to the next line to prepare to display the next row (line 13).

It's time to turn your program over to your MI6 client. Here's a sample output of this program, but your output will most likely be different:

```
2 8 1 6
3 9 3 9
1 5 7 8
```

You can make matrices even more useful by programming them to accept user input. We'll look at how to do that next.

TRY IT OUT 17-1

In Listing 17-1, the numbers in the matrix are stored by rows. First, row 1 is filled, then row 2, and finally row 3. The reason is that we made the r loop (which represents rows) the outer loop and the c loop (which represents columns) the inner loop. Change the program so it fills the matrix by columns first instead of rows.

A Matrix with User Input

Your MI6 client loves the program you built, but now they want to be able to enter certain numbers into the password matrix. You can easily change Listing 17-1 to take input from the user instead of using random numbers. Just replace line 4 with the following two lines:

```
TextWindow.Write("mat[" + r + "][" + c + "]: ")
mat[r][c] = TextWindow.ReadNumber()
```

The first statement prompts the user to enter an element in the matrix, and the second line reads and stores the user's entry. Make this change, and try it out to see how it works.

But matrices aren't only about numbers. You can use them to make some fun, colorful applications too. In the next example, you'll create a colorful grid and animate it.

Animated Squares

Let's write a program that creates a 4×8 grid of randomly colored squares and then animates these squares to fly to the upper-left corner of the graphics window, as shown in Figure 17-4.

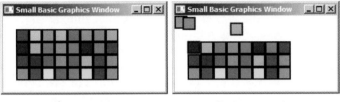

Before animation   During animation

Figure 17-4: Illustrating the output of AnimatedSquares.sb

The complete application is shown in Listing 17-2.

```
1  ' AnimatedSquares.sb
2  ' Creates a 4x8 grid of randomly colored squares
3  For r = 1 To 4    ' 4 rows
4    For c = 1 To 8  ' 8 columns
5      clr = GraphicsWindow.GetRandomColor()
6      GraphicsWindow.BrushColor = clr
7      box[r][c] = Shapes.AddRectangle(20, 20) ' Adds a square
8      Shapes.Move(box[r][c], c * 20, r * 20)  ' Positions it
9    EndFor
10 EndFor
11
12 ' Animates the squares to the upper-left corner of the window
13 For r = 1 To 4
14   For c = 1 To 8
15     Shapes.Animate(box[r][c], 0, 0, 1000)
16     Program.Delay(400) ' A small delay (in milliseconds)
17   EndFor
18 EndFor
```

Listing 17-2: Using a matrix to store shape IDs

The program uses a nested For loop to create the squares (lines 3–10). The outer loop (which creates the rows) runs four times, and the inner loop (which creates the columns) runs eight times (lines 3–4), for a total of 32 iterations (4×8). In each pass of the inner loop, the square's color is set by changing the BrushColor property (lines 5–6), and a square is created by calling AddRectangle(). We save its identifier in box[r][c] (line 7) and then move the created square to its position on the square grid (see Figure 17-4). Let's take a closer look at lines 7–8.

At line 7, the AddRectangle() method takes the width and the height of the desired rectangle and returns an identifier of the created shape. In this example, we pass 20 for both arguments to create a square, and we save the returned identifier in box[r][c].

To move the square, we call the Move() method of the Shapes object (line 8). This method takes three arguments: the identifier of the shape we want to move and the x- and y-coordinates of the position we're moving it to. The squares in each row have their x positions (left edge) at $1 \times 20 = 20$, $2 \times 20 = 40$, $3 \times 20 = 60$, and so on. The squares in each column have their y positions (top edge) at $1 \times 20 = 20$, $2 \times 20 = 40$, $3 \times 20 = 60$, and so on. This is why we use c * 20 and r * 20 in the call to Move().

At the end of this For loop, the box matrix contains 32 unique identifiers for the 32 squares created by the Shapes object.

The program then animates the squares (lines 13–18), using a nested For loop to access the rows and the columns of box. During each iteration, we ask the Shapes object to animate one square (line 15) and then pause for a short time (line 16). The Animate() method takes four arguments: the identifier of the shape we want to animate, the x- and y-coordinates of the destination, and the animation duration in milliseconds. We ask the Shapes object to move each square to point (0, 0) in 1 second (1000 milliseconds).

TRY IT OUT 17-2

Change the program in Listing 17-2 to animate the squares by columns instead of by rows. If you're feeling artistic, try moving the squares to create a pattern in the graphics window.

Using String Indices

The previous examples used integer indices to access the elements of a matrix. Our next example teaches you how use strings for indices. You'll examine an application that keeps track of students' scores in different subjects.

Welcome to Professor Xavier's School for Gifted Youngsters! The class has only three students right now: Scott, Jean, and Logan (the others are on an important mission). The school teaches only three subjects: math, science, and combat. Let's write a program that prompts the user to enter a student's name and then displays the student's average score. The complete program is shown in Listing 17-3.

```
1  ' StudentAvg.sb
2  score["Scott"]["Math"] = 92
3  score["Scott"]["Science"] = 90
4  score["Scott"]["Combat"] = 87
5  score["Jean"]["Math"] = 85
6  score["Jean"]["Science"] = 82
7  score["Jean"]["Combat"] = 92
8  score["Logan"]["Math"] = 85
9  score["Logan"]["Science"] = 95
10 score["Logan"]["Combat"] = 99
11
```

```
12 TextWindow.Write("Enter student name: ")
13 name = TextWindow.Read()
14 sum = score[name]["Math"]
15 sum = sum + score[name]["Science"]
16 sum = sum + score[name]["Combat"]
17 avg = Math.Round(sum / 3)
18 TextWindow.WriteLine(name + " average score = " + avg)
```

Listing 17-3: Using strings for indices

The program starts by initializing the score matrix with the scores of the three students (lines 2–10). Rows are indexed by the students' names, and columns are indexed by the subjects. Figure 17-5 shows a visual representation of the score matrix.

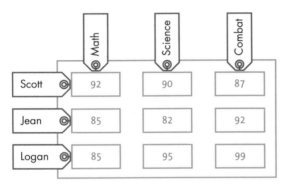

Figure 17-5: The score matrix in Listing 17-3

The program prompts the user to enter a student's name (line 12) and assigns the input to the name variable (line 13). It then pulls that student's math score into the sum variable (line 14), adds the student's science score to sum (line 15), and adds the student's combat score (line 16). Finally, the program computes the average score (line 17) and displays it (line 18).

Here's the output from a sample run:

```
Enter student name: scott
scott average score = 90
```

The string index is case insensitive, which is why the program worked when we entered *scott* with a lowercase *s*. What do you think the output will be if you enter an invalid student name? Run the program to check your answer.

TRY IT OUT 17-3

Update the program in Listing 17-3 to display the score of a student in a given subject. Have the user enter the name of the student and the subject.

Going Interactive

Let's explore how to get the students' scores from the user rather than hardcoding them within the program like we did in Listing 17-3. We'll use two loops to iterate over the students' names and subjects, as shown in the following pseudocode (you'll learn how to translate this pseudocode into real code in a moment):

```
For each student in the array: [Scott, Jean, Logan]
  For each subject in the array: [Math, Science, Combat]
    score[student][subject] = read score from user
  EndFor
EndFor
```

You can save the names of the students in a one-dimensional array, save the names of the subjects in another one-dimensional array, and then use nested For loops with integer indices to access the individual elements of these two arrays. Then you can use the strings (student name and subject) as indices for a score matrix. Check out Listing 17-4 to see the code in action.

```
1  ' StudentAvg2.sb
2  nameList = "1=Scott;2=Jean;3=Logan;"
3  subjList = "1=Math;2=Science;3=Combat;"
4
5  For I = 1 To 3              ' Three students
6    name = nameList[I]        ' Name of the Ith student
7    For J = 1 To 3            ' Three subjects
8      subj = subjList[J]      ' Name of Jth subject
9      TextWindow.Write(name + "'s " + subj + " score: ")
10     score[name][subj] = TextWindow.ReadNumber()
11   EndFor
12  EndFor
13  TextWindow.Write("Enter student name: ")
14  name = TextWindow.Read()
15  sum = score[name]["Math"]
16  sum = sum + score[name]["Science"]
17  sum = sum + score[name]["Combat"]
18  avg = Math.Round(sum / 3)
19  TextWindow.WriteLine(name + " average score = " + avg)
```

Listing 17-4: Reading scores from the user

The program starts by creating the name and subject arrays (lines 2–3). Then a nested loop starts to fill the score matrix. The outer loop iterates over the students, and the inner loop iterates over the subjects.

The outer loop starts with I = 1. Here name gets assigned to nameList[1], which is "Scott" (line 6). Then the inner loop runs three times, the first time with J = 1, and subject gets assigned to subjList[1], which is "Math" (line 8). Line 9 displays Scott's Math score: , and line 10 waits for the user's input. The number entered by the user is saved in score["Scott"]["Math"], and the inner loop repeats for J = 2. Now subject gets assigned to subjList[2], which is "Science". The program displays Scott's Science score: , waits for the user's input, stores the entered number in score["Scott"]["Science"], and repeats the inner loop with J = 3. Now subject gets assigned to subjList[3], which is "Combat". The program displays Scott's Combat score: , waits for the user's input, and stores the entered number in score["Scott"]["Combat"]. This ends the inner loop.

The outer loop repeats with I = 2. This sets name to nameList[2], which is "Jean" and the inner loop works again to fill score["Jean"]["Math"], score["Jean"]["Science"], and score["Jean"]["Combat"].

The outer loop repeats with I = 3. This sets name to nameList[3], which is "Logan", and the inner loop works again to fill score["Logan"]["Math"], score["Logan"]["Science"], and score["Logan"]["Combat"].

Trace through this second version of the program to understand how it works. Thinking through what happens at each step is a great way to learn how matrices work!

TRY IT OUT 17-4

Replace the statements that find the sum (lines 15–17) in Listing 17-4 with a For loop, as shown in the following code snippet:

```
sum = 0
For J = 1 To 3
  ' Add each student's score in the Jth subject to sum
EndFor
```

Common Operations on Numerical 2D Arrays

In this section, we'll develop a useful set of subroutines that can perform common operations on a 2D array made up of numbers. We'll use the sales of a fake company, Duckberg Industries, whose December sales report is shown in Figure 17-6. The company has four stores (Beddy Buyz, UBroke I.T. Emporium, LAN Lord's Cyber Store, and Mother Bored Electronics) and sells five types of products: Exploding Shoes (eShoes), the iShirt Computer (iShirt), Shampoop, Dehydrated Water (dWater), and the Invisible Hat (iHat). The numbers are the sales of each product in thousands.

Duckberg Industries December Sales (in Thousands)					
	eShoes	iShirt	Shampoop	dWater	iHat
Beddy Buyz	50	60	90	85	60
UBroke I.T. Emporium	35	55	75	70	85
LAN Lord's Cyber Store	40	45	85	95	75
Mother Bored Electronics	65	40	60	80	90

Figure 17-6: Duckberg Industries' December sales report

Open the file *Duckberg_Incomplete.sb* from this chapter's folder. The file contains the data in Figure 17-6 in a sequence of statements that looks like this:

```
sales[1][1] = 50    ' Beddy Buyz store; Exploding Shoes sales
sales[1][2] = 60    ' Beddy Buyz store; iShirt Computer sales
--snip--
sales[4][4] = 80    ' Mother Bored Electronics; Dehydrated Water sales
sales[4][5] = 90    ' Mother Bored Electronics; Invisible Hat sales
```

The program also defines the following variables:

```
ROWS = 4      ' Number of rows
COLS = 5      ' Number of columns
product = "1=eShoes;2=iShirt;3=Shampoop;4=dWater;5=iHat"
```

Follow the instructions in the next two sections to complete the program.

Step 1: Add All Elements

Donald, the company's sales manager, wants to know the total sales of the company. You need to add all the numbers in the sales matrix. The TotalSales() subroutine in Listing 17-5 shows you how to do that.

```
1 Sub TotalSales
2   sum = 0                          ' Initializes the running sum
3   For r = 1 To ROWS                ' For all rows
4     For c = 1 To COLS              ' For all columns
5       sum = sum + sales[r][c]      ' Adds number at row r, column c
6     EndFor
7   EndFor
8   TextWindow.WriteLine("Total Sales: $" + sum + " K")
9 EndSub
```

Listing 17-5: Adding all numbers in a matrix

You start by initializing the sum variable (which holds the running sum) to 0 (line 2). You then use a nested loop to iterate over all the rows and columns (lines 3–4). For each iteration, you add the number stored in sales[r][c] to sum (line 5). When the outer loop ends, you display the result followed by K for thousands (line 8).

Add this subroutine to the program, and then add a statement to call it. Here's what you should see when you call the TotalSales() subroutine:

```
Total Sales: $1340 K
```

Step 2: Find the Sum of Each Column

Donald also wants to see the total sales for each Duckberg Industries product. He needs to compare these numbers with those from his competitors to assess his company's market share.

To give Donald this information, you'll use the ColumnSum() subroutine in Listing 17-6 to compute the sum of each column in the sales matrix.

```
1  Sub ColumnSum
2    For c = 1 To COLS            ' For each column
3      sum = 0                    ' Initializes the sum for column c
4      For r = 1 To ROWS          ' Iterates over the rows
5        sum = sum + sales[r][c]  ' Adds number at row r, column c
6      EndFor
7      colName = product[c] + " Sales: $"  ' Name to display
8      TextWindow.WriteLine(colName + sum + " K")
9    EndFor
10 EndSub
```

Listing 17-6: The ColumnSum() subroutine

You start the outer loop to iterate over the five columns (line 2). For each column (each value of c), you initialize the column's sum to 0 (line 3) and then start a For loop to add the numbers from all the rows in that column to sum (lines 4–6). When the inner loop completes, you get the name of the current product (from product[c]), append "Sales: $" to it, and save the resulting string in colName (line 7). In line 8, you display that string followed by the sum you just computed. The outer loop then restarts to find and display the sum for the next column.

Add this subroutine to the program, and then add a statement to call it. Here's what you should see when you call the ColumnSum() subroutine:

```
eShoes Sales: $190 K
iShirt Sales: $200 K
Shampoop Sales: $310 K
dWater Sales: $330 K
iHat Sales: $310 K
```

Arrays of Three or More Dimensions

You've learned that using 2D arrays is a convenient way to represent a table or a matrix. Small Basic also supports arrays with more than two dimensions. You can extend the syntax for creating 2D arrays to create arrays with even higher dimensions. Next we'll explore how to create *three-dimensional (3D)* arrays in Small Basic.

Let's work with a shelf that has five racks. Each rack has three rows and four columns, and each position on the shelf has a box that contains screws of a certain size. Look at Figure 17-7 and imagine boxes of different screw sizes in each column and row (that's 12 boxes). Then imagine that same number of boxes on all five racks. That's 60 boxes in total!

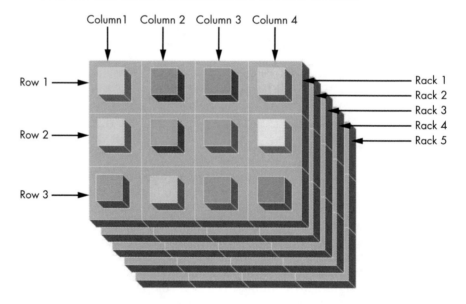

Figure 17-7: Visualizing a 3D array

We'll examine a program that fills each box with a random number that indicates the size of the screws in that box. The program is shown in Listing 17-7.

```
1 ' 3DArrayDemo.sb
2 For rack = 1 To 5      ' For each rack
3   For row = 1 To 3     ' For each row
```

```
4      For col = 1 To 4   ' For each column
5        box[rack][row][col] = Math.GetRandomNumber(9)
6      EndFor
7    EndFor
8 EndFor
```

Listing 17-7: Demonstrating the syntax for 3D arrays

This program creates a 3D array named box. Its elements are indexed with three subscripts: rack runs from 1 to 5 (line 2), row runs from 1 to 3 (line 3), and col runs from 1 to 4 (line 4). This array has 60 elements (5×4×3), just like the shelf in the example. Line 5 uses the syntax box[rack] [row][col] to access the box in rack number rack, row number row, and column number col, and it puts a random number in that box.

Notice that another nested For loop is used, but in this example, we nested three For loops instead of just two (lines 2–4). Generally, you'll need to use one For loop per dimension in your higher-dimension array; as a result, you'll be able to access every element in your array!

In the next section, you'll use what you've learned so far to create an exciting treasure game. Get ready for another adventure!

TRY IT OUT 17-6

Write a program that displays the output of the box array in Listing 17-7. Your output should have the following format:

```
Rack 1:
2 7 3 2
4 3 1 3
1 2 6 4

Rack 2:
8 8 2 1
7 4 2 7
1 5 2 7
--snip--
```

Create a Treasure Map Game

You woke up one morning and found you were alone on an island. A treasure map and an old compass were lying next to you. You could hardly hold back your excitement! You decided to look for the treasure. Figure 17-8 shows a sample map of the island.

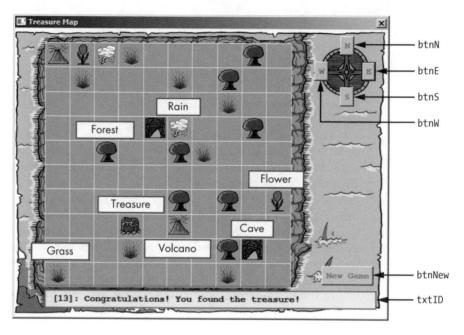

Figure 17-8: The user interface for the Treasure Map game

You can move north, east, south, or west, one block at a time. But because the compass is old, it might lead you in the wrong direction. For example, if you go north or south, there's a 20 percent chance that you'll also move one block to the left or to the right. And if you go east or west, there's a 20 percent chance that you'll also move one block up or down. Each time you move, you'll receive information about your current location. The game ends if you find the treasure or if you fall in the water where the hungry sharks are waiting! Don't think of *Jaws* while you're playing this game! (Sorry, that probably didn't help.)

Because you have the treasure map in your hands, you should be able to guess your location. For example, let's say you're in a forest, and when you click the S button to go south, the game tells you you're now next to a volcano. Looking at the map, you can figure out that the treasure is just two blocks west.

The following sections will guide you step-by-step to show you how to put this game together. Adventure awaits!

Step 1: Open the Startup File

Open the *TreasureMap_Incomplete.sb* file from this chapter's folder. This file contains some comments and placeholders for the required subroutines. You'll add all the code one step at a time.

This folder also contains the eight images you'll use. *Background.png* is a 580×450 image of the game's background, and the seven 32×32 icons are the different objects on the treasure map.

If you run into any problems, check out the finished program TreasureMap.sb, *which is also included in this chapter's folder.*

Step 2: Create the GUI Elements

Add the code in Listing 17-8 to initialize the GraphicsWindow and create the controls (buttons and text shapes) for the game.

```
1 GraphicsWindow.Title = "Treasure Map"
2 GraphicsWindow.Width = 580
3 GraphicsWindow.Height = 450
4 GraphicsWindow.CanResize = "False"
5 GraphicsWindow.FontSize = 14
6 GraphicsWindow.FontName = "Courier New"
7
8 ' Creates a text shape for showing the player's location
9 GraphicsWindow.BrushColor = "Black"
10 txtID = Shapes.AddText("")
11 Shapes.Move(txtID, 60, 415)
12
13 ' Creates the 4 movement buttons and the new game button
14 GraphicsWindow.BrushColor = "Red"
15 btnN = Controls.AddButton("N", 507, 10)
16 btnS = Controls.AddButton("S", 507, 90)
17 btnW = Controls.AddButton("W", 467, 50)
18 btnE = Controls.AddButton("E", 541, 50)
19 btnNew = Controls.AddButton("New Game", 480, 370)
20
21 Controls.ButtonClicked = OnButtonClicked
22
23 NewGame()
```

Listing 17-8: Initializing GraphicsWindow

Lines 1–6 set the properties of GraphicsWindow. Lines 9–11 create and position the text that tells the player their current position on the island, and lines 14–19 create the five buttons (see Figure 17-8). Line 21 registers a handler to process the buttons, and line 23 calls NewGame() to start a new game.

Step 3: Start a New Game

Now you'll add the NewGame() subroutine. This subroutine (shown in Listing 17-9) is called when the player clicks the New Game button.

```
1 Sub NewGame
2   gameOver = 0    ' Game isn't over yet
3   moveNumber = 0 ' How many moves the player makes
4   path = Program.Directory
5
6   GraphicsWindow.DrawImage(path + "\Background.png", 0, 0)
7   CreateNewMap() ' Creates and draws a new treasure map
```

```
8    ShowLocation()  ' Gives feedback to the player
9  EndSub
```

Listing 17-9: The NewGame() subroutine

You set the gameOver flag to 0 because the game isn't over yet (line 2). You also set moveNumber to 0 because the player hasn't made any moves yet (line 3). You then find the program's path and assign it to the path variable. You'll use this variable when you draw the different icons on the treasure map. In line 6, you draw a new copy of the background image to erase the previous map. You then call CreateNewMap() to create and draw a new treasure map (line 7) and call ShowLocation() to give feedback to the player about their current location on the island (line 8). ShowLocation() updates the text message to describe the player's new location after they move. You'll add these subroutines next.

Step 4: Create a New Treasure Map

The CreateNewMap() subroutine builds a 10×10 array to represent the treasure map. Each element in the array stores a number between 0 and 7. The number 0 means clear, 1 means grass, 2 means forest, 3 means volcano, 4 means cave, 5 means rain, 6 means flowers, and 7 means treasure. The CreateNewMap() subroutine is shown in Listing 17-10.

```
1  Sub CreateNewMap
2    For row = 1 To 10
3      For col = 1 To 10
4        map[row][col] = 0     ' Clears all cells
5      EndFor
6    EndFor
7
8    objId = "1=1;2=1;3=1;4=1;5=1;6=1;7=1;8=1;9=2;10=2;11=2;12=2;13=2;14=2; ↵
       15=2;16=2;17=3;18=3;19=4;20=4;21=5;22=5;23=6;24=6;25=7;26=0"
9    count = 1                 ' Points to first element in objId
10   While (count <= Array.GetItemCount(objId))
11     row = Math.GetRandomNumber(10)
12     col = Math.GetRandomNumber(10)
13     If (map[row][col] = 0) Then    ' Cell is clear
14       map[row][col] = objId[count] ' Reserves the cell
15       DrawObject()
16       count = count + 1     ' Points to next element in objId
17     EndIf
18   EndWhile
19
20   rowP = row                ' Player's current row
21   colP = col                ' Player's current column
22 EndSub
```

Listing 17-10: The CreateNewMap() subroutine

First, you set all the elements of the map to 0 (lines 2–6). In line 8, you define an array, objId, that holds the identifiers of the objects you'll add to the map. This array asks for eight grass fields, eight forests, two volcanoes, two caves, two rainy spots, two flower fields, and one treasure spot. The last element in the array is intentionally set to 0 so that the While loop on line 10 finds an empty starting place for the player. When you're feeling more adventurous, you can change the objId array to make the treasure map contain more or fewer objects.

Next, you start a While loop to add the objects to the treasure map. First, you select a random cell on the map (lines 11–12). If that cell is clear (line 13), you mark it with a number that's not zero to reserve it for the next object from objId (line 14), call DrawObject() to draw the added object on the treasure map (line 15), and increment the count variable to point to the next element in objId (line 16). When the loop finishes, you set the player's current row, rowP, and column, colP, to the empty cell found by the While loop in its last iteration (lines 20–21). This ensures the player starts on a clear cell on the map.

Step 5: Draw Objects on the Map

Before you add the ShowLocation() subroutine, you need to add the DrawObject() subroutine in Listing 17-11. You call this subroutine to draw an object at map[row][col].

```
1 Sub DrawObject
2   imgName = "1=Grass.ico;2=Tree.ico;3=Volcano.ico;4=Cave.ico;5=Rain.ico; ↵
    6=Flower.ico;7=Treasure.ico"
3
4   imgID = map[row][col]
5   If ((imgID >= 1) And (imgID <= 7)) Then
6     imgPath = path + "\" + imgName[imgID]
7
8     xPos = 52 + (col - 1) * 38
9     yPos = 25 + (row - 1) * 38
10    GraphicsWindow.DrawImage(imgPath, xPos, yPos)
11  EndIf
12 EndSub
```

Listing 17-11: The DrawObject() subroutine

You define the imgName array that holds the name of the image file for the seven objects in the game (line 2). In line 4, you get the number stored in the map at row number row and column number col, and then you assign this value to imgID. If this number is between 1 and 7 (line 5), you construct the full path for the image that corresponds to this number (line 6) and then draw that image at its position on the map (lines 8–10). The numbers you see in lines 8–9 (52, 38, and 25) come from the background image. These numbers ensure that the objects are drawn in the centers of the cells in Figure 17-8.

Step 6: Show the Player's Location

Now you can add the ShowLocation() subroutine in Listing 17-12, which tells the player their current location on the island.

```
1 Sub ShowLocation
2   locID = map[rowP][colP]
3   If (locID = 1) Then
4     msg = "You're in a grass field."
5   ElseIf (locID = 2) Then
6     msg = "You're in a forest."
7   ElseIf (locID = 3) Then
8     msg = "You're next to a volcano."
9   ElseIf (locID = 4) Then
10    msg = "You're in a cave."
11  ElseIf (locID = 5) Then
12    msg = "You're in the rain."
13  ElseIf (locID = 6) Then
14    msg = "You're in a flower field."
15  ElseIf (locID = 7) Then
16    gameOver = 1
17    msg = "Congratulations! You found the treasure!"
18  Else
19    msg = "You're in the clear!"
20  EndIf
21
22  Shapes.SetText(txtID, "[" + moveNumber + "]: " + msg)
23 EndSub
```

Listing 17-12: The ShowLocation() subroutine

The subroutine uses an If/ElseIf ladder to create a message, msg, based on the player's current location, which is identified by rowP and colP (lines 1–20). The subroutine then calls SetText() to show this message using the text shape identified by txtID. Note how the player's move number, moveNumber, is included in the message so they know how many times they've moved.

Step 7: Handle Button Clicks

This is the final step to finish the game! You just need to process the button clicks. Add the OnButtonClicked() subroutine shown in Listing 17-13.

```
1 Sub OnButtonClicked
2   btnID = Controls.LastClickedButton
3
4   If (btnID = btnNew) Then
5     NewGame()
6   ElseIf (gameOver = 0) Then
7     moveNumber = moveNumber + 1
8
9     MovePlayer()      ' Finds the player's new row and column
10
```

```
11    If ((rowP < 1) Or (rowP > 10) Or (colP < 1) Or (colP > 10)) Then
12      gameOver = 1
13      Shapes.SetText(txtID, "Sorry! You were eaten by the shark!")
14    Else
15      ShowLocation() ' Tells the player their new position
16    EndIf
17   EndIf
18 EndSub
```

Listing 17-13: The OnButtonClicked() subroutine

Because you're using five buttons, you start by finding the identifier of the clicked button (line 2). If it's the New Game button (line 4), you call NewGame() to start all over (line 5). Otherwise, the player has clicked one of the four movement buttons. You need to process the player's request only if the game isn't over yet. If the game is still in progress (line 6), you increment moveNumber (line 7), call MovePlayer() to set the player's new location (line 9), and then check the status after this move (lines 11–16). If the player falls into the shark-infested water (line 11), you set gameOver to 1 (line 12) and inform the player of their bad luck (line 13). Otherwise, if the player is still on the island, you call ShowLocation() to give them information about their new location (line 15).

The last subroutine you need to add in this game is in Listing 17-14. The MovePlayer() subroutine sets the player's next position based on which button (N, E, S, or W) they clicked.

```
 1 Sub MovePlayer
 2   shift = 0                      ' How much to shift direction
 3   randNum = Math.GetRandomNumber(10)
 4   If (randNum = 1) Then
 5     shift = 1
 6   ElseIf (randNum = 2) Then
 7     shift = -1
 8   EndIf
 9
10   If (btnID = btnN) Then      ' North
11     rowP = rowP - 1
12     colP = colP + shift
13   ElseIf (btnID = btnS) Then ' South
14     rowP = rowP + 1
15     colP = colP + shift
16   ElseIf (btnID = btnE) Then ' East
17     colP = colP + 1
18     rowP = rowP + shift
19   ElseIf (btnID = btnW) Then ' West
20     colP = colP - 1
21     rowP = rowP + shift
22   EndIf
23 EndSub
```

Listing 17-14: The MovePlayer() subroutine

We mentioned that the old compass has a 20 percent chance of being wrong. To simulate this, you create the variable shift to alter the player's direction. First, you get a random number between 1 and 10 (line 3). If this number is 1, you set shift to 1. If this number is 2, you set shift to −1 (lines 4–8). Otherwise, you keep shift at 0, which means that you won't alter the player's move in any way (line 2).

You start an If/ElseIf ladder to process the clicked button (lines 10–22). If the player clicked the north button N (line 10), you move them up one row (line 11) and change their current column by using the shift variable (line 12). If shift is 0, the player's current column won't change, and they'll move north. The rest of the ladder works the same way.

Now that the game is complete, you can enjoy it. See how long it takes you to find the treasure without getting eaten by the sharks!

TRY IT OUT 17-7

The Treasure Map game has a lot of room for improvement. For example, you can give the player another chance if they fall victim to the sharks. You can also give the player more clues about their current location. Come up with some ideas to improve the game, and try to implement them. Make an adventure worthy of Captain Jack Sparrow!

Programming Challenges

If you get stuck, check out *http://nostarch.com/smallbasic/* for the solutions and for more resources and review questions for teachers and students.

1. Okla is a fearless warrior known for his courage and wisdom. He's now on a noble mission in a haunted castle looking for the four keys needed to free the puppies that are trapped inside! But there's a problem: the haunted castle is guarded by evil monsters who throw bombs all over the castle. Each time one of these bombs hits Okla, he loses 10 units of energy. You need to help Okla navigate his way through the castle to find the four keys before he loses all his energy.

Open the file *Okla.sb* from this chapter's folder, and run it to play the game. After you play the game and understand how it works, come up with some ideas to improve it, and try to implement them.

2. Open the file *TicTacToe_Incomplete.sb* from this chapter's folder. This game lets you play tic-tac-toe against the computer. The game's board is represented by a 3×3 matrix named board. When the player clicks a square, the game draws an X in the clicked cell and fills the number 1 in its board element. The computer then takes its turn and picks an empty cell at random (the computer isn't that smart). The game draws an O in the cell the computer selected and fills in the number 5 in that board element. The following figure illustrates how the game works.

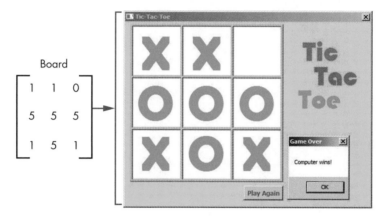

Your task is to complete the CheckWinner() subroutine, which is called after each move. You need to check the sum of each row, each column, and the two diagonals. A sum of 3 means the player won the game. A sum of 15 means the computer won the game. If there's no winner and nine moves have been made (the board is filled completely with the Xs and Os), the game is a tie.

18

ADVANCED TEXT MAGIC

Although pictures of blue skies and green fields are prettier to look at than a screen full of words, many useful programs, such as Facebook, Twitter, and Words with Friends, work with text. That's why Small Basic provides the Text object for working with text. In this chapter, you'll learn how to use the Text object to find the length of a string, extract a small portion of a string, and perform many other advanced string-processing tasks. You'll also write your own string-processing subroutines and apply what you learn to create some interesting applications, like a pig latin translator and a word scramble game!

The Text Object

You've been working with strings throughout this book. To recap, a *string* is a sequence of characters that is enclosed between double quotes, such as "stringY strinGy striNg strIng stRing". These characters can include letters (both uppercase and lowercase), digits (0 to 9), and other symbols on your keyboard (such as +, −, &, @, and so on). You can use strings in your programs to store names, addresses, phone numbers, book titles, names of *Star Trek* episodes, and more. The Text object contains many useful methods for working with strings.

Figure 18-1 shows the complete list of the Text object's methods. We've divided these methods into four groups that we'll discuss in the following sections.

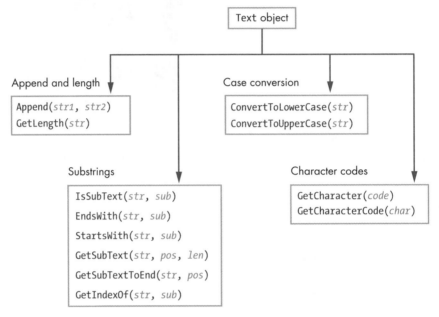

Figure 18-1: The Text object's methods

Appending Strings and Getting Their Length

Combining strings and finding their length is a common task in programming. Let's look at how the Text object can help you out.

Appending Strings

The Append() method can join (or *append*) two strings together, as shown in the following example:

```
str = Text.Append("He-", "Man")
TextWindow.WriteLine(str) ' Displays: He-Man
```

Earlier in the book, you learned how to join strings using the + sign. But the Append() method is useful when you have text that the + sign treats as numbers, as shown in the following example:

```
res = Text.Append("1", "5")
TextWindow.WriteLine(res)        ' Output: 15 (1 followed by 5)
TextWindow.WriteLine("1" + "5")  ' Output: 6
```

The first statement appends the two strings ("1" and "5") and assigns the result to the variable res (short for *result*). The output of the second statement shows that the string "5" was appended to the string "1", resulting in a new string "15". The third statement shows that you can't do this concatenation using the + sign. The + operator interprets its two operands as numbers (1 and 5) and adds these numbers together, which is why the third statement displays 6.

Using Append() is the only way to concatenate numbers in Small Basic.

Getting the Length of a String

The number of characters in a string makes up its length. To find the length of a string, you can use the GetLength() method, as in the following example:

```
1 res = Text.GetLength("")              ' res = 0 (empty string)
2 res = Text.GetLength("Careless Bears") ' res = 14 (the space counts!)
3 res = Text.GetLength(1023)             ' res = 4
4 res = Text.GetLength(-101.5)           ' res = 6
```

GetLength() treats its argument as a string and returns the number of characters in that string. Line 1 shows that an empty string has zero length. Line 2 shows that the length of the string "Careless Bears" is 14, because this string contains 14 characters (spaces are characters too). Line 3 calls GetLength() using the number 1023 as an argument. GetLength() treats this number as a string ("1023") and returns 4 as the length of this string. A similar process happens in line 4 for the number –101.5, where GetLength() returns 6 (four digits, the minus sign, and the decimal point).

TRY IT OUT 18-1

Write a program that prompts the user to enter an adjective. Have the program display the corresponding adverb by appending *ly* to the input. For example, if the user enters *mad*, the program displays *madly*. Will this program work for all adjectives? (Hint: consider adjectives ending in *y*, such as *happy*, or adjectives ending in *ic*, such as *heroic*.)

Taking Strings Apart: Substrings

Just as you can join strings to create longer ones, you can also separate strings into smaller strings, which are called *substrings*. A substring is just a portion of a larger string. The Text object has six methods that let you work with substrings. Let's look at these methods.

The IsSubText() Method

You can use IsSubText() to find out if one string is part of another. This method takes two arguments: the string you want to search through and the substring you want to search for. It returns "True" or "False" depending on whether the substring is in the source string. Here are some examples:

```
1 myString = "The quick brown fox"
2 res = Text.IsSubText(myString, "brown") ' res = "True"
3 res = Text.IsSubText(myString, "BROWN") ' res = "False"
4 res = Text.IsSubText(myString, "dog")   ' res = "False"
```

As these examples show, IsSubText() is case sensitive when it searches for substrings. This is why searching for "BROWN" in line 3 returns "False".

The EndsWith() Method

Use EndsWith() to find out if a string ends with a given substring. Here are some examples:

```
1 myString = "The quick brown fox"
2 res = Text.EndsWith(myString, "fox") ' res = "True"
3 res = Text.EndsWith(myString, "x")   ' res = "True"
4 res = Text.EndsWith(myString, "FOX") ' res = "False"
5 res = Text.EndsWith(myString, "dog") ' res = "False"
```

Again, the string's case matters: the search for "FOX" in line 4 returns "False".

The StartsWith() Method

Use StartsWith() to find out if a string starts with a given substring. Here are some examples:

```
1 myString = "The quick brown fox"
2 res = Text.StartsWith(myString, "The") ' res = "True"
3 res = Text.StartsWith(myString, "T")   ' res = "True"
4 res = Text.StartsWith(myString, "the") ' res = "False"
```

Similarly, the search for "the" in line 4 returns "False".

The GetSubText() Method

To extract text from any position in a string, you can use GetSubText(). This method takes three arguments: the source string to get your substring from, the starting position of the substring, and the length of the substring you want. To understand how this method works, look at Figure 18-2.

Figure 18-2: Illustrating character positions in strings

The first character has a position of 1, the second character has a position of 2, and so on. Now consider the following examples:

```
1 myString = "The quick brown fox"
2 res = Text.GetSubText(myString, 1, 3)  ' res = "The"
3 res = Text.GetSubText(myString, 0, 3)  ' res = ""
4 res = Text.GetSubText(myString, 17, 3) ' res = "fox"
5 res = Text.GetSubText(myString, 17, 4) ' res = "fox"
```

Line 2 gets a substring of length 3 starting at position 1, which returns the string "The". Line 3 fails to get a substring that starts at position 0, because the first valid position is 1. Instead, it returns an empty string. Line 4 gets the three-letter substring that starts at position 17, which returns "fox". Line 5 requests a substring of length 4 starting at position 17. Because that substring extends beyond the end of the string, the length is cut short, and the method returns "fox", whose length is 3.

You can use GetSubText() inside a For loop to access the individual characters of a string. For example, the following code writes each character of strIn on a new line. Enter and run this code to make sure you understand how it works:

```
strIn = "Pirate squids hate hot dogs."
For N = 1 To Text.GetLength(strIn)    ' For each character
  ch = Text.GetSubText(strIn, N, 1)   ' Gets the character at position N
  TextWindow.WriteLine(ch)            ' Displays it on a new line
EndFor
```

The loop counter, N, runs from 1 to the end of the string. Each iteration requests a substring of length 1 (a single character) that starts at position N and displays that character.

The GetSubTextToEnd() Method

The GetSubTextToEnd() method is similar to GetSubText(), except it returns a substring from one position all the way to the end of the string. It takes two arguments: the source string that you want to get your substrings from and the starting position of the substring. Here are some examples (refer to Figure 18-2 for context):

```
1  myString = "The quick brown fox"
2  res = Text.GetSubTextToEnd(myString, 13) ' res = "own fox"
3  res = Text.GetSubTextToEnd(myString, 19) ' res = "x"
4  res = Text.GetSubTextToEnd(myString, 20) ' res = ""
```

Line 2 gets the substring starting at position 17, which returns "own fox". Line 3 gets the substring starting at position 19, which returns "x". Line 4 requests the substring starting at position 20. Because the source string contains only 19 characters, this method returns an empty string.

The GetIndexOf() Method

You pass the GetIndexOf() method the substring you want to search for, and it returns the index position of that substring in the source text. Here are some examples:

```
1  myString = "The quick brown fox"
2  res = Text.GetIndexOf(myString, "The")    ' res = 1
3  res = Text.GetIndexOf(myString, "quick")  ' res = 5
4  res = Text.GetIndexOf(myString, "QUICK")  ' res = 0
5  res = Text.GetIndexOf(myString, "o")      ' res = 13
6  res = Text.GetIndexOf(myString, "dog")    ' res = 0
```

The search is case sensitive, so line 4 returns 0 because "QUICK" isn't found in the source string. Line 5 requests the index of the letter *o*, but because there are two, it gives you the index of the first one it finds. The last line returns 0 because it doesn't find "dog" in the source string.

TRY IT OUT 18-2

A young boy named Franklin Roosevelt once signed letters to his mother backward: *Tlevesoor Nilknarf*. Write a program that displays the characters of an input string in reverse order. (Hint: start a loop that counts from the string's length down to 1, and use GetSubText() to extract each character.)

Changing Case

Sometimes you might want to display strings in uppercase or lowercase letters. The ConvertToLowerCase() and ConvertToUpperCase() methods can do that for you. Run the example in Listing 18-1.

```
1  ' ChangeCase.sb
2  var1 = "Ewok"
```

```
3 lwrCase = Text.ConvertToLowerCase(var1)      ' lwrCase = "ewok"
4 TextWindow.WriteLine(lwrCase)                 ' Displays: ewok
5 TextWindow.WriteLine(var1)                    ' Displays: Ewok
6 uprCase = Text.ConvertToUpperCase(var1)       ' uprCase = "EWOK"
7 TextWindow.WriteLine(uprCase)                 ' Displays: EWOK
8 TextWindow.WriteLine(var1)                    ' Displays: Ewok
```

Listing 18-1: Changing the case of a string

The call to ConvertToLowerCase() on line 3 returns the lowercase string "ewok", which is displayed on line 4. The statement on line 5 shows that the original string isn't affected by the lowercase conversion; calling ConvertToLowerCase() returns a brand-new string whose characters are lowercase. The ConvertToUpperCase() method on line 6 returns the uppercase version of "EWOK", which is displayed on line 7. And line 8 also shows that the original string isn't affected by the conversion.

You can use these methods to make case-insensitive string comparisons. For example, let's say your program asks a user about their favorite *Shrek* character. If the user likes Donkey, they win 200 points; otherwise, they win 100 points. The user can enter donkey, DONKEY, Donkey, DOnkey, or any other combination of cases in response to the question. Rather than checking for all the possible combinations, you can convert the user's response to uppercase (or lowercase) and compare the result with that new string "DONKEY" (or "donkey" if you're using lowercase). Run the program in Listing 18-2.

```
 1 ' StringMatch.sb
 2 While ("True")
 3   TextWindow.Write("Who's your favorite Shrek character? ")
 4   name = Text.ConvertToUpperCase(TextWindow.Read())
 5   If (name = "DONKEY") Then
 6     TextWindow.WriteLine("You won 200 ogre points!")
 7   Else
 8     TextWindow.WriteLine("You won 100 ogre points!")
 9   EndIf
10 EndWhile
```

Listing 18-2: Case-insensitive string matching

The Read() method on line 4 reads the text entered by the user. The user's text is then converted to uppercase, and the result is stored in the name variable. Note how we used the Read() method directly as an argument to ConvertToUpperCase(); this is equivalent to the following two statements:

```
name = TextWindow.Read()
name = Text.ConvertToUpperCase(name)
```

The If statement on line 5 compares the uppercase version of the user's input with the literal string "DONKEY" and awards the user accordingly.

Here's an output example:

```
Who's your favorite Shrek character? dOnkey
You won 200 ogre points!
```

> **TRY IT OUT 18-3**
>
> Write a program that prompts the user with a yes/no question, such as "Can you paint with all the colors of the wind?" Create a program that accepts y, *yes*, n, or *no* using any casing as valid answers. If the answer is invalid, ask the user to re-enter their answer.

Character Coding with Unicode

All computer data (including text) is stored as *binary* sequences of 0s and 1s. The letter *A* for example is 01000001. The mapping between a character and its binary representation is called *encoding*.

Unicode is a universal encoding scheme that lets you encode more than a million characters from many languages. Each character is assigned a unique number (called a *code point*). For example, the code point for the character A is 65, and the code point for the dollar sign ($) is 36. The GetCharacterCode() method returns a character's code point. But the GetCharacter() method does the opposite; when you give it a character's code point, it returns the corresponding character.

Run the program in Listing 18-3.

```
1 ' CharCode.sb
2 str = "ABab12"
3 For N = 1 To Text.GetLength(str)
4   ch = Text.GetSubText(str, N, 1)      ' Gets the Nth character
5   code = Text.GetCharacterCode(ch)     ' Gets its code point
6   TextWindow.WriteLine(ch + ": " + code)  ' Displays ch and its code point
7 EndFor
```

Listing 18-3: Demonstrating the GetCharacterCode() method

Line 2 defines a string that contains six characters. Line 3 starts a For loop that accesses each of these characters; GetLength() sets the upper limit of the loop. Each iteration of the loop reads one character from the string and saves it in a variable named ch (line 4). Then the loop gets the Unicode code point for that character and saves it in the code variable (line 5). Line 6 displays the character and its code point. When you run this program, you'll see the following output:

```
A: 65
B: 66
```

```
a: 97
b: 98
1: 49
2: 50
```

Fancy Characters

Let's explore some characters not used in English. Listing 18-4 shows a simple program that displays the symbols for 140 Unicode characters, starting with the character whose code point is 9728. You can change this number to explore other Unicode symbols.

```
1  ' UnicodeDemo.sb
2  GraphicsWindow.BrushColor = "Black"
3  GraphicsWindow.FontSize = 30   ' Makes the font larger
4
5  code = 9728            ' Code point for the first symbol
6  xPos = 0              ' Horizontal position for drawing a symbol
7  yPos = 0              ' Vertical position for drawing a symbol
8  For row = 1 To 7      ' Draws 7 rows
9    xPos = 0            ' For each new row, start at the left edge
10   For col = 1 To 20   ' 20 columns for each row
11     ch = Text.GetCharacter(code)          ' Gets a character
12     GraphicsWindow.DrawText(xPos, yPos, ch)  ' Draws it
13     code = code + 1                        ' Sets to next code point
14     xPos = xPos + 30                       ' Leaves a horizontal space
15   EndFor
16   yPos = yPos + 30                         ' Moves to the next row
17 EndFor
```

Listing 18-4: Demonstrating Unicode characters

The outer For loop runs seven times (line 8). Each time the outer loop runs, the inner loop displays 20 symbols that are placed 30 pixels apart (lines 10–15). After drawing a complete row of symbols, we move the vertical drawing position down 30 pixels to draw the next row (line 16). Figure 18-3 shows the output of this program.

Figure 18-3: The output of UnicodeDemo.sb

More on Code Points

The Unicode code points for lowercase letters are consecutive integers from 97 (*a*) to 122 (*z*). Similarly, the code points for uppercase letters range from 65 (*A*) to 90 (*Z*). The code point for a lowercase *a* is greater than the code point for an uppercase *A*, and the difference between the code points for *a* and *A* (97 – 65 = 32) is the same as the difference between the code points for *b* and *B* (98 – 66 = 32), and so on. When given the code point for a lowercase letter, which we'll represent as ch, the code point for its corresponding uppercase letter is 65 + (ch – 97). Here's the formula:

```
code for uppercase ch = code(A) + (code for lowercase ch - code(a))
```

Now that you know that each character in a string is identified by a code point, you can perform many useful operations on strings. The following examples show what you can do.

Displaying a Quotation Mark

Let's say you want to display the string "Bazinga" with the double quotes included in the output. If you write TextWindow.WriteLine("Bazinga"), Small Basic displays Bazinga without the quotation marks because the quotation marks identify the start and end of a string. But Small Basic returns a syntax error if you write TextWindow.WriteLine(""Bazinga""). So how do you display the quotation marks? By using the quotation mark's code point, you can append the quotation mark characters to the string, as shown in the following code snippet:

```
QUO = Text.GetCharacter(34)                  ' Gets the double quotation mark
TextWindow.WriteLine(QUO + "Bazinga" + QUO)  ' Output: "Bazinga"
```

The first statement gets the quotation mark character from its Unicode code point (34) and assigns it to the variable QUO. The second statement inserts the string "Bazinga" between two QUO characters to output the desired result.

Creating a Multiline String

You can create a multiline string by embedding the *line feed* character (code point 10) into a string. Enter the following code snippet as an example:

```
LF = Text.GetCharacter(10)                    ' Code for line feed
TextWindow.WriteLine("Line1" + LF + "Line2")  ' Displays two lines
```

When you run this code, the two strings, "Line1" and "Line2", are displayed on two lines. The result is identical to what you get when you use the following two statements:

```
TextWindow.WriteLine("Line1")
TextWindow.WriteLine("Line2")
```

Armed with the knowledge you've gained so far, you're ready to create full-sized programs that use strings in all kinds of fancy ways!

TRY IT OUT 18-4

The following program displays the letters of the English alphabet. Explain how the program works.

```
For code = 65 To 90
  ch = Text.GetCharacter(code)
  TextWindow.WriteLine(ch)
EndFor
```

Practical Examples with Strings

Earlier you learned how to use GetLength() to get a string's length and GetSubText() to access individual characters in a string. When you use these two methods with a For loop, you can count special characters, examine multiple characters, and do several other useful tasks with strings. Let's explore some examples!

Counting Special Characters

Listing 18-5 shows a program that counts the number of vowels in a string. It asks the user to enter a string and then counts and displays the number of vowels in that string.

```
 1 ' VowelCount.sb
 2 TextWindow.Write("Enter a sentence: ")   ' Prompts the user for text
 3 str = TextWindow.Read()  ' Reads text entered by the user
 4
 5 count = 0                 ' Sets vowel count to 0 (so far)
 6 For N = 1 To Text.GetLength(str)       ' Checks all characters
 7   ch = Text.GetSubText(str, N, 1)      ' Gets Nth character
 8   ch = Text.ConvertToUpperCase(ch)     ' Makes it uppercase
 9   If ((ch = "A") Or (ch = "E") Or (ch = "I") Or (ch = "O") Or (ch = "U")) Then
10     count = count + 1   ' If it finds a vowel, increments count
11   EndIf
12 EndFor
13 TextWindow.Write("Your sentence contains [")  ' Shows result
14 TextWindow.WriteLine(count + "] vowels.")
```

Listing 18-5: Counting the number of vowels in a string

After getting the user's input (lines 2–3), the program initializes the count variable to 0, because no vowels have been found so far (line 5). Then a loop starts to check the characters of the input string one by one (line 6). The loop counter N points to the Nth character of the string.

Line 7 gets the *N*th character of the input string using GetSubText() and assigns it to the variable ch (short for character). The code then converts the character to uppercase (line 8) and compares that uppercase letter with the vowel characters (line 9). If the character is a vowel, count increases by 1 (line 10). When the loop ends, the program displays the number of vowels counted (lines 13–14). Here's a sample output from this program:

```
Enter a sentence: Small Basic is fun
Your sentence contains [5] vowels.

Enter a sentence: Giants leave nasty diapers.
Your sentence contains [9] vowels.
```

TRY IT OUT 18-5

Convert the code in Listing 18-5 into a game for two players. The first player enters a word, and the second player has to guess the number of vowels in the word. Then the players alternate turns. A player scores one point for each correct guess. End the game after 10 rounds and display the winner.

Palindrome Number Checker

In this section, we'll write a program that checks whether an integer entered by a user is a *palindrome*. A palindrome is a number, word, or phrase that reads the same backward and forward. For example, *1234321* and *1122332211* are palindromes. Likewise, *racecar*, *Hannah*, and *Bob* are also palindromes.

Let's look at the input number 12344321 shown in Figure 18-4.

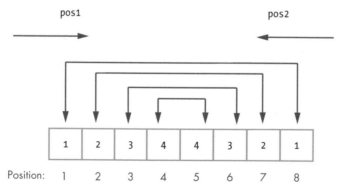

Figure 18-4: Using two variables to check whether a number is a palindrome

To check whether this number is a palindrome, you need to compare the first and eighth digits, the second and seventh digits, the third and sixth digits, and so on. If any two digits in the comparison aren't equal, the number isn't a palindrome. As the figure illustrates, you can access the digits you want to compare by using two variables (pos1 and pos2), which move in opposite directions. The first variable (pos1) starts at the first digit and moves forward, and the second variable (pos2) starts at the last digit and moves backward. The number of required comparisons is at most one-half the number of digits in the input number. In this example, you need at most four comparisons because the input number has eight digits. The same logic applies if the input integer has an odd number of digits, because the digit in the middle of the number doesn't need to be compared.

Listing 18-6 shows the complete program. The comments should help you understand how the program works.

```
 1 ' Palindrome.sb
 2 Again:
 3 TextWindow.WriteLine("")
 4 TextWindow.Write("Enter a number: ")
 5 ans = TextWindow.ReadNumber()              ' Saves user's input in ans
 6
 7 length = Text.GetLength(ans)               ' Number of digits of input number
 8 pos1 = 1                                   ' Sets pos1 to read first digit
 9 pos2 = length                             ' Sets pos2 to read last digit
10 For N = 1 To (length / 2)                  ' Performs (length/2) comparisons
11   ch1 = Text.GetSubText(ans, pos1, 1)      ' Reads digit at position pos1
12   ch2 = Text.GetSubText(ans, pos2, 1)      ' Reads digit at position pos2
13   If (ch1 <> ch2) Then                     ' If not equal, no need to continue
14     TextWindow.WriteLine(ans + " isn't a palindrome.")  ' Shows result
15     Goto Again
16   EndIf
17 EndFor
18
19 TextWindow.WriteLine(ans + " is a palindrome.")
20 Goto Again
```

Listing 18-6: Testing whether a number input by the user is a palindrome

Here's a sample run of this program:

```
Enter a number: 1234321
1234321 is a palindrome.

Enter a number: 12345678
12345678 isn't a palindrome.
```

TRY IT OUT 18-6

Another way to create the program in Listing 18-6 is to reverse the input string and then compare the reversed string with the original. Create a new palindrome-checker program using this method.

Igpay Atinlay

Let's teach the computer a language game called *pig latin*. The rules for creating pig latin words are simple. To convert a word into pig latin, move the first letter to the end and add the letters *ay* after it. So, the word *talk* becomes *alktay*, *fun* becomes *unfay*, and so on. Can you decipher the original title of this section?

Figure 18-5 shows the strategy you'll use to convert a word into pig latin, using the word *basic*.

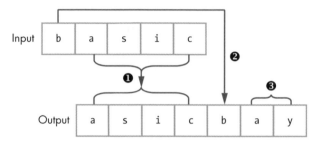

❶ Extract substring (from letter 2 to the end) and assign it to the output string.

❷ Append the first letter to the output string.

❸ Append *ay* to the output string.

Figure 18-5: Translating an English word into pig latin

You first extract the substring from the second character to the end and assign it to the output string. You then add the first letter in the input string to the output, followed by *ay*. Enter the code in Listing 18-7 to implement these steps.

```
1 ' PigLatin.sb
2 TextWindow.Title = "Pig Latin"
3
4 While ("True")
5   TextWindow.Write("Enter a word: ")
6   word = TextWindow.Read()
7
8   pigLatin = Text.GetSubTextToEnd(word, 2)        ' Gets characters 2 to end
9   pigLatin = pigLatin + Text.GetSubText(word, 1, 1) ' Appends first character
10  pigLatin = pigLatin + "ay"                      ' Appends "ay"
11  TextWindow.WriteLine(pigLatin)                  ' Displays the output
12  TextWindow.WriteLine("")
13 EndWhile
```

Listing 18-7: Converting a word entered by the user into pig latin

The program runs an infinite loop to allow the user to try different words (line 4). After reading the input word from the user (line 6), we extract the substring that starts at position 2 (that is, from the second character to the end of the input word) and assign it to pigLatin. Then we extract the first letter from word and append it to pigLatin (line 9), followed by ay (line 10). We display the pig latin word (line 11), followed by an empty line (line 12) and go for another round. *Ongratulationscay! Ouyay inishedfay ouryay rogrampay!*

Fix My Spelling

Now we'll develop a game that displays misspelled words and asks the player to enter the correct spelling. The game creates misspelled words by inserting a random letter at a random position in an English word. There could be more than one correct spelling of misspelled simple words. For example, if the game displays *mwall*, either *mall* or *wall* could be correct. To keep the game simple, we'll ignore that possibility and insist on a particular spelling for the correct answer.

First, we select the word to be misspelled from a predefined array of words and save the selected word in a variable named strIn. We then pick a random character randChar to insert into strIn. The insertion position charPos is a random number between 1 and the length of strIn. Figure 18-6 shows the process of generating the misspelled word hewlp.

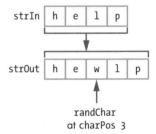

Figure 18-6: Illustrating the process of generating misspelled words

We first extract the substring from letter 1 to the letter at position charPos - 1 and assign it to strOut (because charPos is 3, this makes strOut = "he"). We then append randChar to strOut (this makes strOut = "hew"). We extract the substring from position charPos to the end ("lp" in this case) and append it to strOut (this makes strOut = "hewlp"). Listing 18-8 shows the complete program. Make sure you download and open *FixMySpelling.sb* from this chapter's folder to get the full list of the words we wrote for this program.

```
1  ' FixMySpelling.sb
2  words = "1=mountain;2=valley;...;22=animation;" ' See file for full list
3
4  While ("True")       ' Runs forever
5    strIn = words[Math.GetRandomNumber(Array.GetItemCount(words))]
6    randChar = Text.GetCharacter(96 + Math.GetRandomNumber(26))
7    charPos = Math.GetRandomNumber(Text.GetLength(strIn))
8
9    strOut = Text.GetSubText(strIn, 1, charPos - 1)
10   strOut = strOut + randChar
11   strOut = strOut + Text.GetSubTextToEnd(strIn, charPos)
12
13   TextWindow.Write("Enter correct spelling for [" + strOut + "]: ")
14   ans = TextWindow.Read()
15   ans = Text.ConvertToLowerCase(ans)
16   If (ans = strIn) Then
```

```
17    TextWindow.WriteLine("Good Job!")
18   Else
19    TextWindow.WriteLine("Incorrect. It is " + strIn + ".")
20   EndIf
21   TextWindow.WriteLine("")
22 EndWhile
```

Listing 18-8: Creating misspelled words and asking the player to fix them

The words array contains the words for this game (line 2). The program randomly picks a word from the words array and saves that word as strIn (line 5). Note how we used the array's item count to set the upper limit of the random number. The program then selects a random letter, randChar, from the alphabet (line 6). It does that by getting a random number from 1 to 26 and adding 96 to it; this gives you a random number between 97 (the code point for letter *a*) and 122 (the code point for letter *z*). Next, the program picks a random position, charPos, in strIn (line 7): this is the position where the random character is inserted. Then the program creates the misspelled word and stores it in strOut (lines 9–11).

In line 13, the program asks the player to enter the correct spelling. It reads the user's answer (line 14) and converts it to lowercase (line 15). It then compares the answer with the correct word (line 16). If the player's answer matches the original word, the game displays Good Job! (line 17). Otherwise, the game displays an error message and shows the correct spelling (line 19). In both cases, the program ends by displaying an empty line (line 21), and the loop repeats to give the user a new misspelled word.

Here's a sample run of this program:

```
Enter correct spelling for [mairror]: miror
Incorrect. It is mirror.

Enter correct spelling for [inteorface]: interface
Good Job!
```

TRY IT OUT 18-8

Update the program in Listing 18-8 so the misspelled word contains two additional random letters instead of just one random letter. Also, add more words to the list for more variety.

Unscramble

Now we'll create a word scramble game. The program starts with an English word, scrambles the letters, displays the scrambled word to the player, and asks them to guess the original word.

Listing 18-9 shows the main part of the program. Open *Unscramble.sb* from this chapter's folder for the full list of words.

```
1  ' Unscramble.sb
2  words = "1=mountain;2=valley;...;22=animation;" ' See file for full list
3
4  While ("True")
5    strIn = words[Math.GetRandomNumber(Array.GetItemCount(words))]
6    Scramble()  ' Returns strOut (a scrambled version of strIn)
7
8    TextWindow.Write("Unscramble [" + strOut + "]: ")
9    ans = TextWindow.Read()
10   ans = Text.ConvertToLowerCase(ans)
11
12   If (ans = strIn) Then
13     TextWindow.WriteLine("Good Job!")
14   Else
15     TextWindow.WriteLine("No. It is " + strIn + ".")
16   EndIf
17   TextWindow.WriteLine("")
18 EndWhile
```

Listing 18-9: Scrambling words and asking the player to unscramble them

The words array contains the words for this game (line 2). The program randomly picks a word from this array and saves that word as strIn (line 5). It then makes a call to Scramble() to produce strOut, a scrambled version of strIn (line 6): we'll add the Scramble() subroutine in a moment. Next, the program asks the player to unscramble strOut (line 8). It reads their answer (line 9) and converts it to lowercase (line 10). It then compares the player's answer with the correct word (line 12). If the player's answer matches the original word, the game displays Good Job! (line 13). Otherwise, the game displays the correct word (line 15). In both cases, the program ends by displaying an empty line (line 17) to separate the rounds and the loop repeats.

Now let's look at the Scramble() subroutine, which shuffles the characters of a string into a random order. The caller sets the input string (strIn), and the subroutine returns a new string (strOut) that contains the characters of strIn shuffled around. Listing 18-10 shows this subroutine.

```
1  Sub Scramble                              ' Scramble subroutine
2    len = Text.GetLength(strIn)
3    For N = 1 To len                        ' Loops up to length of word
4      char[N] = Text.GetSubText(strIn, N, 1)  ' Saves each letter into an array
5    EndFor
6
7    strout = ""                             ' Empties the output string
8    While (Text.GetLength(strout) < len)
```

```
 9     pos = Math.GetRandomNumber(len)        ' Picks where to place the letter
10     If (char[pos] <> "") Then
11       strout = strout + char[pos]          ' Adds in the extra letter
12       char[pos] = ""                       ' Empties the element
13     EndIf
14   EndWhile
15 EndSub
```

Listing 18-10: Word-scrambling subroutine

The subroutine saves the length of the input string into `len` (line 2). It then uses a `For` loop to save the individual letters of `strIn` into an array named `char` (lines 3–5). It empties the output string, `strOut`, and starts a `While` loop to assemble `strOut` letter by letter (lines 7–14). The `While` loop runs until `strOut` has the same length as `strIn` (which means that we've added all the letters of `strIn`). Each iteration of the loop picks a random element from the `char` array (line 9). If that element is empty, we loop again to pick another one. Otherwise, we append the selected letter to `strOut` (line 11) and empty that element to indicate that we've used it (to prevent using it again) in line 12. *Ouy fishendi eth egma!*

Here's a sample run of this program:

```
Unscramble [lalvey]: lovely
No. It is valley.
```

TRY IT OUT 18-9

Try to update the word-scrambling game using the skills you learned in previous chapters. Make the game last 10 rounds and then display the user's score: how many words were unscrambled correctly out of the 10? Next, add 28 more words to unscramble so you have a total of 50. Then show the game to your friends and see who can get the best score!

Rhyme Time: The House That Jack Built

Let's finish this chapter with a program that displays a popular British nursery rhyme and cumulative tale. In a *cumulative tale*, an action repeats and builds up as the tale progresses. Figure 18-7 shows this program in progress; more rhyme lines appear each time a user clicks the Next button.

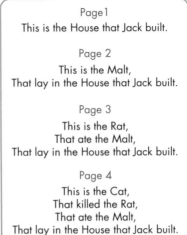

Page 1
This is the House that Jack built.

Page 2
This is the Malt,
That lay in the House that Jack built.

Page 3
This is the Rat,
That ate the Malt,
That lay in the House that Jack built.

Page 4
This is the Cat,
That killed the Rat,
That ate the Malt,
That lay in the House that Jack built.
. . .

Figure 18-7: The House That Jack Built rhyme

Examine this rhyme closely, and you'll notice the common strings among the story pages. Study Figure 18-8 to understand how to create this rhyme by appending short strings at each stage.

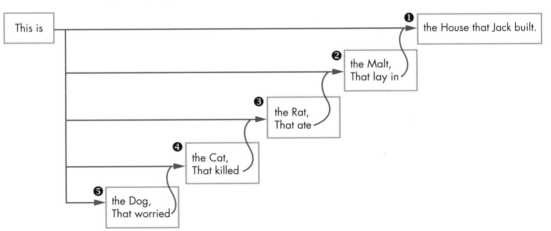

Figure 18-8: The strings that make up the rhyme

For example, let's trace the third row in this figure. Following the third arrow, you'll get the following:

```
This is the Rat,
That ate
```

When you continue with the second arrow, you'll get the following:

```
This is the Rat,
That ate the Malt,
That lay in
```

And, when you follow the first arrow, you'll get the full rhyme that will appear on the third page:

```
This is the Rat,
That ate the Malt,
That lay in the House that Jack built.
```

Open the file *JackHouse_Incomplete.sb* from this chapter's folder. The file contains the main program in Listing 18-11 and a placeholder for the OnButtonClicked() subroutine, which we'll add in a moment. The folder also contains the 11 background images (*Page1.png, Page2.png, . . . , Page11.png*) that we'll display for each page of the rhyme.

```
1 ' JackHouse.sb
2 GraphicsWindow.Title = "The House That Jack Built"
3 GraphicsWindow.CanResize = "False"
4 GraphicsWindow.Width = 480
5 GraphicsWindow.Height = 360
6 GraphicsWindow.FontBold = "False"
7 GraphicsWindow.FontSize = 20
8 GraphicsWindow.FontName = "Times New Roman"
9
10 LF = Text.GetCharacter(10)   ' Code for line feed
11
12 rhyme[1] = "the Farmer who sowed the corn," + LF + "That fed "
13 rhyme[2] = "the Cock that crowed in the morn," + LF + "That waked "
14 rhyme[3] = "the Priest all shaven and shorn," + LF + "That married "
15 rhyme[4] = "the Man all tattered and torn," + LF + "That kissed "
16 rhyme[5] = "the Maiden all forlorn," + LF + "That milked "
17 rhyme[6] = "the Cow with the crumpled horn,"   + LF + "That tossed "
18 rhyme[7] = "the Dog," + LF + "That worried "
19 rhyme[8] = "the Cat," + LF + "That killed "
20 rhyme[9] = "the Rat," + LF + "That ate "
21 rhyme[10] = "the Malt," + LF + "That lay in "
22 rhyme[11] = "the House that Jack built."
23
24 Controls.AddButton("Next", 420, 320)
25 Controls.ButtonClicked = OnButtonClicked
26 nextLine = 11
27 OnButtonClicked()
```

Listing 18-11: The main part of the House That Jack Built program

Lines 2–8 set up the GraphicsWindow object. Line 10 defines the line feed character (for appending new lines to the strings). Lines 12–22 define the rhyme array, which contains the strings for this rhyme. Note how the elements of this array relate to the boxes in Figure 18-8. Line 24 creates the Next button, and line 25 registers the handler for the ButtonClicked event. Then the nextLine variable is set to 11 to point to the 11th element of the rhyme array, which is the first page of the story (line 26), and OnButtonClicked() is called to show the first page of the rhyme (line 27).

Now we'll add the OnButtonClicked() subroutine in Listing 18-12. This subroutine is called when the user clicks the Next button.

```
1 Sub OnButtonClicked
2   img = Program.Directory + "\Page" + (12 - nextLine) + ".png"
3   GraphicsWindow.DrawImage(img, 0, 0)
4
5   strOut = "This is "
6   For N = nextLine To 11
7     strOut = Text.Append(strOut, rhyme[N])
8   EndFor
9   GraphicsWindow.DrawText(10, 10, strOut)
10
11  nextLine = nextLine - 1
12  If (nextLine = 0) Then
13    nextLine = 11
14  EndIf
15 EndSub
```

Listing 18-12: The OnButtonClicked() subroutine

Line 2 fills img with the name of the image for the current page of the rhyme. When nextLine is 11, we'll show *Page1.png* (which is 12 minus 11). When nextLine is 10, we'll show *Page2.png* (12 minus 10), and when nextLine is 9, we'll show *Page3.png* (12 minus 9), and so on. Line 3 draws the image on the graphics window. We then build up the output string (lines 5–8). We set strOut to "This is " (line 5) and then start a loop that goes from nextLine to 11 (lines 6–8). When nextLine is 11, the loop runs one time and appends rhyme[11] to strOut. When nextLine is 10, the loop runs from 10 to 11 and appends rhyme[10] and then rhyme[11] to strOut. Similarly, when nextLine is 9, the loop runs from 9 to 11 and appends rhyme[9], rhyme[10], and then rhyme[11] to strOut.

When the loop ends, strOut contains the entire string for the rhyme at this stage of the story. We display this string using DrawText() in line 9.

Then we decrease nextLine by 1 to point to the previous element in the rhyme array (line 11). If nextLine becomes 0 (line 12), the story is done, so we set it back to 11 to start over (line 13). As a result, when the user clicks the Next button at the last page of the story, the program goes back to displaying the first page. We've finished the tale before it got stale!

Programming Challenges

If you get stuck, check out *http://nostarch.com/smallbasic/* for the solutions and for more resources and review questions for teachers and students.

1. Open the file *Shoot_Incomplete.sb* from this chapter's folder. Run the program to see the following interface.

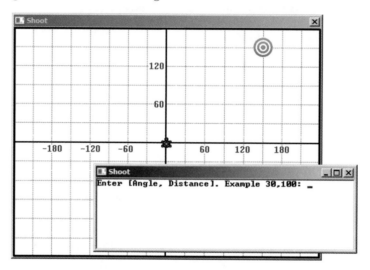

   The goal of this game is to estimate the turn angle and moving distance between the turtle and the target. When a player enters their input, it is saved in a variable named strIn. Your task is to split strIn into two parts: assign the substring before the comma to angle, and assign the substring after the comma to dist. The comments in the file tell you where to add your code. If you get stuck, see the file *Shoot.sb*, which contains the completed program.

2. Open the file *BinaryToDecimal_Incomplete.sb* from this chapter's folder. This program converts binary numbers to decimal numbers and then asks the user to input an 8-bit binary number. It then shows the input number in the graphics window, computes its decimal number, and displays the result of the conversion, as shown in the following figure.

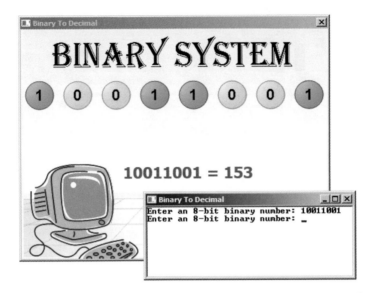

Complete the GetInput() subroutine, which prompts the user to enter an 8-bit binary number. You need to verify that the user's input isn't empty and has at most eight binary digits (so it contains only 1s and 0s). When the user enters a valid input, save it in strIn and return from the subroutine. The comments in the file tell you what to do. If you get stuck, see the file *BinaryToDecimal.sb*, which contains the completed code.

19

RECEIVING FILE INPUT AND OUTPUT

The programs you've written so far in this book took input from the keyboard and sent output to the screen. But what if you wanted to create a virtual phone book and use thousands of lines of data in the program? Working with that much data could make it difficult to write and maintain your program. You'd have to input every name and phone number each time you ran the program!

Fortunately, a program can also receive input from a file and send its output to a file, and both files can be saved on your computer. So all the phone book information could be neatly tucked away in a file, and you'd only have to input the data once. Today, many programs process data that is stored in files.

In most programming languages, working with files is an advanced topic, but Small Basic makes file handling super simple. In this chapter, you'll learn about the File object and how it makes working with files a breeze!

The Case for Files

In your programs, you've used variables and arrays to store data. But data stored in variables and arrays is temporary: all that data is lost when the program ends or when you turn off your computer. When you run your program again, it won't remember the input you entered the last time it ran. If you want to permanently store the data created in a program, you need to save that data in a file. Data stored in files is called *persistent data* because it's retained even after you turn off your computer. It's as persistent as a squirrel caching acorns.

Files provide a convenient way to handle large amounts of data. If your program requires lots of data (like the names of your friends), you can't ask a user to input that data each time they run the program. Most likely, they will get annoyed and stop using the program. If a program can read its input data from a file, a user won't need to enter data by hand and might want to run the program many times. When programs use files, a user could even customize the application by changing the data file. For example, if you write a spelling game that reads its input from a file, the user can set the game's difficulty by changing the input file. For example, they could use short words for an easy game and long words for a more difficult game.

Getting data from a file is called *reading the file*, and the files a program reads are generally called *input files*. Similarly, sending data to a file is called *writing to the file*, and the files a program writes to (or creates) are called *output files*. Storing data to (and reading data from) files on disk is called *file access*. Working with files is called *file I/O*, which is short for input/output.

Before we start working with files in programs, let's look at filenames and how files are saved on your computer.

Naming Files

When you create a new file, you give it a name. You can call it *Fred* or *DontOpenMe* if you want, but it's usually best to name it more specifically, such as *myFriends* or *myLoveStory*.

The Windows operating system is case insensitive and doesn't see any difference between uppercase and lowercase letters in filenames, so *myFile*, *Myfile*, and *MYFILE* would all refer to the same file. Windows also supports filenames with two parts that are separated by a period, such as *myFile.dat*. The part following the period (*dat* in this example) is called the *file extension*. The file extension usually indicates what kind of file it is (such as a photo or text file). Table 19-1 lists some of the most common file extensions and their meanings. File extensions are usually added automatically by the programs you use. For example, the Small Basic IDE adds an *.sb* extension to source code files.

Table 19-1: Common File Extensions

Extension	File type	Used for
.dat	General data file	Storing information about a specific application
.exe	Executable file	Applications
.gif	Graphic Interchange Format	Website images
.html	Hypertext Markup Language website file	Web pages
.jpg	An image encoded with the JPEG standard	Photos from a digital camera
.mp3	Music encoded in MPEG layer 3 audio format	Audio files
.pdf	Portable Document Format file for reading	Ebooks
.txt	General text file	Notes you might write in Notepad

You'll be working with text (*.txt*) files in this chapter.

File Organization

Imagine dozens of books organized in a cabinet with several shelves. Each shelf has a different label (such as Science, Math, Novels, Dr. Seuss, and so on) and is filled with books in that category. Each shelf serves as a container that groups related books together. Similarly, files on a computer are stored in containers called *directories* (or *folders*). A directory can contain files as well as other directories. A directory within a directory is called a *subdirectory*.

The *filesystem* is the part of the operating system that is responsible for organizing files and directories on a computer and providing ways to manage them. When you call a file-related method from your Small Basic program (to create, delete, read from, or write to a file), the operating system's filesystem handles all the low-level details for you, so you don't have to worry whether the actual files are stored on a hard drive, flash memory, a CD, a DVD, and so on. The Small Basic library talks to the operating system to access files stored on various media, as illustrated in Figure 19-1.

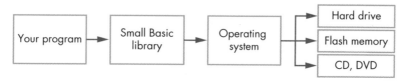

Figure 19-1: How the filesystem lets you access files on different media

The filesystem has a tree structure, like the one shown in Figure 19-2. The top of the tree is called the *root directory* (the drive letter *D:* in this figure). The root directory has a number of files and other directories under it. Each of these directories might contain other files and subdirectories.

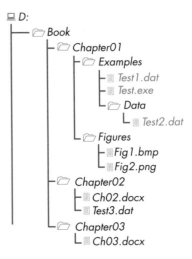

You can locate any file by following a path from the root directory down the tree until you reach that file. The sequence of directories you follow makes up the *pathname* for the file. For example, to find the last file in Figure 19-2, you would look in the root directory *D:*, then in *Book*, and then in *Chapter03* to locate the file. If you write the path using a backslash (\) to separate each directory, the pathname is *D:\Book\Chapter03\Ch03.docx*. You can locate each file on the system using its pathname.

Figure 19-2: The filesystem as a tree

To access a file from a Small Basic program, you need to specify the file's pathname. To learn how, look at the executable file *Test.exe* in Figure 19-2. When you run this file, the running program knows its *current directory* (which is *D:\Book\Chapter01\Examples* in this case). If you want *Test.exe* to access a data file (such as *Test1.dat* or *Test2.dat*), you need to specify the pathname—the sequence of folders, starting from the root, that the program needs to navigate to reach the file. This is also called the *absolute path*. In Figure 19-2, the absolute path for *Test1.dat* is *D:\Book\Chapter01\Examples\Test1.dat*, and the absolute path for *Test2.dat* is *D:\Book\Chapter01\Examples\Data\Test2.dat*.

If you write a program that only you will use, you can save the data files needed by this program anywhere you like and access these files using absolute paths hardcoded in your program. For example, you can write this:

```
str = File.ReadContents("D:\Book\Chapter01\Examples\Test1.dat")
```

But if you give this program to a friend to try, it will fail unless your friend has the same file tree as you. A better solution is to build the desired path(s) in your program at runtime, like this:

```
path = Program.Directory
str = File.ReadContents(path + "\Test1.dat")
```

Now the program will add *Test1.dat* to the end of its current directory, which means it will look for *Test1.dat* in the same folder that the program is in. Then your friend only needs to place *Test.exe* and *Test1.dat* in the same folder; the absolute path will no longer matter. You can just zip your program's folder (right-click the folder, click Send to, and click Compressed (zipped) folder) and send that ZIP file to your friend. Your friend can save the files contained in the ZIP file under *C:*, *D:*, *C:\Temp*, or any other folder of their choice, and your program will work as you designed it.

With an understanding of files and pathnames, you're ready to learn about the File object and how to use its methods to read data from files, write data to files, and perform other file management operations. Let's go single file!

The File Object

Small Basic's File object includes all the methods that handle reading and writing file data, deleting and copying files, and listing directory contents. Because this object supports many methods, this section is divided into two parts. First, we'll explore the methods related to reading from and writing to files. Second, we'll look at the methods related to file management.

File I/O Methods

The File object's most frequently used methods are those used to write data to files and read data from files. Let's explore these methods in detail.

To start, open Notepad and type some words in the editor so it looks like Figure 19-3. Make sure that you don't press ENTER after the last line.

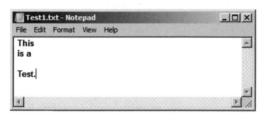

Figure 19-3: An example text file

Save the file as *Test1.txt* in *C:\Temp* so its absolute pathname is *C:\Temp\Test1.txt*. If you don't want to create the file, you can find it in this chapter's folder; just copy it to *C:\Temp*.

Reading from a File

Now let's try reading the contents of *Test1.txt*. You can use the File object's ReadContents() method to read the entire contents of a file at once. This method opens a file, reads it, and returns its entire contents as a string. Enter and run the program in Listing 19-1 to see how this method works.

```
1 ' ReadContentsDemo.sb
2 path = "C:\Temp\Test1.txt"
3 str = File.ReadContents(path)
4 len = Text.GetLength(str)
```

```
5 TextWindow.WriteLine(str)
6 TextWindow.WriteLine("This file has " + len + " characters.")
```

Listing 19-1: Demonstrating the ReadContents() method

Here is the output of this program:

```
This
is a

Test.
This file has 19 characters.
```

Line 2 sets the file's absolute path. Line 3 reads the entire contents of the file and saves the returned string in a variable named str using the ReadContents() method. ReadContents() takes one argument: the pathname of the file you want to read. Line 4 gets the length of the string and saves it in a variable named len. Lines 5–6 display the str and len variables.

But why does GetLength() output 19 characters for the string's length when the string "This is a Test." contains only 15? To understand what's going on, you need to examine the actual characters that make up the str variable. Remember from Chapter 18 that characters are encoded in a format (such as ASCII or Unicode). Add the following code to the end of Listing 19-1, and run the program again:

```
For N = 1 To len
  ch = Text.GetSubText(str, N, 1)      ' Gets one character
  code = Text.GetCharacterCode(ch)     ' Gets the code for this character
  TextWindow.WriteLine(code)           ' Displays it
EndFor
```

This code shows that the str variable has 19 characters. Figure 19-4 breaks down what the program is doing.

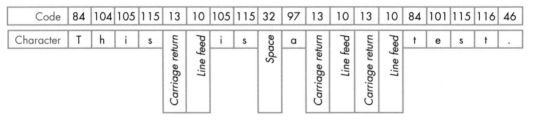

Figure 19-4: The 19 characters of the str variable in Listing 19-1

Notepad inserts two special characters (called *carriage return* and *line feed*, whose ASCII codes are 13 and 10) to mark the end of each line. Think of the *newline* (or end-of-line) marker as a pair of characters produced when you press ENTER on the keyboard. Without these characters, the lines in the file would run together in one long line. The newline characters are *control characters*; they only control the position of the cursor on the screen or the printer.

The ReadContents() method returns the entire contents of the file as a single string, including newline characters between lines in the file.

Writing to a File

The WriteContents() method lets you save the contents of a string in a program to a file of your choice. If you want to create multiple lines of text, you need to insert the newline characters manually. For example, let's write a program that reads text input from the keyboard and writes it back to a file. The program is shown in Listing 19-2.

```
1  ' WriteContentsDemo.sb
2  CR = Text.GetCharacter(13)                    ' Code for carriage return
3  LF = Text.GetCharacter(10)                    ' Code for line feed
4  outFile = "C:\Temp\Out.txt"                   ' Absolute path of output file
5
6  strOut = ""                                   ' Text to be written to file
7  strIn = ""                                    ' One line (read from the user)
8  While(strIn <> "exit")                        ' Until user enters exit
9    TextWindow.Write("Data (exit to end): ")    ' Prompts for text
10   strIn = TextWindow.Read()                   ' Reads line
11   If (strIn <> "exit") Then                   ' If user didn't enter exit
12     strOut = strOut + strIn + CR + LF         ' Appends text to strOut
13   EndIf
14 EndWhile
15
16 File.WriteContents(outFile, strOut)           ' Writes strOut to file
```

Listing 19-2: Demonstrating the WriteContents() method

Here's a sample run of this program showing the user input:

```
Data (exit to end): If Peter Piper picked a peck of pickled peppers,
Data (exit to end): Where's the peck of pickled peppers? I'm hungry.
Data (exit to end): exit
```

Now open the output file *C:\Temp\Out.txt* in Notepad and check its contents. The file contains what the user entered in the text window. Pretty cool, huh? You wrote all of that text without using Notepad!

Here's how the program works. We define the codes for the carriage return and the line feed characters in lines 2–3 and define the output file's path in line 4. We then start a loop to get the user's text (line 8–14). In each iteration of the loop, we prompt the user to enter any text they want (line 9) and read the input text into a variable named strIn (line 10). If the user enters any text other than exit (line 11), we append that text followed by a carriage return and line feed to the strOut string (line 12). When the user enters exit, the loop ends, and we call WriteContents() to write strOut to the output file (line 16). If the file doesn't exist, WriteContents() automatically creates it. If the file does exist, WriteContents() overwrites its contents with whatever is in the strOut variable.

TRY IT OUT 19-1

Write a program that reads an input text file, converts the text to lowercase, and then saves the result to a new output file.

Checking for Errors

Similar to when you work with user input, you can't control what the user saves in a file that your program reads. Sometimes the data in a file might be incorrect due to human error. Many things can go wrong (as you'll see in a moment), and your programs need to be ready to handle these errors.

Fortunately, Small Basic is always prepared! A call to WriteContents() returns "SUCCESS" or "FAILED" automatically based on whether the operation was successful. A well-written program checks the returned string and takes action in case of failure. Let's update Listing 19-2 to check the return value of WriteContents(). Replace the statement on line 16 with the code in Listing 19-3.

```
1 result = File.WriteContents(outFile, strOut) ' Writes strOut to file
2 If (result = "SUCCESS") Then
3   TextWindow.WriteLine("Output saved to: " + outFile)
4 Else
5   TextWindow.WriteLine("Failed to write to: " + outFile)
6   TextWindow.WriteLine(File.LastError)
7 EndIf
```

Listing 19-3: Checking the return value of WriteContents()

First, we save the return of WriteContents() in a variable named result (line 1), and then we check the method's return value. If the method succeeds (line 2), we inform the user that the output has been saved successfully (line 3). If the operation fails (line 4), we tell the user that the program failed to write to the output file (line 5), and then we display the reason for the failure using the File object's LastError property (line 6). This property is automatically updated by WriteContents() if writing to a file fails.

After writing the code to handle the failure case, we need to test the code by making it fail on purpose. Here are some things that can cause WriteContents() to fail:

1. The path of the output file doesn't exist.
2. The output file is already open in another program.
3. There is not enough space to save the file.

Let's experiment with the first possibility to see what happens.

Path Doesn't Exist

Run the short program in Listing 19-4.

```
1 ' BadPath.sb
2 path = "C:\Temp\Folder1\Out.txt"
3 res = File.WriteContents(path, "Hello")
4 TextWindow.WriteLine(res + ": " + File.LastError)
```

Listing 19-4: Writing to a file when the path doesn't exist

You should see this output:

```
FAILED: Could not find a part of the path 'C:\Temp\Folder1\Out.txt'.
```

The program attempts to write the string "Hello" to an output file (lines 2–3). The directory *Temp* exists, but the subdirectory *Folder1* doesn't exist, so WriteContents() fails.

Appending to a File

The AppendContents() method opens the specified file and adds data to the end of the file without erasing its original contents. AppendContents() takes two arguments: the pathname of the output file and the string you want to append to the end of the file. If the operation is successful, the method returns "SUCCESS"; otherwise, it returns "FAILED". If the file you pass to AppendContents() doesn't exist, it's created for you, and the string is written to it. If the file already exists, the string is appended to its end.

To see the AppendContents() method in use, let's say you need to maintain a log file that records actions, errors, and other events in your program. To keep the program simple, let's just record the times when your program is executed. Every time your program runs, you add a record to a log file that includes the date and time. The complete program is shown in Listing 19-5.

```
1 ' AppendContentsDemo.sb
2 outFile = Program.Directory + "\Log.txt"
3
4 strLog = Clock.WeekDay + ", " + Clock.Date + ", " + Clock.Time
5 result = File.AppendContents(outFile, strLog)
6 If (result = "FAILED") Then
7   TextWindow.WriteLine("Failed to write to: " + outFile)
8   TextWindow.WriteLine(File.LastError)
9 EndIf
10
11 TextWindow.WriteLine("Thank you for using this program. And for using ↵
   deodorant.")
```

Listing 19-5: Demonstrating the AppendContents() method

When you run this program, it creates a log string that contains the current day of the week, date, and time (line 4), and it appends this string to the end of a log file named *Log.txt* that is in the program's directory (line 5). If writing to the file fails, the program displays an error message explaining the cause of the failure (lines 7–8). Then the program displays a message (line 11) and ends.

Each time you run this program, a new line is appended to the end of the *Log.txt* file. Here's the output of *Log.txt* after running the program three times:

```
Sunday, 7/19/2015, 12:40:39 PM
Sunday, 7/19/2015, 12:43:21 PM
Sunday, 7/19/2015, 12:47:25 PM
```

ReadLine(), WriteLine(), and InsertLine()

The ReadContents() and WriteContents() methods let you read and write the entire contents of a file at once. Sometimes this is just what you need. But in other situations, reading or writing one line at a time might be better.

The File object provides the ReadLine() method for reading a single line of text from a file. A line of text consists of a string of characters that ends with a carriage return and line feed pair. ReadLine() reads all the text on that line up to (but not including) the carriage return character. This method takes two arguments: the path of the file and the line number of the text to be read. The first line of a file is line number 1, the second line is 2, and so on. If the file contains the specified line number, the method returns the text at that line. Otherwise, it returns an empty string.

The File object also provides the WriteLine() method for outputting a line of text to a file. This method takes three arguments: the path of the file, the line number to write text to, and the text to write. Keep the following information in mind when you're using this method:

1. If the file doesn't exist, WriteLine() creates it.
2. If the file contains the specified line number, WriteLine() overwrites that line.
3. If the specified line number is larger than the number of lines in the file, the specified text is appended to the end of the file. For example, if the file contains three lines and you ask WriteLine() to write new text at line 100, the specified text is written at line 4.
4. WriteLine() automatically writes a carriage return and line feed at the end of the passed text. This means you don't have to append these characters to your strings manually.
5. If the operation is successful, WriteLine() returns "SUCCESS"; otherwise, it returns "FAILED".

In addition to ReadLine() and WriteLine(), the File object provides the InsertLine() method for you to insert a line of text into a file, at a specified line number. As with the `WriteLine()` method, this method takes three arguments: the path of the file, the line number where you want the new text to be inserted, and the text you want to insert. `InsertLine()` won't overwrite any existing content at the specified line. If the operation is successful, `InsertLine()` returns `"SUCCESS"`; otherwise, it returns `"FAILED"`.

As an example, let's write a simple program that creates login names from the first and last names of users. The program will read an input file that contains the first and last names of users, and it will create an output file that contains the login names for these users. The login name for a user is composed of the first letter of the user's first name and up to five characters from their last name. For example, if the user's name is Jack Skellington, his login name is *jskell*. If the user's name is Stan Lee (three-letter last name), his login name will be *slee*. The complete program is shown in Listing 19-6.

```
1  ' LoginName.sb
2  inFile = Program.Directory + "\Users.txt"
3  outFile = Program.Directory + "\LoginNames.txt"
4
5  N = 1                    ' Tracks the line number
6  While (N > 0)        ' We'll set N = 0 when we detect end of file
7    strLine = File.ReadLine(inFile, N)     ' Reads the Nth line
8    If (strLine = "") Then                 ' If the string's empty
9      N = 0                                ' Exits the While loop
10   Else                                   ' We have an entry
11     idx = Text.GetIndexOf(strLine, " ")    ' Finds space in strLine
12     firstChar = Text.GetSubText(strLine, 1, 1)
13     lastName = Text.GetSubText(strLine, idx + 1, 5)
14     loginName = firstChar + lastName
15     loginName = Text.ConvertToLowerCase(loginName)
16     File.WriteLine(outFile, N, loginName) ' Saves to a file
17     N = N + 1                            ' Gets ready for the next line
18   EndIf
19 EndWhile
```

Listing 19-6: Creating login names from first and last names

We start by giving the paths for the input and output files (lines 2–3). We then start a loop to read the contents of the input file, one line at a time (lines 6–19). After reading a line (line 7), we check whether that line is empty, and if it is (line 8), we set N equal to 0 to end the loop (line 9). Otherwise, we process the user's name that is read from the input file to create the lowercase login name (lines 11–15). First, we find the space between the first name and the last name (line 11). Next, we get the first letter of the first name (line 12) and the first five letters of the last name (line 13), combine them to create the login name (line 14), and convert the login name to lowercase (line 15). Then we write the login name to the output file (line 16) and increment N by 1 to read the next line in the input file (line 17).

To keep the code simple, we didn't add error-checking code. We also assumed that the input file was properly formatted: each line contained a user's first and last names separated by a single space. Table 19-2 shows an example input file for this program and the output file.

Table 19-2: Creating Login Names

User's name	Login name
Tina Fey	*tfey*
Jimmy Fallon	*jfallo*
David Letterman	*dlette*
Jay Leno	*jleno*
Amy Poehler	*apoehl*

TRY IT OUT 19-2

Write a program that reads an input file and counts the number of lines, characters, and spaces it contains.

File Management

In addition to the methods that let you perform file I/O, the File object also provides a couple of methods related to file and directory management. Using these methods, you can copy and delete files, create and delete directories, and list files and directories from your program.

Copying and Deleting Files

You can use the CopyFile() method to create a copy of an existing file. This method takes the pathnames of the source file and the destination file as arguments. The source file isn't affected by this operation. If the operation is successful, the method returns "SUCCESS". Otherwise, it returns "FAILED".

If the destination path points to a location that doesn't exist, the method attempts to create it automatically. For example, look at the following code:

```
srcPath = "C:\Temp\Test1.txt"              ' Path of the source file
dstPath = "C:\Temp\Temp1\Temp2\Test1.txt"  ' Path of the destination file
File.CopyFile(srcPath, dstPath)
```

If the subfolders *Temp*, *Temp1*, and *Temp2* don't exist, CopyFile() attempts to create all the directories in the destination path, beginning with the root. When you run this code, you'll have two copies of the *Test1.txt* file: the original source file and the duplicate file under *C:\Temp\Temp1\Temp2*.

If the destination path points to an existing file, that file will be overwritten. So be careful when you use the `CopyFile()` method, because you might overwrite some of your files!

If you want to delete a file, use the `DeleteFile()` method. This method takes one argument: the pathname of the file you want to delete. If the operation is successful, the method returns `"SUCCESS"`. Otherwise, it returns `"FAILED"`.

The deleted file doesn't go to the recycle bin; instead, it's completely deleted from your system. So be extra careful when you use the `DeleteFile()` method!

Using `CopyFile()` and `DeleteFile()`, you can create your own subroutines for moving and renaming files. To move a file to a new location, copy the file to the new location and then delete the original file. To rename a file, make a copy of the file, give the copy a new name, and then delete the original file.

Creating and Deleting Directories

You can easily create or delete a directory. The `CreateDirectory()` method takes a single argument: the pathname of the directory you want to create. If the directories don't exist, the method attempts to create all the directories in the path, beginning with the root. If the operation is successful, the method returns `"SUCCESS"`. Otherwise, it returns `"FAILED"`. Here's an example:

```
File.CreateDirectory("C:\Temp\Temp1\Temp2")
```

If the directories *C:\Temp*, *C:\Temp\Temp1*, and *C:\Temp\Temp1\Temp2* don't exist, `CreateDirectory()` creates them. If the directory path already exists, the function does nothing and returns `"SUCCESS"`.

The `DeleteDirectory()` method also takes a single argument: the pathname of the directory you want to delete. All files and folders under the path are deleted. If the operation is successful, the method returns `"SUCCESS"`. Otherwise, it returns `"FAILED"`. Figure 19-5 shows an example of `DeleteDirectory()`.

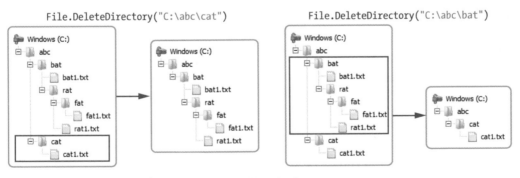

Figure 19-5: Demonstrating the `DeleteDirectory()` method

When you call DeleteDirectory(), all the files and folders under the pathname are deleted. So make sure you don't have any files tucked away that you don't want to delete!

List Files and Directories

The File object includes the GetFiles() method, which lets you list all the files in a directory. This method takes the path of the target directory as its argument. The example in Listing 19-7 shows you how to use this method.

```
1  ' GetFilesDemo.sb
2  path = "D:\Temp"
3  fileArray = File.GetFiles(path)
4  count = Array.GetItemCount(fileArray)
5  TextWindow.WriteLine(path + " contains " + count + " files:")
6  For N = 1 To count
7    TextWindow.WriteLine("  " + fileArray[N])
8  EndFor
```

Listing 19-7: Demonstrating the GetFiles() method

Here is the output after running this program (change the path variable in line 2 to a directory on your computer):

```
D:\Temp contains 3 files:
  D:\Temp\Fig01.bmp
  D:\Temp\keys.txt
  D:\Temp\Test.sb
```

We start by specifying the path of the directory we want to list (line 2). Next, we call GetFiles() with the desired path (line 3). This method creates an array that contains the pathnames of all the files in the directory; we save the identifer of the returned array in fileArray. Then we call GetItemCount() to find out the number of elements in the returned array (line 4) and use a For loop to display its elements (lines 6–8).

NOTE *If GetFiles() fails, then fileArray stores the string "FAILED". In this case, the call to Array.GetItemCount(fileArray) returns 0. So you might not need to perform an extra check on the return of GetFiles().*

The GetDirectories() method lets you list all the subdirectories in a given directory. Listing 19-8 shows an example of this method.

```
1  ' GetDirectoriesDemo.sb
2  path = "D:\Temp"
3  dirArray = File.GetDirectories(path)
4  count = Array.GetItemCount(dirArray)
5  TextWindow.WriteLine(path + " contains " + count + " directories:")
```

```
6 For N = 1 To count                        ' Displays the array's elements
7   TextWindow.WriteLine("  " + dirArray[N])
8 EndFor
```

Listing 19-8: Demonstrating the `GetDirectories()` *method*

Here is the output after running this program:

```
D:\Temp contains 3 directories:
  D:\Temp\Chapter01
  D:\Temp\Chapter02
  D:\Temp\Chapter03
```

But your output will probably look different, depending on what your *Temp* directory looks like. This program is similar to Listing 19-7. We start by storing the path we're interested in (line 2). Next, we call `GetDirectories()` with the path (line 3). This method creates an array that contains the pathnames of all the directories in the specified path; we save the identifier of the returned array in `dirArray`. Then we call `GetItemCount()` to find out the number of elements in the returned array (line 4) and use a `For` loop to display its elements (lines 6–8). Try changing line 2 to access a different directory.

At this point, we've covered everything you need to know about the `File` object. Let's put some of this newfound knowledge to work to create some cool applications!

Practical Programs

We'll present two programs intended to highlight different aspects of file I/O and give you some ideas and new techniques that you can use in your own creations.

The Poet

In this example, we'll modify the Poet program we created in Chapter 16 so it reads its input from files instead of hardcoding the word lists into the program. By doing so, your program will be more awesome and concise, and it will be easy to add words to!

The program uses five input files: *article.txt*, *adjective.txt*, *noun.txt*, *verb .txt*, and *preposition.txt*. The *article.txt* file contains a list of articles and qualifiers; the *adjective.txt* file contains a list of adjectives, and so on. To take advantage of the way Small Basic handles arrays, each of the five files is formatted to make it easy to be read into an array in your program.

Look at this statement:

```
art = File.ReadContents("article.txt")
```

We automatically load the contents of the *article.txt* file into an array named art that contains the five elements shown in Figure 19-6.

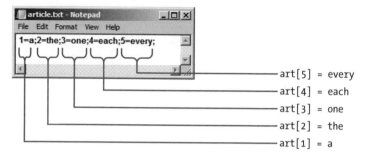

Figure 19-6: Reading the contents of article.txt into an array named art

Open the file *Poet_Incomplete.sb* from this chapter's folder, which also contains the background image and the five input files we'll need. The file has an empty placeholder for the CreateLists() subroutine, which you'll add now. This subroutine is shown in Listing 19-9.

```
1 Sub CreateLists
2   article = File.ReadContents(path + "\article.txt")
3   adjective = File.ReadContents(path + "\adjective.txt")
4   noun = File.ReadContents(path + "\noun.txt")
5   verb = File.ReadContents(path + "\verb.txt")
6   prepos = File.ReadContents(path + "\preposition.txt")
7 EndSub
```

Listing 19-9: The CreateLists() subroutine

Run this program. It should work the same way as before but with an advantage: the user can now change the input files to create their own custom poems.

Math Wizard

In this example, we'll create a program featuring a wizard who seems to know a lot about math. The wizard isn't Merlin, Gandalf, or Harry Potter: welcome to the world of the Math Wizard! The wizard starts by asking the user to think of a *secret* number. He then requests that the user perform some mathematical operations on that number (such as doubling the number, subtracting 2, dividing the answer by 10, and so on). At the end, the wizard uses his magical powers to tell the user the resulting number after performing these operations (although he doesn't know the user's secret number)!

The idea of the program is very simple. We'll save each math puzzle in a text file that has the format shown in Figure 19-7. The first line contains the puzzle's answer, and the remaining lines contain the instructions that the wizard asks the user to perform. This program includes 11 puzzles saved in *Puzzle01.txt, Puzzle02.txt, . . . , Puzzle11.txt.* You can add more puzzles by creating additional puzzle files (follow the format shown in Figure 19-7).

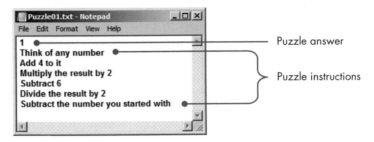

Figure 19-7: The format of a puzzle file

The strategy for developing this program is outlined as follows:

1. When the program starts, we'll list the files in the program's directory to get the pathnames of the puzzle files.
2. For each round of the program, we'll select one of the available puzzles.
3. We read the first line of the selected puzzle's file and interpret it as the puzzle's answer. The remaining lines represent the instructions the wizard displays.
4. The wizard displays the puzzle's instructions one by one until the program reaches an empty line. The wizard asks the user to press ENTER after each instruction.
5. The wizard displays the puzzle's answer.

Open the *Wizard_Incomplete.sb* file from this chapter's folder. This file contains the program's main code, shown in Listing 19-10, and empty placeholders for the DoPuzzle() subroutine that you'll add. The folder also contains the text files for the 11 premade puzzles.

```
1  ' Wizard_Incomplete.sb
2  TextWindow.Title = "MATH  WIZARD"
3  TextWindow.WriteLine("========== MATH  WIZARD ==========")
4  TextWindow.WriteLine("Press Enter after each instruction")
5  TextWindow.WriteLine("==================================")
6  TextWindow.WriteLine("")
7
8  puzzle = File.GetFiles(Program.Directory) ' Stores filenames into an array
9
10 For P = 1 To Array.GetItemCount(puzzle)
11   path = puzzle[P]                        ' File in the app's directory
12   If (Text.EndsWith(path, ".txt") = "True") Then
13     DoPuzzle()
14   EndIf
15 EndFor
```

```
16 TextWindow.WriteLine("The game was won, the math was fun, and the magic is ↵
   done!")
17 TextWindow.WriteLine("There is one Math Wizard to rule them all! Bye!")
```

Listing 19-10: The main code of the Math Wizard program

After displaying the program's title and its instructions (lines 2–6), we call GetFiles() to get a list of all the files in the program's directory, and we save the identifier of the returned array in the puzzle variable (line 8). We then start a loop to process the files we found (lines 10–15). In each iteration, we get one pathname from the puzzle array (line 11) and check whether it has a *.txt* extension (line 12). If the file has a *.txt* extension (which means it contains a puzzle), we call DoPuzzle() to show that puzzle to the user (line 13). The program ends with a message from the Math Wizard (lines 16–17).

Add the DoPuzzle() subroutine shown in Listing 19-11 to the bottom of the *Wizard_Incomplete.sb* program.

```
 1 Sub DoPuzzle
 2   puzzleAns = File.ReadLine(path, 1)       ' Reads answer from first line
 3   N = 2                                    ' Starts from second line
 4   line = "?"                               ' To enter the loop
 5   While (line <> "")                       ' Loops as long as we have instructions
 6     line = File.ReadLine(path, N)          ' Reads the Nth line
 7     If (line <> "") Then                   ' If we have an instruction
 8       TextWindow.Write(line + "... ")      ' Writes instruction
 9       TextWindow.PauseWithoutMessage()     ' Waits for user to press a key
10       TextWindow.WriteLine("")
11       N = N + 1                            ' Prepares to read next line
12     EndIf
13   EndWhile
14   TextWindow.WriteLine("You still have: " + puzzleAns)
15   TextWindow.WriteLine("")
16 EndSub
```

Listing 19-11: The DoPuzzle() subroutine

We read the first line from the file and save it in puzzleAns (line 2). Next, we set N to 2 to read the second line of the file and set the line string to "?" to enter the While loop (lines 3–4). In each iteration of the loop, we read one line from the puzzle's file (line 6) and check whether the program reached the last instruction. If line is not empty (line 7), we display the instruction the program just read (line 8) and wait for the user to press any key (line 9). When the player presses any key, we increment N to read the next instruction in the file (line 11). When the program reads an empty line, the While loop ends, and the program moves to line 14, where we display the puzzle's answer followed by an empty line (lines 14–15).

Figure 19-8 shows a sample run of the program.

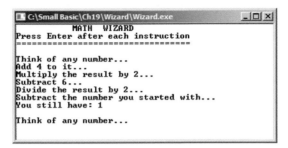

Figure 19-8: Sample output of the Math Wizard program

TRY IT OUT 19-3

Think of ways to improve the Math Wizard program, and try to implement them. For example, add some colors to make the output look fancier or draw something after each puzzle.

Programming Challenges

If you get stuck, check out *http://nostarch.com/smallbasic/* for the solutions and for more resources and review questions for teachers and students.

1. Let's write a spelling quiz game using homonyms. Homonyms are words that sound the same but have different meanings. Use Notepad to create the following text file:

```
In your math class;ad/add;add
Halloween queen;which/witch;witch
Eyes do this;sea/see;see
In the church;altar/alter;altar
A rabbit;hair/hare;hare
A good story;tail/tale;tale
Animals have them;clause/claws;claws
Pencils do this;right/write;write
```

Each line in this file contains three fields separated by semicolons. The first field is the hint you'll show the player, such as In your math class. The second field is the two possible answers that your player will choose from, such as ad/add. The third field is the correct answer, such as add.

In each round, have the program display the hint and the two possible answers to the player, and then wait for them to enter their answer. Have the program compare the user's answer with the correct answer, and then let them know whether their answer is correct.

2. Write a science quiz that tests the student's knowledge of the animal kingdom. First, use Notepad to create the following text file:

```
1=Invertebrates;2=Fish;3=Amphibians;4=Reptiles;5=Birds;6=Mammals
Bat;6
Clam;1
Dog;6
Frog;3
Lizard;4
Peacock;5
Salamander;3
Salmon;2
Spider;1
Turkey;5
Turtle;4
```

The first line contains the possible classifications. Each of the remaining lines contains an animal's name and its correct classification. Display an animal's name to the player, and then ask them to classify that animal by entering the number of the correct class. Then process the player's answer and let them know whether their answer is correct; if their answer is incorrect, display the correct classification.

WHERE TO GO FROM HERE

So you've mastered the basics of programming with Small Basic. Congratulations! If you're itching for more, there are extra resources online that you can explore.

Online Resources

Visit *http://www.nostarch.com/smallbasic/* to download the extra resources for this book. Once you've downloaded and unzipped the file, you'll see the following materials:

Book Programs and Solutions   Download the finished programs, all the images you'll need, some skeleton code for the Programming Challenges, and the solutions to the Programming Challenges and Try It Out exercises. This will save wear and tear on your typing fingers!

Additional Resources   These are online articles that relate to the topics covered in this book. Many of these were written just to supplement the book!

Review Questions   Test your knowledge (or your student's knowledge).

Practice Exercises   In addition to the Try It Out exercises and the Programming Challenges in the book, you can find even more exercises to practice. This is also great for teachers who want more options for assignments.

The Small Basic Website

Visit *http://www.smallbasic.com/* to explore the world of Small Basic and programming. You'll find featured games and programs, documentation, a curriculum for teachers, and much more.

Play Games   Visit the program gallery to check out what other programmers have made.

Join the Community   Post on the forums at *http://aka.ms/ SmallBasicForum/* to ask questions and share your games and programs with the entire Small Basic community.

Learn the Latest News   Find out about new releases, extensions, and featured content, games, and apps at *http://blogs.msdn.com/b/smallbasic/*.

Get Teaching Support   Teachers can join a private network to get personal support from Microsoft on all Microsoft products at *http://aka .ms/MCSTN/*.

Connect with the Team   Email Ed Price and the rest of the Small Basic team at *smallbasic@microsoft.com*. Tell them the book sent you!

Graduating to Visual Basic

You can convert any Small Basic program into an equivalent Visual Basic program, which lets you transition to the full power of a professional programming language. First, you'll need to download Visual Studio for free. Go to *http://www.visualstudio.com/* and click **Free Visual Studio** in the upper right.

Next, go to the Small Basic toolbar, click **Graduate**, select your **Output Location**, and click **Continue**. Visual Studio will open with the code translated into Visual Basic! Head back to the Visual Studio website for getting started documentation on Visual Basic and the Visual Studio interface. And if you have any questions about the graduating experience, ask us in the Small Basic forum.

INDEX

parts of, 14–16
publishing, 5–6
running, 5–6
terminating, 21
writing and running, 6–9
prompts, 75–76
properties
setting and changing, 19–20
working with, 20–21
Properties.sb, 20–21
pseudocode, 52, 248
publishing programs, 5–6

Q

quotation marks, 272

R

Race_Incomplete.sb, 204–205
Raji, Vijaye, xvii–xviii, 2–3
Random2DArray.sb, 243
random matrix, 243–244
random numbers, 92
random selection, 216–217
RandomSelect.sb, 217
readability, 47
ReadContentsDemo.sb, 291–292
ReadContents() method, 291–292
reading
numbers, 74
text, 79–80
ReadLine() method, 296
Read() method, 75, 269
ReadNumber() method, 74, 75, 76
registering, event handlers, 152
relational operators, 100–101, 120
relative motion, 59–60
Remainder() method, 90–91
Rock-Paper-Scissors game, 200–204
announcing winner in, 204
game setup, 201–202
MouseDown handler, 202–203
switching images in, 203
root directory, 290
RotatedPolygon.sb, 67
rounding methods, 86–88
Round() method, 78, 86–88
running sum, 79
running programs, 5–6
runtime errors, 25

S

SailBoat.sb, 29
saving
files, 5
records in arrays, 216
Scribble2.sb, 169–170
Scribble.sb, 156
SeaWorld_Incomplete.sb, 179
selection statements, 97
semiperimeter, 134
sequential execution, 17
SeriesCircuit.sb, 173–176
main code, 172–174
OnMouseDown() subroutine, 174
OnTextTyped() subroutine, 175
startup file, 172
toggling switch in, 174
UpdateUserInterface() subroutine,
174, 175–176
updating interface, 175–176
SetApplePosition() subroutine, 221
SetSize() method, 167–168
SetTextBoxText(), 169
SetText() routine, 258
SetTurtle.sb, 54
SetUp() subroutine, 139–140
shapes, drawing, 30–35, 120–122
circles, 32–34
ellipses, 32–34
polygons, 64–70
rectangles, 31–32
squares, 31–32
star, 65–66
triangles, 30
Shapes object, 120–122, 159, 246
sharing files, 5
ShootArrow() subroutine, 145
Shoot_Incomplete.sb, 284
ShowLocation() subroutine, 256, 257–258
Show() method, 57
ShowWinner() subroutine, 202, 204
Silly.sb, 79–80
SimpleSlot.sb, 205
Sin() method, 94
slash sign (/), 83
Small Basic
blog, 3, 308
forum, 5, 14, 308
goals of, 3
history of, 2–3

Learn to Program with Small Basic is set in New Baskerville, Futura, The Sans Mono Condensed, and Dogma. The book was printed and bound by Versa Printing in East Peoria, Illinois. The paper is 60# Anthem Plus. The book uses a layflat binding, so when open, the book lies flat and the spine doesn't crack.

UPDATES

Visit *http://nostarch.com/smallbasic/* for updates, errata, and other information.

More no-nonsense books from **NO STARCH PRESS**

SUPER SCRATCH PROGRAMMING ADVENTURE!
Learn to Program by Making Cool Games
by THE LEAD PROJECT
OCTOBER 2013, 160 PP., $24.95
ISBN 978-1-59327-531-0
full color

PYTHON FOR KIDS
A Playful Introduction to Programming
by JASON R. BRIGGS
DECEMBER 2012, 344 PP., $34.95
ISBN 978-1-59327-407-8
full color

SCRATCH PROGRAMMING PLAYGROUND
Learn to Program by Making Cool Games
by AL SWEIGART
FALL 2016, 200 PP., $24.95
ISBN 978-1-59327-762-8
full color

LEARN TO PROGRAM WITH SCRATCH
A Visual Introduction to Programming with Games, Art, Science, and Math
by MAJED MARJI
FEBRUARY 2014, 288 PP., $34.95
ISBN 978-1-59327-543-3
full color

THE LEGO® MINDSTORMS® EV3 DISCOVERY BOOK
A Beginner's Guide to Building and Programming Robots
by LAURENS VALK
JUNE 2014, 396 PP., $34.95
ISBN 978-1-59327-532-7
full color

LEARN TO PROGRAM WITH MINECRAFT®
Transform Your World with the Power of Python
by CRAIG RICHARDSON
DECEMBER 2015, 320 PP., $29.95
ISBN 978-1-59327-670-6
full color

PHONE:
800.420.7240 OR
415.863.9900

EMAIL:
SALES@NOSTARCH.COM
WEB:
WWW.NOSTARCH.COM